The Journey to Transform Culture

What Leaders and Teams Need to Know

By Steven W. Jones

(1st Ed.)

Copyright © 2024 by Steven W. Jones

All rights reserved.

No part of this publication may be reproduced, distributed, or transmitted in any form or by any means, including photocopying, recording, or other electronic or mechanical methods, without the prior written permission of the publisher, except for brief quotations embodied in critical reviews and certain other noncommercial uses permitted by copyright law.

First Edition, 2024

Published by Steven W. Jones

Publishing platform: Kindle Direct Publishing

Cover art: Kindle Direct Publishing

Dedication

For my beloved mother, Anna, and father, Carl, whose love and guidance helped to shape me into who I am today.

Acknowledgments

I am very grateful to the leaders, instructors, coaches, and colleagues at every level in numerous organizations, sports, and businesses who have contributed significantly to my personal and professional development for over thirty-five years.

My enthusiastic appreciation goes to my family: Miranda, Tyler, Kala, Dave, Jacob, Jessa, Lilly, Aiden, Kaylee, Brantley, Everly, Braxton, Josie, Sharon Gilman, Jim Rees, Christy, Rob, Michelle, Babs, Todd and lifelong friends for their support and encouragement, particularly during the challenging phases of writing.

I wish to extend my special thanks to the United States Air Force for its foundational professional development, for instilling an adventurous and curious spirit, and for inspiring in me the confidence to reach beyond my grasp to serve people.

Authors Note

This book is the culmination of a life that includes the guidance of organizational improvement across numerous organizations for over two decades. As I reflected after 2021, I recognized that I would have to live over three thousand years to help numerous organizations across cultures realize similar breakthroughs by going from organization to organization. My solution was to write this book to help guide and educate anyone to begin realizing their transformation personally and professionally. I have witnessed plenty of suffering by leaders and team members alike, who struggled to find and sustain resolution to the challenges they faced. Writing this book has been a labor of love, which has taken me most of my lifetime to compile. Inside, you will find insights, solutions, wisdom, and steps that can be taken to begin long-term or rapid transformation immediately. This work is a tribute to those who have struggled, those who have suffered, and those who desire to elevate their performance.

Table of Contents

Table of Contents	1
Chapter 1: Introduction	4
Chapter 2: What Do You Care About	10
Chapter 3: Why Can We Trust You	16
Chapter 4: What's Love Got to Do with It	42
Chapter 5: The Great Reset	51
Chapter 6: Dealing with Our Own Human Nature	56
Chapter 7: First Do No Harm	61
Chapter 8: Self-Significance	67
Chapter 9: You Can Only Control You	69
Chapter 10: Personality	75
Chapter 11: Embrace Functional Change	92
Chapter 12: Pay Now or Pay Later	111
Chapter 13: You Think You Know You	115
Chapter 14: The Dysfunction in Life	120
Chapter 15: Deception	127
Chapter 16: Boundaries	133
Chapter 17: Make Peace with Your Past	143

Chapter 18: We Are Not Just Here for the Party	152
Chapter 19: Scoreboard Mentality	154
Chapter 20: There is Always Cause and Effect	159
Chapter 21: People, Environment, and Motivation	163
Chapter 22: Anchor Points	169
Chapter 23: Vision is Important to the Organization	170
Chapter 24: Find Ways to Have Fun	172
Chapter 25: Resourcefulness	179
Chapter 26: Backsliding	182
Chapter 27: Head and Heart	183
Chapter 28: Persistence	187
Chapter 29: It's About We	194
Chapter 30: Problem-Solving and Creating	197
Chapter 31: Tools, Techniques & Insights	203
Chapter 32: The Rebellion	210
Chapter 33: How Do You Prevent a Rebellion	213
Chapter 34: Organizing Improves Performance	219
Chapter 35: Systematize Your Policies, Processes, and Procedures	228
Chapter 36: Artificial Intelligence	239
Chapter 37: Friend or Foe	244
Chapter 38: Conclusion	248
Negative Behaviors	251

Good Behaviors	253
Conflict Resolution	260
Bibliography	277
Appendices A	281

Chapter 1

Introduction

When we think of how grand the cosmos is, the depth of questions like, 'What is infinity?' and 'Where do we come from?' can feel overwhelming compared to the absoluteness of our daily routine to survive each day. Most days, we hope to have a little energy left over to find some joy, distraction, and rest enough to start all our routines again tomorrow. The day's drama consists of difficulties in our lives that we experience, like ocean waves under a boat that bobs all over the place. Still, every new day upon those waves stands out compared to the one before. Aside from the variable movement of our lifeboat upon the water, most of our human condition is predicated on what we do, what is being done to us, and what pleasurable experiences we can sneak into the gaps of the extremes. Human reality is more like a grand zoo with a fence kept so far away that our consciousness, which resides at its center, gets little or no attention. Like a rare forgotten bird that finds itself penned in, we only notice our inner self in those rare moments when life slows way down. We catch ourselves staring longingly into a sunset or sunrise, releasing that bird to fly freely before our awareness of the mundane of 3D life: an abrupt horn, a whistling teapot, a child's cry, or an irritated spouse looking for lost keys, and an infinite number of other distractions return our spirit, that free bird, to its cage. Most of us regard anything grand or the vastness of our cosmos as exciting, dismissing our distant connection to it as less than a priority in our lives. In the same way, we may believe that an ant is not thinking much about an erupting volcano nearby; we humans march ahead, focused on the linear tasks and perhaps the few important ants in our circle. However, we humans are not that linear or thoughtless. Somehow, deep down, we humans know better, right?

What if we are wrong, though? What if the immediacy of tasks that saturate our natural world and our time on them is the real dream? What if our tremendous cosmic journey is the only thing firm about our human experience? Our daily grind would then be the fantasy, the dream we created to occupy the boredom that the ant must endure. Ants do well in filling their time constructively. Perhaps we made this dream from a desire to learn, grow, and seek out wisdom and truths that will grow all humanity. Wouldn't it be a waste of a dream not to enjoy the unraveling of it, unscrambling ourselves, and rebirthing this dream-escaping the maze in favor of a grander version of our inner ideal? Wouldn't we then be the solution that breaks us free? Perhaps we are in this dream solely to get through the maze with love intact, more robust, thriving, and protected. What if love is the only key we refuse to pick up that unlocks every door and would allow humanity the chance to grow further than we ever thought possible? It would not be so fantastic to think we could create anything in the future in that dream.

All humanity works with only a part of truth all the time. Humans can only see .0035 percent of all known light (NNSA, 2018). For those with sight, our visual sense can only see twenty percent of everything we experience. Over ninety-nine percent of all reality then is real yet invisible to humanity. Our human audible perception only operates in the 20-20,000 Hz range (Hill, 2021). We are only aware of one-millionth of the highest usable sound frequencies. The amount of what we are unaware of in our reality is frightening. Yet, we want to trust our senses. We need our senses to survive. The complexity of the invisible is so far beyond what we can comprehend that it serves as a reminder of our infant-mindedness when it comes to how accurately we think we experience the world.

Medical science shows us that our awareness and cognitive abilities "unfortunately do decline as we age" (Cherry, 2010, p. 160). I call this the cognitive curve. This decline happened to my father, who had cancer, and my severely diabetic grandfather as he aged until his death. Now, my mother's mental abilities are in noticeable decline. Many aspects of our health and aging significantly affect the cognitive curve in our lives. Moreover, with the vast proliferation of electronic devices, our TVs, phones, pads, and video games distract us from real human connections. People are becoming more informationally aware yet are more numbed to the emotional reality of people in the same room. Some are triggered at the drop of a pin yet quickly self-proclaim their expertise as armchair foreign policy gurus. I am amazed at the 'absolutes' from those mouths who have traveled little beyond the hometown they grew up in. For all the possibilities that our electronic devices give us, they pay us nothing for our investment in them. Some parents obfuscate their parental duties directly to these same devices. How much will this increase the chasm between human connection now and well into a developing person's future? For decades, the behavioral struggles of youth have been a cry for help. It is a cry that has followed some into adulthood to become parents who now live their best childhood out loud on social media. Perhaps throwing the first stone at the responsible party only means we would be throwing it at ourselves and our parents first.

Distraction has slowly lulled humanity to its greatest uselessness on the one hand, while some have made significant innovative strides at a steady rate on the other. Still, the distracted masses have a fantastic opportunity to awaken and unlock many important contributions and discoveries. It will require greater cooperation, creativity, awareness, problem-solving capability, and focus. The result is the possibility of overcoming some of humanity's most significant challenges: disease, famine, clean drinking water, homelessness, education, and more. These are vital to everyone.

The top of Maslow's hierarchy of needs is crowned appropriately with the concept of self-actualization, the highest stage of human development (Mcleoud, 2024). How do we, communities spread throughout the world, broken into land masses, countries, states, and organizations of all types, provide a future where everyone will have an opportunity- an environment to become self-actualized? Consider what would be needed to make people understand the benefit of self-actualization. It would mean empowering people to affect the richness of their lives by taking steps forward with enthusiasm to grow and build it, accepting that fundamental transformation is complex, at first, for everyone.

A pragmatic example of transformation would be when we want to get into better physical shape to improve our health and fitness. Your first thought is, what must I do to get in shape? After that, following your understanding of what is needed to get into better physical condition, your next step is getting off the couch, walking around your house, and then stretching. Maybe the next day, you go outside, walk around the block, and this continues until you gain sufficient momentum and confidence to do the little things each day until, eventually, you find yourself on a track, on a treadmill, or in a weight room with a conditioning coach, for example. Similarly, transforming organizational culture requires the same building of momentum, where each stage has minor levels of discomfort combined with growth as you progress. For organizations, people like me would be the coach or guide, helping people learn how to maintain and grow in their abilities confidently. As a coach, it is inherent that we are truthful about where our development is and what is needed to succeed. Then, we help guide and inspire you to be independent and confident until you support and coach one another. Ironically, my job is to work myself out of a job.

Another example of making changes would be that of a loved one or teen who stops smoking and lives another decade or two to see their child or grandchild graduate from high school. A decade or two later, they see them getting married and eventually, as an elder, see their entire family flourish exponentially—all this possibility, from one habit change. The same goes for doing other good things daily, not just changing one toxic behavior. Choosing to do good builds positive momentum in your life. Furthermore, that transmits to others you meet along your life path. When it happens, real growth is infectious and cannot be hidden. Changes become new habits that then open your life to new opportunities.

Transformation is improving by intentionally trying every day. When we transform our lives and those of others, we demonstrate that we are here to protect love. If you need a reason to bring about a global transformation of cooperation to realize good, that is it. The math and all the dots connect to reveal that simple cosmic truth. If you love and care about someone or something, you are doing something to protect that love. In so doing, you protect love for others even if you do not understand it. This is customer service.

We are on this tiny blue ball we call Earth, a life raft we all share, hurtling through space at an unbelievable speed, protected by the sun and moon. Where are we going? Where are these cosmic ocean tides taking us? To ponder the question deeply is overwhelming. What if, though, on this voyage of human development and discovery, we are supposed to be getting prepared, learning, and planning like voyagers of old to arrive generations from now, or maybe -tomorrow, somewhere? Would we arrive at our destination prepared? Would our homework be complete, class projects to learn from relationships -finished, quizzes of kindness in life experienced, and courses of fairness passed successfully? Perhaps we should cooperate to evolve instead of letting our pride and ego divide and distract us. Maybe we should not continually rebel against the common good that drives us further from ultimate cooperation. What if our one mandate on our cosmic journey was to protect the fire of love so everyone grows, thrives, and learns? What if we were not allowed to arrive until these lessons were complete? If we arrived at our destination tomorrow, would we have failed? Let us hope we succeed at our one mandate: to protect love.

Through this book, I will reveal some insight from experience and offer advice to help you unlock and improve your organizational culture. You may find the information personally helpful as well. Increasing our knowledge as leaders, team members, and people means we honor the privilege of riding this life raft, this tiny blue ball-Earth, across the cosmos cooperatively while you journey through these pages. While on this raft, I will relay from up in the crows' nest what I have seen, heard, unraveled, and witnessed so you can navigate the waters of transformation with deeper awareness. This book is a resource for you from one human to another.

Chapter 2

What Do You Care About

Typically, people fall into more predominantly left or right-brain categories of their chosen behaviors (Cherry, 2024). This is not about a literal physical description but rather about behaviors. People have been differentiated differently by personality types throughout history. We could add eye-opening realizations about life path numbers, zodiac signs, enneagrams, and many myths, beliefs, dogmas, and religious influences on the behavior equation. In that case, you see the algorithmic complexity that nature and nurture have passed down to us through the ages. Like a hall of mirrors, we must find true reflection about ourselves to find our way. Boiling down personality types, in the end, will always be about the math of our humanity. The algorithms of behavior from the ancient tribal traditions have followed us into the modern-day workplace and culture. In truth, behavioral influences have always been with us. The association of the left and right brains helps us somewhat simplify the correlation between our logical and creative minds for discussion. Few people have extreme left or right-brained behavior. Most of us tend to be a varied mix of both. The highly logical mind may be more comfortable in environments with systems, while the creative mind may like a more accessible, more open, and inspired artistic approach. That said, because both extremes operate in those modes, their desire to work outside of them may be greater than we expect. The logical-minded may secretly want to belt out into song and have more creative control, while the creative-minded may thirst for a more grounded structure to maximize their potential. Interestingly, I have seen this in relationships and stories where a traditional person dates a highly creative person and vice versa. We have heard this described as opposites attract. Longevity and happiness, personally and professionally, are much more profound levels of human math, not so cutely simplified. Suffice it to say that it is like creating a flavorful stew; you get out of it what you put into it. We know this about ourselves; we must make friends with our strengths, continue to build upon our weaknesses, and test ourselves outside our comfort zone. We must make friends with where we fit along the left-right-brained spectrum. Evolving ourselves, our team, and our organization means appreciating everyone's gifts and talents. It is our uniqueness that lends flavor to the stew that is our team.

What pleases us? Is it arriving at the destination or the journey that satisfies us most? Is it both? Who is pleased with our efforts? Is it just the customer's need or the pleasure of making the art that the artist enjoys? Is there more going on that drives a person to perform to an excellent level? Irrespective of mere survival, what are the intricacies of our talents and approaches that move us? Many enjoy connecting and working with people and being a part of something bigger than themselves, contributing a verse to our human experience, being seen, and being valued in life.

Forming bonds in foxholes is the lesson of military service. The civilian world has always been slow to catch on to the fact that it is much better to care for one another in the foxhole than to compete for the opportunity to throw each other out of it. Recognizing and nurturing the soul of your peers is not about competing with them that bind us, but ultimately competing for them that bond us. One only needs to ask anyone who has served how they regard their brothers and sisters at arms. Family, remember that. Compete for those who love and those who seem to hate you. If that kind of genuine care is your only awakening, you will see a transformative energy in your environment. Like it or not, everything you do is essential. You are giving yourself and all of us meaning in life by extension of yours when you value people moving through your day. You form bonds in the human collective when you value connection with everyone. See people with your heart through the veil of the trivial and past the arduous to witness their treasure of being that glows inside like a star.

How we live is our highest expression of thankfulness for each other and expresses love. Ultimately, you care about humanity, even if you hate it, which sometimes irritates you. Hating something is just another bell that rings that should tell you that you do care. Otherwise, you would have no feelings at all. We may not always express the deeper 'why' that allows hate to force its way to the surface. Dig down far enough, though, and you will find a fear, medium or small, surrounded by a shroud of helplessness that our soul fights. The question we must resolve is, can humanity heal deep frustrations while simultaneously healing others' fears that pop up and become an orchestra of chaotic agony? It is the ultimate 'can we walk and chew gum at the same time'?

Remind yourself how important you are, and everyone else is, too. Remind yourself each morning when you wake up. My Dad would set his feet on the ground before standing when he awoke every day and say a prayer of thankfulness. He was not a man known for faith, but within him lived a universe of love, gratitude, and faith expressed in how he put people at ease. A humble approach that helped shape me. You can have strength and be vulnerable under a cosmos you cannot see the end.

How enthusiastic we live and work says a lot about how much we care about our customers. People fight obsessively for the newest shiny material objects. People get caught up in the toxic drama surrounding them in the workplace and their private lives. Some people fight to endure it, while others seek to create it. In the flurry of the drama, we ask, "Don't I deserve to be acknowledged and appreciated in the story of my life?" The answer is yes, you do. You deserve more of the most real: Love, acceptance, and appreciation -to be seen, valued, and respected. How do you realize that in your life and then show it to other people? What shiny objects, experiences, distractions, and things are you running toward to 'feel good' only to feel a void where love and appreciation are concerned? How many people are alone asking themselves that same question? We must first love ourselves and the value we bring to the world to make the ripples necessary to serve. Those ripples will then become the waves of change that affect our team, our culture, and everyone for the better. We must become people who live, risk, love, cooperate, and contribute collectively.

When you take part and engage with the rest of the human family, you unlock a love that binds all of us mysteriously. It is an energy, a feeling like a blanket of protection, a warm reassurance, a comfortable shield, a rope that pulls us from the trouble of disconnectedness. Love is a formless attribute that we bear inside us first and then give intentionally. Love is important. In nature, flowers bloom, and birds sing with the rising sun, honoring and being thankful for everything love has created around us. We are all worthy and want to be a part of that sunshine; we yearn for it from our depths, no matter what labels, paradigms, or dogmas others have placed upon us. Moreover, we are accountable, no less than nature itself, to do our part.

If we keep our heads down or worry about the day's expectations too much, we forget why our actions are so important to us. Despite what we do, everything we do, we do for love. In every moment, someone somewhere is lying in a hospital bed or a nursing home near dying. Their life is a final compression of all the love given and received. Love has been poured out of and into them by everyone, in grand and minor ways. This is what the culmination will one day look like for most people. The narrowness of our life span is another reason we must spend our time, our life's capital, being accountable to express love through our thoughts, words, behaviors, and actions. Life is fleeting and temporary. What will your contribution to humanity be? Indeed, helping one another through it with love, instead of trying to dominate and oppress one another, is a valid path to begin walking regardless of when in life you start. Happily, a new baby is born every moment, bringing new love, hope, and possibilities. A new life is the butterfly effect that emanates from everyone and affects and touches everyone's life in the future. Between the birth of new life and our death, we are compelled to learn, grow, and love, and we must be in a steady state of doing that repeatedly. It takes time to get good at being a good human, much like it takes time for a jagged rock to be smoothed out into a beautifully rounded skipping stone that can glide effortlessly across a glassy stream.

We must ask ourselves, 'Am I saying the words I am out of love? 'Am I taking the actions I am taking from a place of love?' If not, who are you hurting when you are not speaking and acting from a place of love? Why do you want to hurt or divide anyone? Hurting or helping, every moment is a test for us all. With every test, we can realign our compass toward what truly matters: doing what honors love, what honors ourselves. Then, everyone who receives love will feel good, lighter, and happier, knowing the journey is fruitful. We can be an active bridge connecting the sublime to everything practical and pragmatic. Simple chores can be unique when you are connected to love as your purpose. Love can inoculate the hurt and fuel you if you let it. If you care about the importance of love, you will not be able to hide it. Love will be a prominent part of who you are that no one can ignore -and a power no one can take from you. When you genuinely care from a place of love, you can accomplish anything, like being truthful, accountable, forgiving, forgetting, letting go of past wrongs, and freeing yourself. Can everyone see and hear what you care about? Do not be afraid to show how good you are at what you do, how you care, and how you love by the expression of how you live.

Chapter 3

Why Can We Trust You

There are no wrong choices; everything is learning. You may be asking yourself, Steve, why should we trust you? Are you an Ivy leaguer who considers himself a 'know it all'? How can you understand my concerns and that of my organization? How do you know anything about all the people contributing to our success? How can you understand what I go through as an employee? How can you begin to grasp what I deal with as a leader in my organization with all the challenges I face each day? How can you understand my frustration and employee concerns? How can you perceive the level of office politics, narcissism, and sociopathy that exists in my organization? How can you grasp how little I care after being exhausted trying so hard to fix an organization that does not seem to care? What have you done? Who are you? Can you help my organization find where the rubber meets the road? Despite everything you tell us, how can we trust that what you will say to us is not just some pipe dream?

The first mistake is to think anyone is perfect or to expect perfection from anything. If the 80/20 rule holds firm, the best outcome I could ever hope for is that forty percent of you would be motivated to enrich your lives by what you learn here. However, if twenty percent of you are highly motivated, it would be enough to significantly improve organizational culture and culture overall.

I have met people in organizations and my walk-through life who were inundated by the same concerns, fears, disappointments, frustrations, and anxieties that everyone, including me, has had in our lives. Let me assure you that I have met and helped many people and organizations overcome them. That said, the road to personal and professional excellence is a road that ensures you never arrive -because we are not perfect, there is always room to grow. We should constantly be evolving. This is a powerful lesson; the realization we must make friends with is that the journey is the destination.

What is my motivation? I value our futures. I value the success of organizations and the success of all cultures, and I believe that each human being should have the opportunity to grow and thrive together as a collective. To make successful progress, though, we must transform together in simultaneity. Organizations must build and sustain healthy cultures. Doing this requires us to grow as people. This is not a 'chicken or the egg' proposition; it is the chicken and the egg. We must intersect our expanding human capabilities to catch up to and integrate with the expanse of our technology. We must seize the opportunities we have now to grow. The fate of humanity may depend on it. Look at the world around you. Isn't it boldly clear that division and lack of cooperation overwhelm virtually everyone and everything? Isn't it evident that our human behavior is more erratic, less predictable, and less safe than at any time in our modern past? Business, as usual, needs to be fixed for humanity's benefit. What does this mean? It means we must change, with heart in hand, peacefully, and with respect. When I say change, I mean grow and transform to lift everyone through growth and development. By everyone, I mean all team members, leaders, and owners together. Together, we can succeed in our efforts to transform. By following, I mean we get onto a path of constancy to continuously grow in our knowledge, skills, and abilities that will positively affect our results in all areas. If we stay satisfied with the divide and dysfunction in organizational cultures, we will only see stagnation and failure, leading to global cultural decline. In everything we do, there is always a choice. The opportunity we have is to choose to steer history consciously toward a future where thriving is normal. Imagine if nearly everyone had a waking expectation to succeed and to help others thrive. We indeed have systems of learning from the trades to the highest collegiate levels. Now, let me ask you what digging a ditch at any point in your life was like. Have you painted a room? Have you changed a tire? Have you changed out a doorknob in your house or apartment? Have you raked leaves? Have you found and checked out a book in the library? Have you ever changed the oil for your vehicle? Have you changed out the heating elements in your water heater? Have you removed the back panel of your dryer and removed the lint that could burn your house down? None of these require higher education, but they need you to know how to learn and be motivated and able to do the necessary tasks. Life is full of tasks and actions you will never learn about in school but will only experience through living. Are you motivated to learn and do tasks? Can you teach others to do them? Now you understand what the essence of education is about. Taking on a necessary task shows you are motivated, that you care about what is essential, and that it is important enough to help others learn how to do it. Learning is healing. Continual learning is healing and transformation.

Organizations must swap the mystery of transformation for open transparency about it. They must delve into their shadow, uncovering impactful core issues and challenges that hold the entire team back. I have experienced uncovering core issues, dragging them into the light, acknowledging them, and then collaborating with the team to begin the healing process. I know that sometimes organizations must be humble, drop back, take a knee, own their fearfully held mindsets, work to repair and build better solutions, and then surge confidently forward.

I assure you that my efforts have not been about me. The answers and solutions discovered have always lived within the hearts and minds of the people you have on your team right now, no matter who you are, the size of your organization, or its scope of influence. However, unlocking your synergistic abilities requires seeing and understanding what affects people on your team. What I am presenting will be different from a vehicle walk around to size up the status of your car, 'kicking the tires' as it used to be called. The process and topics presented will require us to look under the proverbial hood, dissect and inspect the parts, explain what is wrong, what is or what may be broken, listen, and learn to be able to zero in on what is afflicting your 'vehicle,' your organization. We will expand by examining where the wear and tear has occurred. We will discuss what is worn out and what must be repaired and replaced and suggest new approaches. Leadership, too, must know how to drive and maintain their organizations more effectively by being present, having and enforcing accountability, and doing so with genuine care. This process will be intimate, not unlike a doctor giving you an extensive physical or a race car mechanic looking at your 'daily driver,' your vehicle. You will find out things about yourself and your team that you need to learn about. You will be presented with realities to help you change your 'driving' behaviors and approach to taking care of your vehicle 'your organization.' Because of this, you must know who I am, what has influenced me, and what my experience is in helping organizations.

 I will cover the events that affected my life's journey, helping people so that you have a picture of who I am and why you can trust me. I was born in Truckee, California, on April 23rd, 1968. My Father worked for the US Forest Service; my mom was a housewife until they divorced when I was almost two years old. I have no conscious memory of my parents living together. My mother then worked three jobs, and I alternated between grandparents and a babysitter who watched me who had acreage in northern California as a small child. I am an only child. At an early age, my grandparents, aunts, and uncles from both sides helped raise me and teach me the dos and don'ts. However, half of that village was conservative-leaning people, and the other half was liberal-leaning, where politics and perspectives were concerned. I was exposed to life through a unique lens of seeing more than one side of everything. I could find agreement and faults with all of them. Like the middle class, I was ignored due to the volatility of the extremes of a changing society of the time. However, in the early 70s, I enjoyed the peace of mind of not being too bothered by what I considered the mediocre thinking of adults then. If I were a visitor from another planet, my introduction to life in American culture would not be awe-inspiring. Again, I found gain and fault in the mindset of extremes who were too preoccupied with problems and conflict to solve problems or end conflict. That said, as opposed to now, my young perspective viewed differences then as separated by degrees, not universes. When I was young, both sides of the family got along and had respect for each other, irrespective of differing viewpoints. One of my grandfathers had an orchard and would give fruit every year to my other grandparents. I was not highly aware of my family situation as a child, but what impressed me was the depth of cooperation, respect, and consideration. I never heard a sideways word from either about either. I was not impressed with this until I got older and realized that this kind of harmony was not common in the world.

We lived in Auburn, California, during the Vietnam era when I was a younger child. I found culture diverse; it seemed all ethnicities were getting along. At the time, the media challenged institutional thinking, corporate manipulation, and corruption in many forms, no matter the source. I just enjoyed the music on the radio that emerged from the natural cultural tensions during that time. Mom was very musical and always had music playing at home. She played the clarinet growing up and led the high school marching band. My grandfather, my mom's father, served as a marine during the Korean War; he boxed while in the Marines, played the guitar, flew on aircraft, hunted, fished, worked in a hardware store later, and eventually owned an A&W restaurant. None of my grandparents went to college, yet their work ethic, dedication, and pride left an indelible imprint on my mind. As a kid, I gravitated to superheroes, science fiction, sports, and a fascination with space and time travel. In my later teens, the movie 'The Right Stuff' captivated me and made me want to be an astronaut. However, my higher math skills were weak then.

I have always been drawn to movies that break down thematic elements and their messages. I found it easy to break a film down, and I loved heroic movies with multilayers and plot twists. My grandparents watched a lot of Westerns then, so the classics, Big Valley, and others were the hit of the time. And like so many of us, I enjoyed the idealized Superman and clever Batman TV shows. I liked the hero helping the helpless, fighting for the underdog, truth, justice, serving the suffering, and helping those unable to help themselves. Serving others has always been a prime and constant motivator in my life, and yes, at times, I have allowed it to work to my detriment. The village did most of the work disciplining me when I was a little guy; my grandmother chased me through the garden because I was pulling radishes up out of the ground and eating them raw, running barefoot -she could never catch me, at least I do not remember her catching me.

Like a dog playing keep away with its owner or a young Tarzan boy, which was me as a little kid. As I grew out of that, I would help older adults in my mother's apartment complex. They would give me cookies and baked goods as payment, a great way to spend a Saturday morning. It felt good to help people. And as it turned out, I like food.

1978, I was ten years old, and we moved to North Idaho. We lived with my aunt and cousins for a year until we moved into a postage stamp-sized two-bedroom home. My best friend still refers to it as 'the shack.' I got involved in soccer and baseball and fell deeply in love with basketball. Basketball was my obsession. My friends Eric, Clay, Brian, and John, among others, played basketball all the time, anywhere we could -even in the snow. In America in the late '70s and '80s, sports heroics seemed to be a norm no matter what sport you were into. National sports heroes influenced us. Playing sports was where I was exposed to the 80/20 rule. Twenty percent drove our success, Twenty percent slowed our success, and sixty percent held their own by showing up. Though I would not learn about the 80/20 rule until later in life, the constancy of the math was sound. At age fourteen, I ran a race at the YMCA Superstars event. It consisted of twenty events that each contestant would participate in for a combined score. Winning the trophy for the fourteen to sixteen-year-old age group at fourteen was a personal breakout motivating moment. I was the youngest in my Group, running a two-and-a-half-mile river race to clinch it. That was a critical moment for me psychologically because I had to come from behind to win the victory, passing my close friend Eric on the final turn. That experience taught me that I could overcome myself and push the limitations of my mind. If something mattered enough to me, I could push to achieve it.

    As a younger man, I Was no child prodigy. We were poor. I was lucky if soda crackers were in the cupboard when I got home from track practice after school. People thought I was working out intensely as I grew. The reality was that I was starving. I could not get enough food. And because of this, I was very lean. I would spend the summers going to my dad's home in Oregon. He had a few small acres of farmland. I did the usual farm work you would expect when you have animals: changing field sprinklers for alfalfa and chickens, pulling weeds, hay, and more. As a kid, I hated a lot of chore work-who didn't? The freedom of riding my bike, experiencing nature, and adventuring with my cousins during summer meant we would ride all over the countryside after the chore work was done. Riding our bicycles around the orchards of Hood River Valley, Oregon, connected me to nature with a backdrop of Mount Hood watching over us.

Dad had his degree in sociology. He was the only college-educated person among his nine other brothers and sisters. He was methodical. Dad had a large and deep timber to his voice that housed a kind authority without effort—slightly less timber in his voice than that of James Earl Jones, the actor. There was surety in his words. Dad could see the movement in thinking and decision-making in groups of people. He predicted that the Berlin Wall would fall when I was a teen. I do not know if I was too young to grasp it or just distracted and surprised entirely. Six years later, the Berlin Wall fell. At the time, I credited his prediction to his education. Much later, I realized that Dad had a sixth sense, a forward-thinking inner intellectual intuition I did not understand. There were always nuggets of gold in his words when he casually posed things. Much later, I found my forward-thinking intuitiveness, perhaps more silver, less gold. Thankfully, that intuitiveness helped me to help people in my way, often asking the right questions in the moment that pulled out key insights that would serve as breadcrumbs to solutions later. If we all have a gift or talent, mine has been to tap into the struggle that others were going through and channel solutions. Then again, maybe years of being a military instructor, improving operations, and having site leader experience helped the mechanics of that process; nurture over nature or both coming together, I suppose.

In the 70s, Dad ran for sheriff and commissioner in Hood River, Oregon, after he had been crushed in an avalanche in Death Valley while he was serving in the U.S. Forest Service before my birth. As the story goes, Dad died on the operating table for one minute and forty seconds. He recounted a near-death experience where he was floating above his body in the hospital room. I was sixteen years old when he told the story. I had no idea what to make of this. Now we know it is called an (NDE) a near-death experience.

When my dad recovered from his accident, he said he went from being a 'lunch pail worker,' as he put it, to becoming a voracious learner after his accident. He could do math very quickly with high Accuracy, computing figures and solving problems at a strangely rapid rate. His thirst for knowledge and learning propelled him to become the only college graduate among his nine siblings and parents. Dad did not have to work hard to reason with me. Dad had a calm, pleasant, and jovial way of conveying a point. You felt like you had just eaten a comfortably filling meal after a conversation with him. I finished his sentences in my head, though I never told him that. My parents benefited from me being an innately pretty good kid. To this day, Mom will say I raised myself. No one raises themselves. Back then, though, I was very bored as a young person. I had diverse interests. I had groups of friends who enjoyed sports, others who enjoyed the outdoors, and others who enjoyed science fiction and being creative. I did not and still do not fit in any one of these societally restrictive boxes - well. Having nonlinear diverse interests has kept life interesting, however. My most significant flaws, as I know them, were being too much of a people pleaser and being interested in learning and doing so many different things that, at one point, I had no idea what I would do when I grew up. I have since resolved that the lesson was not to grow up in the heart fully but to keep a young, adventurous, curious, and open mind. In my youth, I was drawn to more intelligent adults who verbally traveled through an incredible landscape of words I could visualize as they spoke. Ideas, imagination, and the 'possible' have always pulled me forward. My insight and creativity have been part of a growth pattern all my life. I was no genius, however. I learned a great deal from everyone in my life. Some lessons were hard, especially when the manipulative and the nefarious struck, while others were 'ouch, a hot stove.' I took some calculated risks in line with helping people; one was to date and then marry a woman who was pregnant, raising our eldest daughter to live a life of service as a nurse. I would learn that sometimes life presents you with something; it is up to us to alchemize love and hope into it, into them for this example. She, like my other children, has a happy family of her own. These and less significant life events are not always planned. We must shine and grow a garden where others only see weeds. I knew families who were growers of orchards, gardens, alfalfa, flowers, businesses, and more, so why wouldn't I alchemize and grow life, too?

I love Mom; she has a huge heart and is a selfless, self-sacrificing giver who influenced my heart. However, Mom has also been the most linear-thinking person I have ever known, and my first challenge dealing with linear-thinking people who resist change. Although a believer, I think Mom believes God created Diet Pepsi and chocolate. Maybe. Mom was a constant source of positive affirmation about how smart I was when I felt like a speck among stones. Mom influenced my self-talk early, and this helped build confidence in sports and life. I am confident the words about 'being smart' were less about the talk and more about affirmations of never giving up and often learning by doing, failing, and trying again. We all need someone to believe unquestioningly in us; Mom has been that person for me -despite my corny jokes and off-the-wall humor when I visit her in the nursing home.

In school, I enjoyed writing and playing sports. When I graduated from high school, I left home two weeks to the day after graduation. I took a bus; my stepdad and Mom sent me to Dad's house in Oregon. My stepdad passed away six months later due to aggressive cancer. The bus station was the last time I saw him in his presence. My mom would lose the house.

I took the bus to my dad's house as he had promised to give me his 74' Vega. It was in pristine condition. I drove to California to become a resident to go to college there. And like every good story with a pinch of intrigue, there was a girl. Isn't there always a girl or significant person who motivates you, drives you out of your nest, and seemingly disappears out of your story like the wind with the heart you dragged out of the nest with you?

I moved everything I could fit into my car and drove to Lancaster, California. There, I slept on my cousin's hard floor for four months while I worked two part-time jobs. The local basketball coach from Antelope Valley Community College called me while I was at work and asked me to try out for the team; I was unknowingly playing with his former players at the park and made an impression. I made the team tryouts successfully, though I had to get financial aid as a walk-on. The school waived me for a few months, and I began to practice on the team. Financial aid did not come, so I had to quit. This was heartbreaking. Later, some engineers invited me to a weekend football game between defense contractors. It was a 'friendly' rivalry. Being in that innovative air and energy inspired me and bruised me simultaneously. They were building an aspect of the B1 Bomber. A few decades later, I would refuel them during air-to-air refueling while in the Air Force, flying on KC-135s.

My stepdad passed away shortly after I moved to Northern California to live with my grandparents. Strangely, while working alone at the time at the mercantile, a man who looked just like him when he would dress to go rock-hounding walked into the store, said nothing, and made no eye contact. He walked down the primary wall, looking at fanny packs. I kept looking down the aisle, amazed at how uncanny he looked like my stepdad. As quickly as he entered, he exited, said nothing, and walked down the lot without a car or ride. Sometime within the hour, my grandmother called and told me he had passed away. I have no explanation for it. It was a beautiful day, though.

While living with my grandparents, I paid them rent each week while working at Auburn Mercantile, where my experience in customer service began. It was an outdoor outfitter. I would learn how little the public educated themselves about the products they sought. I would get residency in California and attend Sierra College in Rocklin, California. Due to my schedule, I had to drop the full-time job and work three part-time jobs. After two years in California, I moved back to Idaho, or I went back to Idaho to visit Mom and friends during the summer of 88' and ran out of money. It was a great summer with friends, but I was now stuck back in my home area with Fall and Winter ahead of me.

I got a job at a newly opened dog track in the evenings and a retail store in the mornings, marking products with a pricing gun. Yes, it was monotonous and uninspiring work. During this time, I was barely surviving. I never had more than one-fourth of a tank of gas in my car. I always needed money to do something. At that time, there were no real opportunities to break out. I knew a change needed to happen when I was alone at the home where I was renting a room; eating a peanut butter sandwich, I began to choke to death, and my only act before passing out and exiting my earthly plane was to attempt giving myself the Heimlich maneuver over the back of a chair. I knew that if I failed, it would all be over. I spun around to the back of the chair I was sitting in. I fell over the back of the chair abruptly as it thrust into my abdomen area. It barely opened my airway, but it was enough for me to start getting air through a small gap I created. I was able to clear my airway coughing. I am pretty sure it was during this time that, like so many of our lives, the universe was nudging me to do something different. During this time, I decided I would join the Air Force. I worked with a retired Air Force guy who refueled aircraft for twenty years.

This guy was so genuinely at peace and just happy every day. He told me about the Air Force. He was so satisfied with his Air Force experience that he didn't have to say words; I picked up on his satisfaction, which was enough for me. I have learned that you cannot fake or hide happiness or goodness for long. My intuition picked up his sincerity, too. I valued these traits in those I served during my Air Force career, enhanced by an environment of commitment and loyalty. The Air Force was a win for me. The math of joining the Air Force made sense: earning a salary, getting full benefits, a thirty-days-per-year vacation package, playing a multitude of sports in multimillion-dollar advanced fitness complexes, traveling, learning marketable technical skills, and getting your college degree paid; every bit of what I did in the Air Force. I learned later how difficult it was for many people to qualify to get into the Air Force due to drug use, health issues, parental restrictions, and legal hurdles. I am bow-legged; the Doctor walked around me three times and finally said I was okay. Wow, that was a close call, I thought, at the end of a line of other guys trying to join. You do not realize until you look back at how significant some of these events are in your life. What did the universe or God whisper into that doctor's ear? Was it, 'he's okay,' or perhaps more like, 'I wonder what the wife put in my lunch today?' Whatever it was, it set my life on a course that allowed me to thrive. I have since regarded my own and others' decisions similarly. Nothing is insignificant. What we think, say, do, and our choices affect others, whether we realize it or not. That sounds simple and perhaps lacks profoundness at first glance. However, if you allow all these micro-to-macro moments in life to sink in, dots connect, and some become clear about why they do not connect.

    I had an excellent work ethic before going into the Air Force. The rules, standards, and expectations were spelled out clearly; confusion and misunderstandings were rare. The core values in the Air Force are:

'Integrity First, Service Before Self, and Excellence in All We Do.' I would learn decades later that the civilian professional world struggles with core values. I enjoyed a couple of decades of Air Force life free of most things that thwart civilians. The Air Force could have been better, but good can seem perfect against the backdrop of arguably okay, in contrast.

I worked on F-16s while in the Air Force. I worked on weapons systems first, then became an instructor, and later, I volunteered to be a recruiter. After 9/11, I became a boom operator and an instructor on KC-135s. My roles themselves did not necessarily play a significant part in my journey as the things I did during the time I had those roles. I was an instructor for a third of my career. I learned how to learn. I learned new paradigms and how to instruct, teach, and coach. I coached the men's base basketball team before retiring.

Early in the Air Force, a manufacturer sent wired equipment defectively during Desert Storm. I worked around the clock for a week to rewire and prepare two hundred of these units so that we could be operational. I was awarded a medal for doing that. However, I was the customer fixing what the manufacturer failed to produce correctly the first time. This failure was another marker that would be a valuable lesson to refer to later.

A year later, I was trained in Total Quality Management, TQM. This quality model says that everyone downstream from you is your customer, and you are the customer of those upstream from you in any process. To simplify it, everyone is everyone's customer. Later, the TQM model would fall from favor as it seemed to open to too much cross-communication in an organization. This was an excuse. It is one of the most potent approaches any organization can implement for rapid change and consistency. It did not rely on solving problems at the lowest possible level enough for the Air Force. Taking a philosophy to its extreme and then arguing against it is a sophomoric technique that happens with a bias toward investing in or against investing in tools of all kinds. How it would have benefitted the customer is the only real question. Beware this lesson: Is the decision being made based on inaccurate bias or accurate information? The nail gun does not invalidate the usefulness of the hammer and vice versa. Which tool works best in this situation is the most critical question.

My career was filled with experiences of overcoming problems that I was sure others must have encountered before my time as a junior member of the Air Force. Apparently not. I often wondered if challenging situations were seeking me out. I found later that many people sought me to help work on their problems. Next, I got orders to go to Misawa, Japan, for three years. In Japan, I quickly became an evaluator, training personnel, writing and administering tests, performing flight line evaluations, and formally inspecting aircraft. As part of the standardization team, I learned how critical each step in a process is to ensure the outcomes are the same each time. Accuracy meant life and death. Later, I would be surprised to know how much dissociation there was in the civilian world regarding process discipline, the negative impacts on product safety and quality, and preventing loss of life.

I received orders to Arizona. Again, I was selected to be an evaluator at Luke Air Force Base in Phoenix. I was a weapons standardization crew chief on the exercise evaluation team. The Group would hire me to train the base cadre for F-16s. Again, I lived a life of standardization. If something was done a particular way in Arizona, it was done the same way on the other side of the planet. When I say standardized, I mean more standardized than most will experience on Earth in their life. This level of standardization meant we had to communicate very well and have an extremely high level of situational awareness.

I was pleased with the Air Force. I got the idea to become an Air Force recruiter. Three Chiefs I worked for recommended that I don't citing it would be a career killer. They were right where achieving rank was concerned. Do you know the old saying about making lemonade from lemons? That is what I did. I had worked my way up from turning a wrench in the Air Force to becoming an instructor and then evaluator and was now going to sell the Air Force life. In one way, those Chiefs were right; comparatively, special duty roles get promoted at a lower rate. However, as a recruiter, I ran my storefront in the community, which helped my overall communication, and more importantly, I helped lead others to find their way to success of their own. In recruiting, among other things, you learned how to engage and establish rapport, a vital skill that helped my entire career in building teams. It also exposed me to the community, poverty, tragedy, and hopelessness that many people have in life, which is no small catalyst to writing this book now. I made it a part of my mission to motivate those who could not enter the Air Force, too. When I spoke to local schools, I challenged people to push forward, not to give up, and to overcome their circumstances. I took a lot of pushback from those who thought people in the military were terrible, pre-9-11. No matter where you go, there will always be a few bad apples. You cannot let them be the reason you give up on doing your best or expect less than the best from others. We cannot make others our excuse. During this time, I was still a competitive basketball player, and I coached basketball as well. I Taught, recruited, coached, and trained as a bedrock in my development along with those I helped develop. These experiences helped me later as an operations and plant management leader once I retired from the Air Force.

Eight years before I could retire, I decided to fly on KC-135s at Fairchild AFB in Washington State. It would take six-plus months to complete the training once I received orders. However, a month after making that decision, 9-11 happened. Ironically, I was scheduled to fly to my grandmother's funeral in California that same day. We did not make it to her funeral. I would deploy often. I was not formally trained yet, so I took over scheduling for our squadron and was surprisingly good at it. I would take on flight, ground safety, and other supervisory duties. Later, while being deployed, my inquisitive nature drew me to accounting issues around fuel transfers, and I discovered that deployed units were dumping over fifteen million pounds of fuel each year into the atmosphere unnecessarily. Ultimately, it was due to over-planning. I received a medal for this discovery, which resulted in fifty-three million dollars saved for the Air Force per year. The officer who supervised me at the time sent me a check for twenty-five dollars for an improvement that had a max of fourteen thousand dollars for the award. I suspect I did not get the total award because it would mean that a general or two would take a hit for unnecessarily polluting the atmosphere with all that fuel. My award was two-tenths of one percent of the max award. I never got rich off public service. Yet this experience helped me see through the lens of the workforce how they are and are not heard and how they can be disrespected by poor leadership. I was proud of saving all that toxic fuel from being dumped into the atmosphere needlessly. I can only imagine how much environmental damage was done. This occurred because of over-planning and a failure to communicate well. The Air Force is not perfect, nor was anyone in it, which is why it takes a team. It also takes good people to stand up, see through what might appear normal, and ask more profound questions. Later in my career in the civilian sector, I would find similar amounts of under planning, much assuming, and similar communication drop-off issues. By then, I had become much better at knowing where to look.

In 2005, I volunteered for a tour to become a full-time instructor in Oklahoma. After two years as an instructor, I led the Current Operations team as the Noncommissioned Officer in Charge. My first project was to help the Air Force improve their flying schedule and reduce excess costs -

as they spent millions on excessive overtime due to poor schedule coordination. I returned ninety days after coordinating with organizations base-wide, supplying them with a new scheduling plan and a guide that allowed them to align their training times that looked a lot like a Chinese food menu. This improvement effort saved the Air Force another thirty million dollars a year. Again, I received a medal for this improvement. During this project, I was able to use tools from many disciplines. I realized it was not about a silver bullet approach but understanding and using the best tool for the job. During that time, I recovered another hundred thousand dollars in bookkeeping errors when I oversaw fuel accounts. My Colonel was very appreciative of the work I performed. I found it fascinating that my predecessors could not solve these challenges previously. Again, it was as if these challenges were waiting for me to find and fix them, a universal doorbell awakening me to my innate gifts and talents. Moving forward, my ability to find solutions became increasingly second nature, more puzzle than work and more challenge than a problem. Dare I say fun.

Looking back, I was unaware of the large amounts of dopamine that surge through us when we find significant breakthroughs and get wins for our team. The great feeling I got from doing projects began to rival how doing the same in sports made me feel when I played or coached well. Almost as if I was tapping into something beyond what I could explain, my ability to improve organizations was becoming effortless. Coaching our base basketball team for two years before retiring in 2010 also had a seamless flow. We played against other branches of the armed forces and a local college. I enjoyed strategizing, getting all the players to work together successfully, and applying what we learned from each experience. More than that, I enjoyed finding ways to tap into and inspire the team to give their best effort.

Once I retired from the Air Force in 2010, I moved to Tennessee and began working for a defense contractor. What I quickly discovered after the Air Force was that I could not count on the conduct and behavior of people at work. A few had bad attitudes and displayed negative behaviors, clearly bogging down productivity. It was not that these civilians were terrible people; some didn't care. Being self-aware was not a part of the question in my head at the time. Consistency had been a challenge. At one point, I had six programs. Later, I discovered that these contracts required one person to do my job for each contracted program. This was exposed when I asked for a pay raise for carrying six more programs than I was getting paid. Nervously, they hired a few more people instead of paying me congruent to the workload. I knew this work was a temporary stop on my professional journey. I made some longtime friends there. The manufacturing manager was a significant enabler that allowed me to flourish. I learned more about human nature in my education. I rallied support and increased project completion times on their vehicle systems by thirty percent. The question that lingered was, 'Were these peoples' attitudes eroded by a system, or did they lack professional self-motivation?' Did they give up or give in? And if so, how could this be possible? After improving these programs, I decided to strike out on my own as a consultant. I had seen enough. If a defense contractor of this caliber had this volume of organizational issues, private businesses would suffer greatly and could use my assistance. I would be right.

    I garnered a contract to work for a family-owned company as a consultant at a local industrial park in Tennessee. Their primary issue was getting the team to work together cohesively within operations. Within three months, I was able to eradicate over a million dollars in wasted time and trained personnel across three sites and two states. Shortly after completing that project, I was offered an operational leadership role over three of their sites. My work to streamline continued, along with organizing the operation by building their infrastructure. This allowed the team to achieve its first-ever ISO certification for all three sites on the first evaluation. Keep in mind that this family-owned operation needed more operational documentation for policies, processes, and procedures and needed to be standardized. One of the site leaders let on that another site was running its machinery at half speed to accommodate break times. I marshaled that issue forward without firing one employee and significantly increased production efforts. After a few years, I moved to help another company make water booster pumps in Florida, a startup this time. I lived on the beach, which was nice for a time. I led the team to more than quadruple their production performance in four months while simultaneously cleaning up the plant, creating a Kanban system, 5S-ing the facility, and reducing build times for electrical control panels. Our abrupt increase in production speed shocked the sales team, who struggled to grow the customer base to keep up with our improved capabilities, a common theme: organizations that focus on improving productivity to meet customer needs that don't apply more thrust to grow the customer base. Organizations that do not do the long-range planning needed to improve actual sales cause the entire team more trouble later. Giving sales teams a six-month head start is wiser unless you are already past due by large quantities. You may train employees on continuous improvement tools and lean manufacturing techniques to sustain productivity. Make and improve upon those gains. I did this partly to give the sales team time to gain the proper momentum. They were not expecting exponential improvements in a few months. This would be an ongoing challenge in my civilian career, getting the sales teams to ramp up the sales rate, to believe, to be true believers where they had been the most cynical Group in the organization about the organization's ability to achieve breakthroughs. My teams were able to transform and rapidly improve productivity in between three to six months. Ironically, the sales teams always led with complaints about low productivity when I arrived, who always staggered to keep up. Regardless, this pattern revealed itself. Rather than poke them in the eye, I worked to allow them the space to be inspired by the production teams. This works, but a caution to sales teams:

- Put your track shoes on.
- Drink your energy drink of choice.
- Get rest.
- When you awake on that new day, put all excuses in your locker and hit the ground running like your life depends on it. Your ability or inability will directly affect the lives of your organization's people and their families. Let that sink in.

I took a sabbatical to move across the country to take care of my Father, who was dying from colon cancer in Oregon. Later, while looking for another leadership role, I took on a project for a food powdering company, doing continuous improvement and supervisory work. After significantly improving their full clean turn time capabilities across their production lines, a large but older corporation reached out to hire me. They had seventeen sites. Due to their size, I figured there would be a lifetime of work potential with them. They represented a long-term challenge for me. The division I initially worked in had five sites. And while they hired me to lead continuous improvement efforts, I was also given leadership over maintenance and manufacturing. Again, I found myself doing the work of many, getting paid for one. I improved productivity by 40% in the first six months. It was the first time I had ever had a CEO ask me if we needed to produce that fast. Again, the sales team was riding the struggle bus. A month later, I was able to ISO certify that operation. However, during that process, I discovered that the engineering team at that site was operating under old standards.

Luckily, their specification standards were more than three times the minimum, so safety was unaffected. Over-production waste added cost to their process, so their efforts were to improve efficiency to overcome this cost/waste and become more competitive. This was wonky. However, the industry requires great costs to re-certify new products and update old ones when changed. And they had a myriad of products, which would have been an extravagant cost to synthesize the product to an adequate level. Worse, this operation was not working from current and relevant procedures or processes; ragged, decade-old documents were archived and were not being referenced. I cleaned up these and over fifty pages of OSHA safety write-ups. For me, engagement with the people on the team was vital. Getting to know everyone and building a relational bridge opened communication that allowed the team to get to the actual root cause of their issues. The team did not appreciate the plant manager, but I could not fault him; his background was not in leading manufacturing teams previously. We got along well, and he allowed me access to improve his site. I saved his site a lot of money by covering three management roles simultaneously to resurrect their reliability. I created an operations plan for him before the ISO certification, which would bring continuity to his entire operation. Doing this saved about two hundred and fifty thousand dollars in waste by year's end. We were on track for four hundred thousand dollars, except I had to go to Ohio for a month to help fix another plant struggling with shipping. During that time, the plant manager struggled to sustain our progress in reducing the scrap rate. This is why engagement cannot be taken for granted. A team will not appreciate you more when you engage less. Genuine and intentional engagement is critical to sustainment and training those in key leadership roles in continuous improvement tools and techniques. You cannot be successful in transforming your organization without training your team. It can be detrimental if you do not provide excellent training.

I volunteered to help other sites within the broader organization with their improvement efforts. I led a kaizen event in Ohio. I led a team that increased shipping capacity by forty-eight thousand dollars more each day. That company has yet to rival this level of improvement before or since by one continuous improvement effort. That site was two and a half million dollars behind on shipping orders.

Approaching the end of 2018, one of the sites in North Carolina was struggling. Their plant manager walked out on the plant. He and his core leadership team quit. This happened so fast that the company's president needed more time to arrive and work out the issues with him. Later, I would hear that he had left a four-page resignation letter. I was not privy to the letter, but I assume he called out everything under the sun as a reason to go. The division president had me come down for a day to survey the plant and assess what I thought about its status. I did this and provided him with a four-page report, ironically, a couple of days later, about what was not working. While there, I engaged with people who knew what was happening, what was being neglected, and what should be happening. According to people locally, the CEO had not visited the site in over five years. A few weeks later, the company's president asked me if I wanted to run the plant. I said yes and gave him a two-page report on my game plan to improve the site, and within a month, I wound up in North Carolina to run the site. The North Carolina site was second to last out of seventeen facilities in the broader corporate fold. I mobilized the team to erase over two hundred thousand dollars in backlog orders and improve productivity. Our performance raised our status from fifteenth to fourth in three months. This got the attention of the owners, who thought they would have had to shut the plant down previously.

While in North Carolina, I applied all the methods in this book. The corporate accountants said the plant had not seen an operational profit from that site in many years. The North Carolina site was underwhelming regarding the tools, the machines, and the infrastructure available and intact. The site was the worst working environment I had ever seen. It looked like it had been abandoned after a bombing raid. It was dark, dank, and neglected. The manner of the people resembled the site condition; hopelessness was written all over their faces. The entire operation was in a sorry state. I learned that a person died a few years earlier, sucked into two massive belt rollers. Knowing that walking through the site was awful to me. However, that site had a coachable and hungry pool of employees who, at their core, had hearts as big as the moon. Applying all the necessary tools of daily management, continuous improvement, and lean manufacturing, the energy and effort of those people -following the vision I laid out produced the success that they achieved. I told the corporate sales team to put on their Acme rocket roller skates and get ready for an increase in our productivity. The corporate sales team ignored me. I instructed my internal customer support representative to reach out on a usual basis to let the customers know we had more capacity to produce if they needed more products. This worked; who knew that old-fashioned communication and a fearless desire to serve would garner positive results; we did. The CSR and I had a weekly morning conversation to find which customers to contact. The corporate sales leader would go on about how awful the site was despite our clear month-over-month improved standings. Deep down, I knew something was off about all of it. My team improved their performance until the corporate sales team ran out of steam to keep the orders coming in. This gave ownership no choice but to sell off the site. I discovered that they wanted to shut that plant down all along. Connecting the dots, I realized they did not expect me to turn that plant around. And I figured they told the corporate sales team to drag their feet. If so, that is a disingenuous way of treating people who work hard on teams. Why can you trust me? Because I will fight for your wins no matter what external challenges affect you and your team. I will give you the truth, hold you accountable, and you will always know where we stand. I do not play politics or games dealing with people's lives. And it all comes from my heart. If those folks had read my resume, they would have known that I had never failed before to turn a fledgling operation into a reliable producer. Imagine if their efforts aligned with mine to make that site a long-term success. They would still be making a profit from it and other sites. However, we would not be talking now, would we?

I returned to the original plant I was servicing in Tennessee at the start of 2020. I was promoted to corporate continuous improvement leader. I serviced a few more kaizen projects, but as I returned to the Tennessee site after being away for over a year in North Carolina, I noticed that the other leadership teams had not maintained the improvements I had led for them over the previous two years. Their employees were unhappy with them, and the organizational culture was eroding. This was odd and in stark contrast to the North Carolina team. The North Carolina team had many more obstacles working against them, yet even in a sell-off state, they steamed with conviction like a locomotive.

When COVID hit, that company prepared for the worst, working people a few days a week, slashing projects, and people of which I was one because I was the last one added to the corporate fold, ironically. I was the first convenient sacrifice at the corporate level. The site leader told me that either that or the local plant would have to lay off five long-term employees. The cutbacks became a blessing in my life, and I am thankful. Helping improve organizations throughout my career has taught me much about people, their sociology, psychology, organizational culture, and motives.

Developing people in organizations to empower themselves has been a cumulative lesson over the past thirty-plus years. I have been where you are, and despite the sometimes-austere roads traveled, the wisdom and lessons I have experienced and learned will bear you good fruit. However, I realized I would have to live another three thousand years to improve organizations using a linear site-to-site approach. With that in mind, I am choosing to follow a different path to help as many people as possible by providing what is needed to allow everyone to transform their organizations and develop their teams. Organizations offer unique products and services, but let's be frank: a value stream is a value stream. For me, it has all been about the math of our humanity playing itself out when we give it a chance by steering it positively instead of letting it swerve everyone off the path into the weeds, leaving us dazed and confused as to why and how it all happened. My approach is simple: make everything work more effectively so everyone can be more fruitful. And this approach goes into every area of life we humans may experience.

This is a top-view look at the experiences of my life. There is considerably more. More profoundly, intrinsic moments like the birth of my children and grandchildren, love, adventure, and heartbreak have all educated and informed my life's journey. This is true in all our lives. Like matter, though, there is more space than substance between the particles. In that space, life has been a reflective experience of learning, doing, reflecting, appreciating, loving, changing, growing, and being thankful. This is truly why you can trust me; I care.

Chapter 4

What's Love Got to Do with It

What is needed before you embark on a journey to improve your organizational culture? First, have an even-handed, fair, loving, and kind balance in your nature. As a leader, you must bring your highest and best energy. You can only have high expectations of people by consistently presenting your best. Consistency with our attitude can be challenging. We all hit walls of frustration. That is ok; take a breath, listen, understand the drivers, and perform what I call 'energy judo.' Turn your problem into 'our problem'. Because when others have problems, guess what? They are your problems, too. It's just the way it is. People mentally put an electric fence around others' issues as if they were not their own, so they are unaffected. There is only partial truth to this. If you are part of the team, any problem is everyone's problem. If you are an organization of one person, then this does not apply. Everyone else, it does. You cannot benefit from success and insulate yourself from the challenges. You just cannot. That is what it means to take full accountability and ownership. You own your team and what they value, and they own you and your struggles, too. This is why you must be doing what you love. Performing well requires that we love what we do. You will not always love everyone on your team, but you can love that they have a family and make an impact for the good in the world, and that is worthy enough to keep trying and building.

Making great products and providing excellent service is your purpose. Properly aligning with your purpose can bring your highest energy and love to the team, the customer, and the organization. Your team must align with the same purpose, as illustrated in Figure A5. When out of alignment with purpose, sustaining the benefits of transformation will be a struggle, and customers will lose. Many have generalized people in the military negatively, as militant. This is not so. Military members perform at high levels because they are empowered, developed through training, and accountable for their conduct twenty-four hours a day. Few in the solar system beyond law enforcement and the medical community have lived with that social responsibility. Further, and most importantly, they have a passion for freedom, health, and life that pulls on their highest motivation - their purpose to serve humanity. Doesn't everyone feel the same accountability toward their families? I suppose there are examples we can imagine: the educator doing illegal drugs, the county administrator who steals office supplies, the retiree hacking into your internet, and the mail carrier who steals and cashes your checks, all random examples of things that would shock us until they show up in our news at night. However, don't we always see this in the news, someone always willing to go too far or do far worse? This is why it is so important that your passion and your motivation to follow it must be strong because you will get bored otherwise and venture down dangerous, irresponsible pathways; like the drunk driver, once you cross that line, there is no coming back if an entire family's life is turned upside down in a collision. This can be anyone, and do not miss hearing me; people in the military are just as susceptible to failure as anyone. But not everyone reminds themselves how important living toward your passion, toward love, is. So, I am doing it now; I am reminding you. Life is no fairytale, but living and growing toward your ideal can be so much more incredible when you feel it inside of you. If you need a motivator to hold you on a path, do it for your family, friends, community, and culture. Be a hero to anyone doing anything from giving someone thirsty -some water or holding a door, sharing a smile, offering a thank you, or listening to someone tell you about their demanding day. You do not have to cure cancer tomorrow to make a difference, but you do have to work on curing yourself, cutting out what does not matter and strengthening what is weak. Each day, we must prove it, be consistent and persistent, and seek out the possible.

You are the puzzle piece to our collective puzzle that brings everyone's existence into clarity when you play your part. How do you know if you are playing your part? Your customers are served, appreciative, and thankful for what you do. If you are a buyer, ensure you are voicing and affirming appreciation and building and growing your organizational connections. Remember, your customers, your team, and the health of your organization are your grading scale to measure your motivation and the capacity of what love looks like because you are taking part. We get what we give. Are we giving enough from our hearts? Only you can answer that question. Only you move the momentum of love you can control, and we need you. The world needs you.

Before measuring your organization's current state, you must establish your internal state and determine your leadership team's current state. It would help if you made the hard choice to release any toxic team members. It would help if you allowed those not aligned with your organization's purpose to depart respectfully. Anyone thwarting your customers' ability to grow and thrive is the answer to that question. Similarly, suppose your organization is toxic, and its product and service hurt customers. In that case, you must separate your good self from anything nefarious, manipulative, or hurtful, as in any toxic personal relationship. Why would your professional life be worth any less to you?

So now you might be asking what love has to do with it. Especially if we must let go of those who, by actions, words, and deeds, have chosen not to bring their highest good -their highest self to the organization. Let us be clear: We are not talking about requiring perfection. But the love we must show by what we do must protect the journey of those who want to be on our team first. Anyone hurting your family would not be allowed to stay in your home, so why would it be any different in your organization? Love is a choice; reform all who make that choice and let go of those who do not value what the team values. To grow a healthy organizational culture, we must lead with love. The lesson is that some will have to develop more love in their lives, perfecting, not perfection. Love is in the coaching, and love is being coachable. A team must embody the attributes of love and be bound together with respect, hope, humility, and grace.

Let us now establish what genuine customer service is about. First, get a blank piece of paper, an easel, or a whiteboard and write a large C in the middle of the open area. Around that large 'C,' then write smaller 'c's in a clock-like position around the large 'C' in a circular manner, as shown in Figure A6. Explain to your team that the large 'C' represents your primary customer. These customers use your product and or service. You and your entire team must understand that every ounce of effort and energy is put forth to ensure that your primary customer's quality needs are met. Furthermore, stress to your team that all deliveries will be on time as requested or ordered. Let your team know that no excuse, past, present, or future, is acceptable for letting down your customers. Have them focus on ensuring that all proper prior planning and execution occur to fulfill that as a daily standard. This theme will also drive your daily management walk, starting with your daily management board, as illustrated in Figure A8. Next, draw your team's attention to the smaller 'c's around the larger one. Ask your team by show of hands; how many have kids? Ensure they leave their hands raised. Next, ask how many of them have parents. Again, have those people also leave their hands raised. Then, ask, how many of them have grandparents? Next, how many contribute to private civic and or religious organizations? Then, ask how many people support someone ill in a retirement home, home, or hospital. Then ask, how many of them support the community? Then, ask, how many of them impact the livelihood of each team member by performing their jobs well? Let your team know that everything and everyone is connected and that what they do matters! We may not acknowledge it every day. When we perform well, we rise. This is how we demonstrate love. Let your team know they serve customers every moment they spend in service in your organization. Love starts as a motive for our desire; good outcomes occur when we act on it. The story of our humanity has proven this out in instances where humanity has risen above the Frey.

Assessing and then taking proper actions as leaders should also originate from a source of love. Think of your Love for family, community, and social connections. Think of what you appreciate in your life. Empower and liberate your team to show how creative they can be and how well they can do. Leaders who operate on cruise control or for selfish, self-serving motives project the energy of lack (never having enough), which also sends a carrier signal to everyone that 'we are in a state of lack.' A big part of the lack is the need for more appreciation for what they and the team have already accomplished well. Build on your wins, not on the malaise of negativity. The world offers plenty of negativity without systematizing it. Over time, after feeling punched in the face with negativity daily, your team loses a little more passion and patience for everything. Take heed; do not become a caricature of ignorance in your organization. Some leaders think they are struggling because they have not figured something out. Figure your attitude out before you start making or expecting attitude changes to appear in your organization magically. Create momentum by constantly inspiring, growing, encouraging, and mentoring your team. Meld this approach into your daily interactions. That is the best first thing to do where no outside tools are required. A sense of humor goes a long way. Free your team by having some fun. If your team performs well now, put them at ease, get to know them, and discover their challenges. Then, help and encourage them. If you have pets, children, or parents, or if you grow a garden, the key to growing them is to feed them. Feed them your kindness, care, energy, and, at the core, your love. It is the same in your organization if you desire to grow beyond your past achievements. You cannot serve two masters. Leaders must choose everyone else first. This is the attribute of all the best leaders in history.

If we love our primary and secondary customers, then it is blatantly clear that answering the question of what love has to do with it -is this; 'love has everything to do with it.' It is your reason and purpose and should be your prime motivator as a leader or team member. We need it to sustain or grow. If we want to transform anything, we must choose the love inside us as our primary emotive force. The love story aspect of developing a healthy organizational culture should feel intuitive. It requires us to see love in other than just romantic ways. It means seeing love as the embodiment of good growth and the critical life force that pulls our humanity forward. It is what we need and want more of to grow every aspect of culture and everyone in it. A premise we should follow is that it is not good if it is not suitable for everyone. A good idea does not hurt people. In an inverse sense, love is the healing antidote we need. Love can transform everyone and everything for the better. However, love also seems to get ignored over every other codependent distractive solution that can be imagined. If we want this love story, our lives, to mean something, we must align our thoughts and behaviors toward good outcomes. Negative expectations and apathy bring about hardship, betrayal, pain, suffering, and oppression. Isn't it time we give love its day and get great results? Let me take this time to remind you that love costs you nothing. Even the biggest cheapskate ever likes 'free.'

Being seen, acknowledged, respected, and cared for helps us push away everything that distracts us from our path. Take your most cynical friend to a heartwarming, teary, emotional movie where brokenness finally ends in victory and where love is shown. Your friend will be internally realigned for a time -in touch with their heart. Later, though, outside, after you leave the theater, negative forces in the world trap your friend's ego by getting your friend's attention, then realigning them to their cynical norm. Someone cuts them off in traffic, and your friend is now depleted of that open, loving force that so enveloped them just prior. Who has not been here personally at some point in life? Imagine yourself holding love inside you as a cheerful companion, letting it speak as your new inner voice. We are human; you will not always feel love. Give yourself a chance to recover a 'good' state of being by understanding that anything, good or bad, is an opportunity. This does not mean we should do bad things or have bad attitudes by choice. It means that when caught in a moment of weakness, recognize it as a weakness and make an adjustment. Opportunities often come to us in disguise. Negative actions can be a source of pain ignited by moments of emotional weakness. Do not pay anger forward by cutting someone else off in traffic. Instead, with intention, recognize it, center yourself, go for a walk, take a deep breath, and remove your emotions from the situation. If you consciously choose to be a loving human as a norm in life, the results will be seen, and the effects will be felt in significant ways with constancy over time.

Everything is a choice. Transforming an organization will take intentionality to lead or be led. Team members will find value in intentionally manifesting excellent outcomes by making good choices daily. We do not achieve and sustain our successes personally or professionally alone. Transformation is more than just a physical and process change; it is an immersive way of thinking and feeling the collective humanity of your team all the time. If you are wound too tight trying to scrape off lofty ego and pride, you need to unwind at the gym, go for a walk, take a run, swim, meditate, do yoga, get counseling, or whatever it takes for you to engage and contribute to a centered partnering way.

Hold these images in your mind and heart: the birth of your children and grandchildren, the love of parents, siblings, spouses, partners, friends, pets, sunrises, nature, and ice cream, to name a few. Who can be mad or upset while eating ice cream? That is right, no one, unless you drop it, of course. There are many things you love in life. Keep them close to your heart and in your head as a continuous reminder. Let them move you in good ways. These are your sources of joy and happiness. They make everything you do possible. I think of my grandparents and people who loved me and have passed away, as well as my family, children, grandchildren, and friends whom I carry with me as if they are adventuring life alongside me. They are a living conscience that helps me to keep my compass pointing as true north as possible. While deployed, I would think of my family and all the families counting on us to do our jobs right and get everyone home safely. I had one particularly harrowing experience over the ocean, and the first thing that came to mind was the families of the crew I was refueling, getting the aircrew home safely. Thankfully, I was able to fix the problem, and everyone returned safely.

Pragmatically, sadly, we must acknowledge that some people love fighting with other people and love to hate. Their inner pessimism, cynicism, and criticism haunt them, and they love sharing it. The past plagues them, all the failures and all their hurts. Naturally, we must empathize. We must empathize as they transform, overcome, and then integrate their behavior and shadow, not inflict that pain upon everyone else. We cannot belabor those who do not choose to integrate their shadow. Otherwise, they will continue introducing toxicity to your team, whether ready or not. Those fighting their shadow must be encouraged to fight their shadow. They must ask for help if needed and be intentional on their transformational journey, where they are clear that the 'we' is a priority over the 'me' because I am working on my own 'me.' For all customers.

Chapter 5

The Great Reset

Before shifting to improve your organizational culture, reset and forget past performance. The baggage of the past is too heavy to carry. Instead, see the past as data you have already collected to help you go forward knowing how you once were so that you will see how you improved. Communicate to your team that from this day forward, all that matters is what all of you do right now -going forward. Remind them that what matters is that we recommit to our efforts to serve our primary customers to the best of our ability. Let your team know that despite their many concerns, potential doubts, and need for resources, you will diligently drive to fix what is broken. You will help to improve and support the team. Let your team know what some of those things are. Then, tell your team not to let you forget these things for accountability. Let your team know that 'we must all be accountable to one another in everything we do.' This may sound elementary. Sometimes, your solutions are as simple as being vulnerable, honest, and trustworthy to your team to get them to be open, honest, and reliable. If your 'care' factor is not high, or worse, if you are fake, your team will fake it to make it and play a role, act as if in a drama, to get through whatever you are telling them. You must genuinely care and have a passion for your organizational mission. That demonstration is how you provide a space for your team to be authentic and inspired so they can respond kindly to customers. This way, your team won't feel like they must pretend to be kind and care about customers and the team.

Place four easels or four large 30-inch sticky notes in the corner of your lunchroom or large meeting room. Larger organizations may need more than one meeting if the number on your team is large. Place these large sticky notes on the walls. Have your team form into lines in front of the sticky notes on the wall. Have each team member write a bullet statement about an improvement they feel is needed, wanted, or desired. Have your team members sign their initials shortly after the bullet statement. Everyone should contribute at least one idea. This is their chance to publicly submit what they think is important in front of their peers. This gives your team a voice to be heard constructively in the open. If anyone on your team has been in high complaint mode everywhere except where it counts, your team will see if the notorious complainers put their complaints on the sticky note. This will boil out notorious complainers and drama magnets when they are seen not stepping up to express themselves. There is no need to comment or discuss ideas during this collection time. This time is strictly to collect their inputs, which you will review later. Build this around a large team, introductory, or team training already scheduled.

Why don't we discuss all their ideas in an open forum? There is a time for that; this is not that time. We can all agree that open complaining without a solution keeps everyone in a puddle of lack and pointless discord. You do not want to create a forum for pointless complaining. Do everything constructively. Observe who does not write an idea. Anyone self-dismissing without engaging in this process will likely be those with a deep emotion around not being heard in the past. Later, give them a chance to contribute by conversing with them. Do not be punitive. This is a reset, a restart, a new beginning. You want to know what people think and believe. You will get a different perspective, a nugget of truth, and perhaps a great idea. While addressing your entire team, tell them they need to increase their pace safely by just a little going forward. They already know that the organization needs to improve; asking them is a way to ensure backsliding does not happen further. If you never asked, you never asked them; therefore, you don't want them to increase their cadence. Ensure they know this is not a trade-off for the customer's expected quality. Let them know that anything preventing this will be the first constraint you remove. Use your leadership team to ensure it gets done immediately. Do not linger on removing constraints; be highly engaged in that process. Once constraints are removed, productivity and quality can improve, and results can be monitored and followed up. At your next meeting, show appreciation to the person or people whose ideas immediately impacted the value stream. Ensure you communicate proactively to your team so that planned downtimes occur smoothly and quickly. Your team should understand that every minute wasted, you can never get back. This is as true in life as it is in work.

Ensure your proactive and aggressive maintenance team keeps equipment inspected, serviced, and operating well. Use radios for immediate and swift resolution of issues. Radios are used to provide resources quickly and report the status of repaired equipment and other issues. Radio can help resolve other matters swiftly by reducing wasted time searching for people or answers. If leadership teams are in meetings and issues arise functionally in your organization, fixing those issues takes precedence and priority where critical decision-making is required. Downtime is a waste. Be proactive, persistent, and diligent.

If you have members on your team who, for whatever reason, have seemed to lose hope in the organizational change effort, reassure them and engage regularly by incorporating a Gemba walk, which will allow you to reassure, encourage, coach, and praise your team. Praise often as praise is worthy. Praise should not be your weakness. Giving praise is powerful. However, do not use praise too frivolously so that it loses its value. Be honest, be genuine.

The ideas I spoke of earlier that you collected from your team in the meeting:

1. Put those into spreadsheets so you can track your progress to resolve those.
2. Prioritize that list.
3. Weight your priorities in this way: Safety, productivity, and morale.

Do not put morale items last; you will never address them, and people will stagnate. Additionally, this sends the wrong message about where your priorities lie. Instead, work both constraints of productivity and morale with equal exuberance. Work on your list and provide regular updates. Your updates to your entire team should be with kudos to those who find breakthrough solutions. They can be individuals or small teams within your organization, such as a Kaizen team.

The feedback and how you collect it can take place in many ways. A straightforward way is to use a WINS diagram, as illustrated in Figure A7. Divide a blank page into four quadrants. In one quadrant, you will have your team write down organizational weaknesses. Have them write down three to five bullet statements. You will have three more quadrants to fill. The next quadrant should be improvement opportunities. The next quadrant will be needed resources. The last quadrant will be strengths List three to five each. Provide these to employees to complete after a safety or other planned meeting. Do not hand them out to be taken and brought back later. Afterward, you will collect and add these to a risk assessment matrix. The WINS diagram is a qualitative data collection device. Have supervision, department management, functional team members, and the rest of your leadership team complete these. Have everyone put the date, print their name, and sign the sheet before handing it in. This information can be grouped, analyzed, and addressed after you prioritize them. Prioritize according to the number of like bullet statements, grouping them from most to least. There will be topics and issues raised that you should fix immediately. Do not cross-share the individual sheets among your team members. Once prioritized, the issues on a spreadsheet can be shared with the team. Compare to see if your leadership team's bullets align with the team's. You will get insight quickly if there are interpersonal issues that you should resolve independently. Manage these gently, sincerely, and with the intent that all parties heal and grow forward together. You may find an opportunity to create allies where once there were those in conflict. Be creative and fearless; ask your team what they would do differently knowing what they now know. This is a great data collection opportunity. Some people will give you gold, some filler, but you will undoubtedly find gold in the form of more opportunities to mine out success.

Hitting the reset button means no punitive actions for past mistakes in conducting and executing operational plans. Doing this will open your team up. The team will now have nothing to hide. All of you can own missed opportunities and failures. You will create a new team bond. It is essential that taking ownership and accountability is not penalized. Let the team know that revealing what was swept under the rug in the path is healthy if your team is to have a positive reset that lasts. Finding out about things later will be a step backward. You can only have a solid foundation if the facts are known, and past issues are resolved. If your team backslides, do not panic. Regroup, resolve, reset, and take off again.

Chapter 6

Dealing with Our Own Human Nature

Dealing with our human nature and the many fractals that make up who we are can be wonderful and frustrating. We must take ownership of the fact that at any given time, we can be uncooperative with each other. We can give less than our best to those who know us well. We can all fall short of being positive. We can destroy what has taken years to build in a matter of moments. However, each of us must contend with ourselves and own our emotions. We must choose our attitude and behavior continuously, from sunup to sundown. We are continually assessed and evaluated by our behaviors and attitudes. Sitting in our chair quietly, a person's mind will flow to the current events that encapsulate our lives. A teenager, a spouse, pets, neighbors, and even late-arriving mail can draw us into a dystopian maze through which we must find our way. The filter of goodness inside each of us protects us from mental breaks that are a marvel to humanity. Though I'm not sure, we know what that filter is. We humans have a long way to go in dealing with our collective human nature. The high use of legal and illegal substances that people use to numb themselves to life's realness only serves to kick the collective can down the road, where dealing with core human issues, needs, and suffering is concerned. Even those who overly task saturate their lives are running from something. Sadly, watching sports, movies, and television distract us from each other. Spouses, friends, parents, families, communities, schools, and organizations can also find clever ways to distract themselves and us from reality. Slow down and ask a simple question: Is what I am doing now distracting me from a greater priority, concern, or life necessity? If yes, stop, breathe, and think about what is bothering you. Then, formulate an approach where everyone can win, address it, and overcome it healthily.

Everyone chooses to respond to each other and our world differently. Some people may be enraged when cut off in traffic and yet remain indifferent when an ambulance flies hurriedly past doing the same. Our inner values and ethics about fairness and what is just are sometimes inexplicably subjective. Common rights are plain, or are they? Our thoughts, words, deeds, and resulting actions are choices that create outcomes. Our response to those words and actions also has consequences. We are all climbing a tree with many branches with fruit at the end of them. We are always presented with a choice in what we say and do that allows us to either attain the fruit on our branch or prevent us from getting the fruit that opens us up to ascending to the next higher branch. We should be steadily progressing up the tree. The choices we make determine our progress. Some of those choices are overcoming our fears. Some of those choices are helping others to be fearless. On the darker side, some need to get out of others' way and stop blocking people from happily pursuing the fruits that reside on the branches of their lives. Still, some sit on the lower branches, consumed in toxic codependent or addictive behaviors that numb and swallow up their lives, preventing them from progressing toward greater fulfillment. Not choosing to progress past the restraints that reside in the self is the self-sabotage and stuck-ness that traps people. It boils down to making a choice: control the horses of ego and pride by taking the reins or let them drag you by your feet across rocky terrain until you have nothing left. What will you choose? Apply this beyond function and to the behavior of the heart and mind. Life assures that you live it and provides you with intertwined tests and opportunities for rebirth, second chances, and more to see the sunrise on the fruit you seek.

Are you a catalyst for yourself and others in life? If you are not this way in life, how can you be a catalyst for others in your organization, family, community, and onward? Perhaps no one has been a catalyst for you in your life. Set your vision on who you truly want to be and how you want to contribute, and just be that. You will eventually manifest your life once you are aligned with what you want to be, even if you have not become it yet. See it in your mind's eye and become what you imagine. There is no less truth about this with your organization, how you want your team to thrive, and more. Everything must first come from the vision you set in your mind.

We are all in this interconnected loop of constantly choosing our attitudes and behaviors. We are not a natural rock of constancy but rather a bucket of water that we must keep balanced and stable so that the waters of life do not slosh out of control while we navigate the road of life. Some have only walked a few feet, keeping their water calm and stable as they moved their bucket in a straight line on level ground. Others with experience have walked over mountains, through jungles, swam oceans, and more with their bucket. Who would you discern to be wiser about leading you? How are you becoming a better leader walking only in a straight line on level ground? Who do you think you are helping? This same analogy applies to a team member; whom are you helping to be too linear in your self-development? It is easy to judge someone else by pointing at the water; is it sloshing or not? However, see the context of the journey of that individual or team, and instead of criticality, show empathy and help. For owners, invest in your teams and sites, and you will see progress. Course corrections are vital for us when the journey and the ability to maintain stable waters are out of alignment. Finding alignment is no less true professionally than it is in personal relationships of any kind. One might discern deception and disloyalty, where selfishness is the greater truth. It depends on which branch you are observing and what ideals are realistic to expect. Now observe yourself, figure out what is realistic for you, and does that align with who you want to be? Does this vision align with your team? Does it align with your relationships? What needs to change? We can discern too lightly sometimes and fail to take advantage of an opportunity to correctly identify the root cause, conflict, or problem. If you string too many hasty judgments and fail to discern situations accurately, you will find that greater issues arise from those hasty judgments. Use Figure A4 to determine where some conflicts may be, and some suggested starting points to understand and then resolve them.

We have a choice to make about our attitudes and our behaviors. We have an option to avoid judgment and the frustration that follows. We must wisely see beyond the veil of what we think we understand about people. If an employee shows poor behavior or questionable behavior, leaders also have a choice to make about the attitudes and responsive actions they take. If the leader holds heavy judgment to squash an employee at the drop of a pin, this will affect the team worse than the result of the initial infraction itself. This is why using a light touch when dealing with non-catastrophic problems is important. Employees may be falsely enticed to create a flawed narrative of leaders, too. That is why judgment is not always just. That is why we must choose our words and behaviors wisely, irrespective of our role on the team. We must guard ourselves from being enticed to judge because failing to see the opportunity in every situation is a trap.

It is nearly impossible to prove if an organization's failures are primarily employee or leadership driven. It is best not to obsess over it. Both will create a losing condition for the entire team. A team's failure to correct themselves after coaching stands out as most egregious. Every team has one chance to do it right every day. Every organizational member must let go of yesterday's hurt and instead choose patient optimism and hope as a steady state within.

What do toxic attitudes and uncooperative actions say about us? Are we struggling to dislodge the primordial ooze off our genes? Will we blame everything wrong on our parents and societal conditioning forever? It is time to own our default nature, good, bad, or indifferent, and decide to do what is right without excuse. What is right to a child raised to be a thief by a sociopath? The climb out of our conditioned nature, whatever it is, is a mountain each of us must ultimately climb alone. Growth means that even sociopaths, narcissists, obsessive-compulsive, and lazy people have a long personal journey to understand their nature and answer the big questions. Questions like why do I do and act the way I do? Seek help if you need it.

Are some people faking it? Are some people blending into the group just slightly amused that the more extreme team members in organizations are creating micro-chaotic events? If you want to know where those pay raises went, they went up in smoke with your team's apathy about dealing with insidious organizational chaos. It is time to pay attention and question your nature. What is it about you, irrespective of your role, that is not helping your culture improve? If you are one to hide and not speak up, perhaps it's time to speak up. If you want a just work environment, how about maintaining fairness for all, not just those you fear or the fear of creating disharmony? If you want harmony, sometimes you must fight a little for it. That doesn't mean literal fighting but communication, negotiation, and rational discussion. If we want a better culture, irrespective of what scale we are referring to, we must start changing how we live intelligently from the heart. We must stop running and defending the superficial tendencies within the nature of our internal malware and make being human with the ideals we strive for reality. Correct your code and improve your internal software if you need an analogy -there's one.

Chapter 7

First Do No Harm

First, do no harm. In early Latin, it refers to it being better to do nothing than harm (Riggs, 2021). In everything, there is an immediate choice presented to us. You may find people and organizations that could be a lot better. Some are a mess at a level below what can be seen with the naked eye. This can be in paperwork and communications, for example. Others may be upside down because they don't organize workflows well. Some have insidious behavioral issues interacting in teams. Some organizations have environments that resemble hospital-like conditions to the naked eye, with an undertow of disorganization. If you are the leader of that organization, your frustration level may have topped out. You may not see clearly through the mayhem, becoming angry, upset, or worn thin. You may be ready to quit. Your team members may worsen situations by mirroring the leadership team's frustrations. Teams may think the leadership team is the problem and have given themselves private permission to freestyle their work. Depending on your situation, your entire team has a choice. That choice is to respond reactionarily to make matters much worse or slow it all down and see the lesson presented in these moments. Then, make a second choice: to be wise and decide that you must first choose to do no harm. This is much easier said than done. Other people can interrupt us in the flow of our day. Some people operate in reactionary mode as a norm while others are plagued, constantly being gut-punched by surprise -on cue after solving the last problem, then walking into the next one. Some of you have been broken down in installments over time by overload and overwhelm, grasping for any solution in reach. Are we surprised by the high employee turnover rate and the revolving door of leadership changes?

It is essential to apply 'Do No Harm' to us first. Who benefits if we give up on ourselves? Who benefits when we give up on other people at the height of emotion, in the moment? We must slow it down and build our understanding of the situation at hand, understand why something occurred, and take intelligent, methodical steps to correct and prevent what has just occurred from happening in the future. Afterward, we may have to unravel or peel the onion to reveal where we may have failed our team and understand why some problems or mistakes occurred in the first place. We should take an internal personal and professional inventory to know how our part could have alleviated the conditions that allowed errors to occur, even errors of others. Leaders at all levels must evaluate, own, and rectify. This same process must be a team-wide mindset. However, this mindset is not a light switch we can turn on or off. We must be able to learn to do it. We will only serve well if we ease up on ourselves and own our part along the path of making small and large mistakes. While we do not want to crucify ourselves, taking ownership and accountability is a growth mindset that frees you to create conditions you want in the future. A person may require correction, training, punitive repercussions, pay for the damage, or conversation to delve further into the 'why' something occurred. Which of these sounds the most humane and the most effective to you? What approach would you prefer? What would you and your team appreciate and respect? First, do no harm thinking allows fresh air to blow into an organization, allowing healthy problem-solving and innovation. This will enable us to understand how people think, what they value, where they failed, and where we may have failed them.

Do we assume too much? We hired this team, right? So, who failed? Giving in to your reactive emotions and leaping to the termination stage means you both lose; neither of you learn or grow from the lesson of a situation. Organizations have used a 'failing forward' model to build their standards, a default approach. When someone makes a mistake, the organization creates new steps and policy directives to prevent it. Over time, a policy catalog has been built on the buried bones of people who were let go, fired, and discarded. How necessary was that? What does that say about organizational leaders' ability to grow, train, and develop their teams? What does it say about organizations that don't take the time to look ahead? How many careers could have been saved with a bit of forethought and an ounce of preventive planning?

Some create a go-no-go scenario where letting people go has become as routine as the guillotine removing the head off the chicken. No one gives it much of a second thought anymore, finding it easier to turn employees into devils starving for direction and growth at their core. The chain reaction of this type of approach also means that customers turn these organizations out by the same guillotine process. The organizational leaders continue to suffer the same fate; the cycles are constantly repeating. Wouldn't it be nice to stop this merry-go-round effect?

If the bad stuff used to roll downhill in the past, indeed, it rolls oddly twice as fast uphill, where leaders are handicapped by their ineptitudes and inability to grow and develop themselves and their teams. This hurts the customer. We do not have to take this long-term route if we first center ourselves and realize that 'Doing No Harm' allows us to explore, delve, grow, reform, and repair situations, leaving the guillotine to rust in museums that display our social evolution. Nearly everything we do, and encounter can be teaching moments. Reflecting on my time in the Air Force, I'm reminded that if your standards and expectations are clear from the start, you avoid most overt employee mistakes. We must remember and communicate that organizations are not employees' daycares or personal psychologists. There is a giant leap from a daycare to a college or university where people want to be there because they want to grow and develop.

Like it or not, organizations are a place of higher learning. Organizations with an employee development program, a system or operational plan that lays out how the organization works and explains the standards and expectations, are as organized as most institutions of higher learning. If leaders feel like they are running an adult daycare, their employee engagement level is too low or lacks meaningful purpose. While running an organization, you should regularly receive proactive communication from your employees in a constructive way. New employees may see giving constructive feedback as the same as whining and complaining. It is more than that. New employees must know your system for communicating issues, problems, or constraints. Funnel your employees' emotions into constructive, intellectual, documented feedback to help your organization. If no one will write it down and sign their name, you must ask how important an idea is if no one claims or owns it. Further, you must ask if bringing something up was to solve an issue. Delineate between the constructive contribution of ideas and distractive complaining. Those who want to perpetuate drama alone will hate documenting issues. The ego requires unresolved issues to pile on so that a modest harmony never occurs and ensures the team never delves below the water line of the superficial aspects of group interaction. Everyone must leave their egos at the door. Leaving your ego at the door will get you many suggested improvements and give your team the breathing room and head space necessary to resolve serious matters. Leaving their ego at the door for your team means what they say will be taken seriously and not seen now as whining or complaining. Implement what is practical, but never discard any ideas from your team. You will need them. Transforming organizations means we must break old cycles, update old methodologies, and replace them with new approaches.

Value ideas. We cannot transform if we are not disciplined enough to keep from doing intentional harm. First, do no harm to your organization or anyone in it. Sounds simple, right? Conversely, it is essential to remember that just because something is uncomfortable or different does not mean it will turn out badly. We cannot run from conflict or difficulty. Avoiding it creates an unhealthy snowball. Humans are emotionally and spiritually complex. If you are unprepared or just two-dimensional in your thinking and approach, failure will be there to gobble up your organization's culture and effectiveness. Let me be clear: Don't stay in toxic situations, either.

Clarity is king. Being open, respectful, honest, and accepting is a positive first step. If this is not reciprocated, you have done your due diligence to set the stage, and from there, you can choose to evolve or resolve any conflict or situation in the organization. This applies just as acutely to leadership. Leaders must exemplify the standards they expect the entire team to abide by. The result of inconsistent leadership team behavior is a fertilizing of office politics and power struggles that will only disrupt your organization from achieving its purpose day to day and in the long term. Likewise, the entire team must be cohesive. Ensure everyone agrees upon the behaviors and goals the team has prioritized. There is no room for individuals to conduct their parallel agendas. The entire team must first do no harm by leaning into the purpose and focus of the organization. This means that the team must be proactive and self-motivated. If a leader must drag the team around and constantly wait for members to show up late for meetings or projects, then the team member is doing harm. If the team members are not doing what they are supposed to be doing, they are doing harm. If everyone is not doing all due diligence for the customer, harm is being done. Consciously place the thought in your head as you perform in the day or respond to your team, 'Am I doing harm or about to do harm?' Take inventory of the thoughts you think and the words you speak as a prelude to the actions you take. This way, you are less likely to do harm. Do not get me wrong, misunderstandings are possible. However, to do no harm, we cannot assume it was intentional because everything I do afterward in response will do more harm -and on and on the wheel turns everyone harming everyone by reacting instead of owning the mistake, correcting what was said or done, and moving on healthily. All this can result from a misunderstanding if we do not manage it with care, like adults.

Chapter 8

Self-Significance

We may not admit it, but we measure ourselves against other people. People compare their lives to family members, friends, community members, peers at work, different social groups, and leaders. They compare and justify how successful they are or are not and how happy their lives appear to be, marking their success by their abundance over others in the community. This is an illusion. Some of the happiest people are thankful, appreciative, loving, and have extraordinarily little. They have found true wealth in their lives, which allows them to manifest anything they want if they genuinely want it.

For most of society, each day starts with a cumulative report card about us. Depending on what we hyper-focus on: relationships with family, friends, significant others, professional relations, organizations, customers, and suppliers- we assess ourselves using everything and everyone as a mirror. We fall into a fallacy of self-judgment on the one hand or jealousy on the other. Both are wrong because both serve to bite into our confidence, break us down internally, play on our feelings of worth, and, depending on what behaviors are gravitated to, a self-affliction, self-victimization prevents them from living fully from their heart. Instead, a superficial mask is donned to ensure the heart and de facto the heart of essential matters, personally and professionally, are never addressed.

Self-judgment in harsh emotional ways is like losing control of a car while driving on an icy road. If we overcorrect, we make the result much worse. This is why we do not let our ego nature inside us drive the car unsupervised. When ego controls, we lack full self-realization. Ego and pride are linked. Your pride is that which thinks it knows everything already and seeks opportunities to self-congratulate or be congratulated by others. At worst, ego and pride prevent us from learning emotional, heartfelt lessons that lead to high levels of self-significance. Conversely, genuine, sincere, and healthy regard for one another's needs can help achieve exceptional self-significance. They see their part in the turning of the infinite loop of life. This is not to say we should not critically review past mistakes; we should. However, we cannot obsessively internalize and weaponize our mistakes against ourselves. When we do, we miss the point; we miss the lesson and value of what we learned by making the mistakes we made. We must refrain from making them again. Because when we hurt ourselves, we hurt others. Instead, make healthy, conscious, and genuine efforts to improve in all areas. Doing so will yield the best results for your personal and professional life. It is okay to make strides. Start with baby steps. Steps, then strides, will eventually lead to healthy leaps toward significant progress.

Your self-image is based on what and how others perceive you, which is reflected in you. How do you see yourself? What are your strengths, and where is your value? Refrain from speeding past that question; make a list. You bring a lot to this world as a unique human being. You have gifts and talents that the world has not seen. Make a list and believe in your worthiness and how much it is rooted in the love you have inside of you. When you see yourself through the lens of love, let your attitude, thoughts, words, and actions flow truthfully and humbly from that core place where good things in your life are born. Then, like a mirror, reflect that into the world.

Chapter 9

You Can Only Control You

Everything we can control starts with first controlling ourselves. Why? Well, look around; who is trying to control you? Here are a few simple ones: Advertisements, corporations, political parties, politicians, government officials, religious leaders, and the unscrupulous are salted and peppered throughout the culture. Simple things like tasty, unhealthy food, useful but unnecessary technical gadgets, and social media are also vying for control over your life and attention. What is the point? Why control you? Controlling your money, time, and attention means you are giving to their needs, security, profit, and, for the egoic, their emotional needs instead of yours and your family's. Reprimand a child and take their electronic device. See what tantrums ensue. Adults, too, get fidgety when their device is outside their reach. In our culture today, our values are not aligned. You do not need much more proof than someone who prioritizes texting over their desire to drive safely, utterly unaware of their next victim up ahead. This is the painful reality. Our priorities and what we value are not always aligned with the greater good; in this example, the people around you are all the other drivers.

It is not just the politicians who manipulate our time, money, and attention. Artists, too, are vying for our time, money, and attention. They are willing to do nearly anything to get it. You get the point; everyone is competing for your resources. Across the spectrum, everyone, in some way, has become an intellectual and emotional supply for other people and systems happy to control your resources in any way possible.

So, let us look inward and ask, who do you control? Are you a person who manipulates others? Are you using your spouse? Are you manipulating your friends? Are you manipulating your family? Are you manipulating your coworkers, your subordinates, or your boss? How about people in your community? How about businesses in your community? Are you manipulating people in your church or civic organizations? Do you subvert others? Do you only subvert those you compete with? Are you obvious about your control? Are you covert, the victim of yourself and others, to get what you want? Are you stealing time, money, and attention - conveniently unaware consciously that you are doing that? Only you know how you come across in the eyes and lives of others around you. Perception is reality. Do you have self-awareness about what your role in the world is? Look in the mirror; who are you? Who are you really? Are you the protagonist or the antagonist in your life story? Are you a friend, or are you the foe? Are you the result of your conditioning? Are you the driver of your own life or the puppet of harmful people and traditions? Have negative experiences jaded you? Have negative experiences made you a negative person, a hopeless person? Have your negative experiences helped you to justify hurting others because you were hurt? Are you self-serving? On the glideslope of existence, do you find yourself on the selfish and self-centered low road, or are you on the nurturing, caring, and supportive high road? If you are on that high road, what are you doing to help those struggling on the low road? Are you a force for good, or are you hiding in the shadows, letting your gifts and talents rot away? These are the important questions we must ask when looking in the mirror to ensure we lean into the good winds of life. We cannot babysit each other; we must grow up. We must improve our organizational culture. Even if you are not struggling directly with the fallout from these behaviors, you may be, indirectly. Regardless, strengthening ourselves and helping our teams improve is a noble cause.

The reason the team rejects external systems is that many of those systems are cold, lack humanity, and come across as superficial. They try to improve productivity without regard for people, their challenges, emotions, suffering, or their struggles. The team quickly comes to an unspoken conclusion that they are being patronized. The team also concludes quickly that the team members, not leadership, are being singled out as the 'problem.' The truth is that the entire team must own all the problems that are ailing the organization. The reaction of the team to reject a new system comes from the head and the heart. It only takes a few naysayers within the team to upset the entire team's trust. Fears come out as doubts, igniting concerns in most of the team. Concerns then escalate into stronger and weightier fears. There is a cognitive dissonance between wanting to improve and not wanting to do what is needed to improve. Transformation is the beginning of the birthing process. You cannot have just the head or only the body come through in the birthing process. The entire body needs to be unified for your team's transformation to be successful. The whole body must endure the process. You must fight through your fears and trust each other as one.

Team members in organizations may 'go along to get along' due to their needs, debts, and survival. They may stay for the paycheck by extension. Some team members leave organizations when the pursuit of excellence is replaced by lip service alone. Team members leave because leadership does not act genuinely toward the path of excellence. It is worse if leaders blame employees while simultaneously dragging their feet toward organizational excellence. When the team sees more care for short-term gains versus long-term growth, red flags begin to be seen by the team. Those with low leadership stamina then lose traction quickly as well.

Leaders may be doing well. However, if team communication is poor, they may have to climb out of a widening and deepening pit of opinion. Leaders may be the benefactors of false projections by a disgruntled team. The converse can also be true. The gravity of our fundamental human nature is to resist change. The desire to avoid being in the eye of why that change is stalling out may elicit unpredictable behaviors as some scramble to avoid taking responsibility. It is always easier to own the current state, the mistake, and the failure and then grow forward from that point. Anything else is just a waste of time and energy. How leaders communicate change is important. Everyone will learn from those lessons if the team is vulnerable and ready to own past failures. Transformation and change require everyone to set their ego aside. The words spoken and the actions taken are your choice alone because only you can control yourself. A question to ask yourselves as a collective team is: Do you see victory as a one-time thing or an ongoing transformation- a lifestyle change or an ongoing approach? The steady approach to transformation will bring you a stream of victories that will help your team well into the future.

The entire world will try to control you if you let it. Your words and deeds are your responsibility alone. No justification exists for sour, manipulative, nefarious, or toxic words and actions. There is no excuse for betrayal, neglect, or lack of support for or from your entire team. Leaders who commit in fractions will hire those who emulate those fractal behaviors and struggle. If you know who your change agents are, they will help you overcome most of the fractal behaviors. Fractal leaders need to be educated, mentored and coached out of the career rut they have dug for themselves. Neglect, bad foresight, and bad situational awareness will erode the organization, creating a team that mirrors that neglect in their performance. If leaders cannot teach, instruct, mentor, coach, or grow people on their team, they will be in big trouble. It would be like hiring a pilot who is afraid of heights but fails to tell anyone until just before takeoff.

Remember that a struggling organization does not mean the employer is abusive or the employees have nefarious intent. This is why we must check our bias at the door and let the reality of what is going on be what we work as a team to overcome. The solution is training and increasing awareness. The complexity of that solution, however, is that the training paradigms of the past may have only dug superficially into the human experience, mildly into human motivation, and barely into the question of what drives us as humans to thrive in organizations. It is superficial to say people are 'just lazy' or 'just do not care' or are 'ignorant' or 'were raised poorly' and more. There may be truths in the shadow of these statements, but only on the surface due to deeper issues that must be dug into by individuals and teams with healing in mind.

Be warned: Employees can create toxic environments without any leadership influence except for taking their hands off the wheel and doing nothing. These bubbles should be burst by people in them, given the choice to transform and reform. No matter the scenario, failing to speak and function as one team instead of worsening an 'us versus them' or leadership versus employee paradigm means you are creating walls of division that will only grow higher. You cannot serve two masters. The customer should be the personification of everyone in the organization, ensuring the team's purpose remains undivided, giving your team the best chance to succeed.

When you control yourself, there are no excuses. There is no turning back once you begin walking this path. We must distinguish challenges when they arise. We cannot start questioning our purpose during our struggles. You control you; it is up to you to guard your speech and actions. When angry and upset, choose words to give you and others an out. Do not assume that there is always nefarious intent. Do not assume someone is taking advantage of you. Do not assume negative things are not going on as well. Let reality show you what reality truly is. Do not assume you understand your team or that your team understands you. Listen to your team, expect them to listen, and reciprocate the respect you give each other. Be clear and find common ground. This is where all your solutions Lay. Do not perpetuate division between anyone, no matter their role. Be professional, be respectful, and expect the same in return. We can have different opinions and approaches. We need a diversity of perspectives to help solve problems when they arise. Be a better planner and be prepared before difficulties come your way.

Everything is a choice. You can choose not to cooperate and fail to engage with your team. You can have a divided purpose and treat people poorly by not training them. You can breathe higher levels of toxicity and reward that toxic drama. You can drive down your personnel retention and waste while endangering the safety of the people on your team. These, too, are choices the team makes every day. Not choosing, not being aware and responsible -is also a choice. It is vitally important that you are not just a reaction but a result of the world that you are interacting in. It would help if you controlled your personal and professional life. You must deliver the best possible outcomes to the world by word and deed. We all need love, respect, creativity, innovation, and hope. Irrespective of background or beliefs, we must rise above our differences and agree to unify ourselves for the future. Along that path, we will find excellent possibilities that lead everyone to thrive in culture. We must stop believing that 'my problems,' 'my fears' are somehow worse or more important than 'your fears' and 'your problems.' We cannot let inefficient, expensive, ineffective thinking, combined with poor behaviors at cross-purposes, stifle growth for anyone.

Chapter 10

Personality

I will not be diving deeply into the psychological influences that arise from underdeveloped cognition of people or disorders that play a part in personality development. The spectrum of good or bad behavior is compared to selflessness versus selfishness. As a primer, I will introduce overarching thoughts and questions we can ask ourselves as individuals and teams. They may seem abrupt and are meant to be direct to help us formulate growth strategies.

Suppose you were to assemble a team of one hundred people using professional skills criteria. How many people with these disorders and challenges might you rhetorically find on your team or teams you have been on?

Anxiety, social phobia, panic, PTSD, OCD, pathological lying, bipolar, mania, antisocial, substance abuse, personality disorder, borderline personality, eating disorders, paranoid personality disorder, avoidant personality, dissociative disorder, anger management, mood disorders, ADHD, narcissistic personality disorder, acute stress, dysthymic, bipolar disorder, cyclothymic, schizophrenia, body dysmorphic, dependent personality, depressive, avoidant personality, relational problems, sexual dysfunction, sleep disorders, irritability, housing problems, marital problems, gambling, impulse control, and many more (Warren, 2021, pgs. 30-340). These are meant for you to reflect on yourself and your team with empathy.

It is good to be simply aware of some of the existing disorders. We do not have a clear picture of what people on your teams are dealing with inside themselves. We do not know what teams deal with in their families and within their other relationships. To say we have unknowns regarding people is putting it mildly. To the extreme of these, the medications themselves may also have an unknown severe impact on behavior choices. We are all so different. Our reaction to medicine is different. Our behaviors may be vastly different as well while taking medication. How people internalize pain, stress, and suffering may be received in many ways. We do not know everyone's ability to cope. Why does one person lose control under life's pressures and others do not? It is the elephant in the room. Our lack of acknowledgment and conversation about horrific mass murders and their root cause, for example, is dreadful. Humanity is no closer to preventing the genesis of these events from happening again. At the same time, society marches on, no closer to resolving those issues, much less the many less hostile infractions of poor behavior occurring daily in organizations with far less personal harm. Does the personality shaping of a person truly ever end? Cultivating a healthy organizational culture would seem to resolve many adverse outcomes where supplying a systemic caring approach is feasible. Has caring ever not cured or helped? This seems like an excellent place to start. Everyone who has worked has likely known someone who has not cared or those who could care less.

When disorder meets disorder in the workplace, how does the leader, manager, or functional team leader untangle and build unity where the far easier choice is to fire someone or fire everyone involved? Conversely, leaders who neglect employees and create environments where chaos can flourish -supply the excuse to terminate employees built into their hands-off approach. This must be its own disorder, avoidance by leadership. What are they avoiding? The choice to take the easy out is to cut team members instead of investing in and developing the team by providing a healthy cultural environment for them. Is it too much work? Too much strain to do the right thing? Remember, there must be a reciprocation of effort and commitment, or it is not a relationship, professional or otherwise.

We can choose to engage either in confrontation or in cooperation. However, we cannot ignore the high organizational conflict, costing U.S. organizations 359 billion dollars annually in productivity loss (Pollack, 2023). Organizational leaders are struggling to overcome, unify, and heal teams. What is our expectation of the current pool of leaders? Should we be hiring doctors capable of managing organizational health? Our expectation should be to develop these site leaders to better deal with human beings. In the meantime, who are you owners and CEOs handing these struggling sites to? Do you think educated number crunchers and engineers were pining away to lead human beings? Play to the needs and align strengths; otherwise, do not be shocked to discover human problems overtaking your appointees. If you are the site leader, what are you doing above and beyond to expand your knowledge about people? What got you into the chair of responsibility in the first place? Are you learning more to build your culture 360? Are you sharing with your peers and staff? Are you stepping out to grow all organizational sites? Are you getting out of your comfort zone? We have all heard the saying, 'Be the change you want to see in the world.' How about 'Be the change you want to see in your organization'? Education is healing. The underprepared leader sinks the livelihood of teams as well as organizational health.

There is a cognitive dissonance between wanting to improve as an organization and avoiding doing the work to achieve it. Neglectful organizations are forever caught in a loop of organizational self-sabotage. People who neglect themselves and their own needs stifle their development and the development of the larger organizational whole. Organizations will mirror that stagnation as a collective if we are not becoming more whole as people. In these organizations, complacency, lethargy, denial, and avoidance will be apparent.

We must consciously acknowledge that our level of wholeness directly affects our organizational health. The power you must understand about yourself is to look more deeply into your personality, self-assess why you think and act the way you do, and understand the inner and outer drivers that propel your life. Learn to let go of what is not helpful and grow. Choose to flourish; choose your attitude, choose your words, and choose your actions intentionally. Doing so will change your results for the better in your personal and professional life. Your organization will also begin to benefit because delving deeper leads to thriving.

We cannot skip superficially to the end to achieve sustained results. We must work to iron ourselves out on a journey through the valley of our self. Worn parts break the machine and must be cleaned, repaired, and maintained regularly. In this case, 'broken' or less than whole elements in an organization means the organization wears out faster and can result in a catastrophic breakdown. We are all vital parts of the whole. Take care of the parts; take care of your 'team.'

"Saint Augustine, a bishop in Northern Africa in the fourth century, gave this answer to the question: What does love look like? "It has the hands to help others. It has the feet to hasten to the poor and needy. It has eyes to see misery and want. It has the ears to hear the sighs and sorrows of men. That is what love looks like" (Augustine, 0430). So now, what does love look like if I fire people versus develop them besides making myself look foolish, incompetent, and vile? What does love look like if I work at half speed and do not do what is expected of me as a team member besides making me look lazy? What does love look like if I am taking part in rumor and innuendo or slandering other people and my team's character besides making me look like a narcissist or a sociopath? We must grow the garden that is our organization with love, compassion, and passion to achieve our goals. The lack of love is evident in broken organizations where these questions fit. Love does not look like superficiality, shallowness, high levels of sarcasm, negativity, people working in silos, walled-off or hiding leadership, fear, and distrust.

Personality is potent. We are a mixture of many external and internal influences that shape our personality. We are our sculptors daily, building a 'us' that is never finished. We should be developing our weaknesses into strengths. We are responsible for acknowledging and strengthening our weaknesses, bad habits, and ugly traits while disrespecting no one. These weaknesses are the generators of all codependent behaviors, be they physical, substance-related, or emotional. It is not easy. Conquering them will make the most significant difference in your life. Organizations are a cultural collective of 'us'. We cannot speed through our day to such an extent that we resemble skipping stones, skipping across the water, and avoiding our depths. Instead, choose to calmly appreciate the steps you will take to dive into what behaviors you show throughout your week. Understand what drives you and take back control to overcome yourself in areas where you are weakest when dealing with anyone. Do not give fear power over who you are, who you are becoming, and how you conduct yourself. Leave heaviness behind and let your heart be as light as a feather.

People saturate themselves with codependent external experiences and substances to release dopamine. Dopamine artificially quenches and masks fear for a while. What fear are we talking about? The fear that a person will not be loved nor accepted. The reality is that we all fear something. Finding real love is the main driver for most of our seeking lives. The love could be the love of family, love of friends, love in the form of appreciation in the community, or love for a happy and secure life that also includes prosperity. However, codependency (Raypole, 2021) is tied to a boomerang of guilt and expectation that we silently internalize, originating from our and others expressed poor behaviors. We revert to being like frustrated children who become mad that we did not get the treat we wanted. We then hate the treat we wanted and anyone who kept us from it. Now, much of life for some people is either subtle or overt vengeance playing itself out. How do people and their psychology deal with these acts of revenge, whether large or small? They mask it with substances, obsessions, habits, emotional and physical addictions, and so forth. Revenge and the act of 'getting even' has a cost. The cost is an anchor of codependence that then affects relationships, physical and psychological health, and work performance. Remember that passive aggressiveness I spoke about earlier? Yes, this is just a manifestation of vengeance. That vengeance could be with parents who wronged a child early in life, and now that child is an adult, even a professional, someone educated and experienced enough to know better in the ways of treating people well, who gets caught up in acts of vengeance- bewildering the rest of the team. Some people may implode out of nowhere inexplicably. Well, now you know explicably. When vengeance is conducted in passive-aggressive ways, you can be sure that unrequited love deep down, emanating from personal and professional relationships around cooperation, is a likely culprit.

At the physical level, stored-up cortisol from stress manifests as poor health (Nelson, 2019). Are we somehow made sick if we seek love or acceptance and do not find it? Yes. Our inability to love and display that in our behaviors is like everyone having the cure to heal everyone else. Instead of giving it to those who need it, we withhold it from others while we simultaneously pine for it from the people we will not give it to. Isn't that a sickness? Further, our inability to be okay with ourselves -having depleted self-love also weakens us. However, we are unaware of this simple formula, so we are happy to believe that ailing health originates randomly without reason. Masking daily pains of stress and fear is what truly drives people to get their fix rather than nurturing love as a critical component of health. The fantastic thing is that organizations and institutions that want great productivity and quality also withhold love in their approach to their teams, actively ruining their ability to cultivate and sustain healthy organizational environments. When we believe love is not essential in life, we cause tremendous grief in our lives. Our behaviors are a direct indicator to everyone we know at the conscious and unconscious level about how much we love ourselves, others, and everything we do.

Those obsessed with thrill-seeking, for example, participate in activities that distract and mask the depths of our internal emotional real life, too. Humans can easily see and are always predictably running to or away from something. Some people are running away from accountability and responsibility and dashing into the arms of distraction and codependent addictive behaviors. Again, like a stone, we skip across the water, away from the past and toward something in the future, constantly distracted from our depths. We must deal with personal and organizational issues now. Masking by ignoring problems only serves to prolong healing in your organizational culture. One only needs to look at Facebook or other social media sites to see how people market their outgoing nature. We repeatedly find that we have opted for the superficial over the real. One person may have many personalities: a superficial one at work, an unjust one at home, a pleasant one out with peers, and an outgoing one on their social media site. One person, many personalities, many masks. Maintaining fragmented identities must be truly exhausting and stressful. That sounds like another reason to get a 'fix.' Some give up on other people entirely. The overuse of the feeling or reaction of disgust may be its own codependent behavior: the need to feel disappointment so I can react from a place of woe is me, to have oppression validated that I created in the first place. Some people become easily manipulated over-givers, who have been so emotionally enslaved by people in their personal lives that they emulate that submissiveness in the workplace, hoping for appreciation and validation that never comes. These team members are in a codependent loop of never-ending neglect, as if they are ghosts. However, givers will never seem to give up until they have honestly had enough. When they are done, you will hear the door slam and the words fly from a mile away. Moreover, it is forever when it happens. Too much self-sacrifice and over-giving is seen as a weakness, mainly by those obsessed with modulating their sacrifices for the greater good; they race out of the workplace parking lot at high speed. Hopefully, they will not be emulating their same half-efforts elsewhere. A collective result of an unhealthy organizational culture is the unwritten code to keep the bar low no matter what excellent new methods or tools are introduced. There is no judgment to acknowledge that struggling leaders have these blind spots. We are far less evolved than we give ourselves credit when we remove our rose-colored goggles. Personal or professional unresolved issues grow to become your next catastrophe at work, midlife crisis, personal tragedy, or product failure. Nothing is undiscussable where a lack of love, acceptance, or healing is vacant amongst a team.

Being aware of our fears, guilt, and lack of acceptance may seem bad, but they are necessary lessons to learn, irrespective of age or experience. What we do with those lessons is most important. First, you must ask yourself, 'Am I covering hurts, betrayals, distrust, and more with codependency on substances, habits, obsessiveness, and a hyper-outgoing nature? Am I healing the hurts I have in my life?' Is my life in balance? Do I feel harmony in my life? If so, great. If not, keep digging, keep healing -and be kind to yourself in the process while being a helping hand to others who are suffering and struggling. Lend them a hand.

The choice is this: do we free ourselves from ourselves, from our conditions, from the control of others, from false expectations, from our frustrations, from guilt, and the limerence we project onto the world personally and professionally, or do we keep ourselves in predictable codependent boxes? It is true that relaxing and being our authentic selves requires so much less energy; less wasted energy means more enjoyment in life. However, problems arise when we confidently ignore choosing to free ourselves from codependence, fail to realize we have them, make excuses for them, or become a social wrecking ball in other people's lives because we have neglected to deal with them. People suffer more when organizations compound the problem by throwing people away instead of developing them. We are smart enough to recycle plastic but have not overcome ourselves to recycle problems into solutions with the same effectiveness where people are concerned.

The choice a person makes either begins the clean-up of codependent issues or kicks the can down the road, never acknowledging and never healing them. Codependence creates a seed that grows many branches of poor behavior that blooms into a poisonous tree of turmoil and chaos in organizations. Owning and conquering codependence can help turn hurting people into self-healing helpers of others—those whose personal lives may require it. Creating healthy boundaries and a healthy healing environment where communication flows freely must be the most innovative first step.

Beware not to project guilt from a damaged ego into your own heart when the time comes for a person or organization to take accountability. Do not over-internalize harsh or direct feedback; that will also create unnecessary guilt. If you cannot love yourself, you cannot love others. If you have poor self-love, you cannot take direct and sometimes blunt feedback. Those who pass on their internalized pain due to poor levels of self-love only harm other people.

We must remember that everything is connected. Connection is your lifeline. Otherwise, you will fragment yourself, harden your heart, fragment your relationships, and skew your perception about everyone and everything. Suppose people who were examples in your life growing up could not love themselves and others and instead chose to gravitate toward toxicity and drama. In that case, you have zeroed in on what is or has influenced your thoughts, behaviors, and actions. Now, look at your team, leadership, and organization; what do you see? What is influencing the team, the leadership, and the organization now?

Everyone wants more love in the world. How much hurt and suffering are we willing to let go of within ourselves first to allow love and goodness to reign within culture? This is a question of individual and collective ego. Are we becoming, with each day, a collective of manipulative narcissists, or do we want to be collectively a more feeling, loving, and empathetic people? We must choose. We cannot let superficial distractions continue. Shallow consumerism distracts everyone all the time. What is more important to you, a new pair of shoes, a new car, a home, an outfit, or tools? Is your health and safety not more paramount to the bigger picture for everyone? Because this will be the cumulative result of improving the health of culture, be it organizational or otherwise.

Are we here to protect love? We are. Now, what are we willing to do to prove it? Few give the love and acceptance they want to receive. Because let's face it, to be loving is work. Demonstrating love in the world then is a lot of work. Who would use so much energy? Hopefully, those who want love want to give love back, not seeing it as an obligation but rather as an opportunity to share the best spark we have to offer within us; more remarkable than our intellect, more significant than our physical strength is our ability to love when we choose to do so. Lack of love affects everyone at every level in our relationships, communities, and organizations. It is not hard to see how codependence has snuck their way into the lives of so many people who both lack love and use codependency to mask the hole where love has not been allowed to flourish. Because the question then becomes, if I accept love, I become vulnerable to it and bound to pass it along in how I empathize and support others. I'm not asserting that no one has love. I am saying that far too many people modulate love as if the supply of it within each of us is finite. It is not; it is infinite. It is the greatest thing we have to offer and to be affected by in life. So, in every moment and decision, we have a choice to choose love, choose good, or choose what is not good, depriving and driving people away toward their codependency of choice. A visual analogy would be to imagine having an infinite number of band-aids in the presence of an endless number of people with cuts all over them and then withholding them. That can be humanity when we are unaware of our healing capabilities in people's lives.

Starting and raising families before understanding who we are is a gamble that distracts people from discovering who they are and why they behave the way they do. Throughout history, humanity has needed to procreate to ensure the species' survival. This is no longer the necessity it once was. What is the driver now? Ego? Tradition? Has starting a family become another codependent ego-driven possession that couples use to put between themselves as a trophy or an excuse to distract themselves from deepening their relationship? There is plenty of work to do to love one's partner without making children compete with your devices and things for your time. If a couple's relationship is not developed to a healthy state, should children be brought into the center arena of their relationship? Are you inviting a child into a world of lack, reminding them of it by their living conditions, and then turning them into adults who live lives of lack?

Does the child become an angry adult in a world that just looked on apathetically? It is something to consider and perhaps change. The sperm's evolution to struggle through the obstacles to life never ends, even after a child arrives. The miracle of that child in a world sideways to its arrival will become that child's entire life. Perhaps a new social literacy, one that is not defined but expects and protects our ability to contribute, to control our behavior, to think through rather than avoid problems without inflicting vengeance or pain, to get along, to cooperate, to be peaceful and act for our own and others highest good with love, should become our new vital norm? Combining low social literacy with high consumerism injected into the veins of the population has damaged people's lives with layers of hurt and neglect they cannot see. Layers of pain distract them into living lives of survival instead of lives of meaning and purpose. What legacy can be left by those who do not prioritize and protect love for all life? Are we doing enough to protect love?

Who benefits from a legacy of parenting that obfuscates oversight of youth to electronic devices? Was it the goal to find new and creative ways to neglect the emotional development of another generation of children? Perhaps the last couple of generations have succeeded? Everyone gets a trophy. Society and culture do not benefit from parents who do not actively engage with and develop their children. Indeed, the result has been to fragment child development and divide people, society, and culture. The spoiled child is now the spoiled adult. When the reality of life and the true north of that discovery is boldly apparent, it rips at self-entitlement like a person prevented from eating pure sugar foods after decades of living on it. Can you say withdrawal? Are we surprised that substance abuse is so prolific? People who resist victimizing themselves can transform and grow out of self-entitlement conditioning and become functioning and contributing adult humans. This is also true for team members and leaders in organizations just before they embark on their transformational journey. Waking up, having organizational self-awareness, being transparent, and taking extreme ownership of reality -is organizational maturity. It is undoubtedly a part of individual maturity to understand that it is.

Who suffers when organizations throw away employees instead of developing and training them? The answer is everyone, but mostly the children of the next generation who grow up in self-justified cults of poverty who have been ingrained with organizational mistrust, a default' us' versus 'them' way of thinking that conveniently indoctrinates each generation into distraction by embedding into them a mindset of social class; ego incarnate. Division only stagnates growth and prosperity, perpetuating an 'us' versus 'them' environment in organizations. All of this only serves to polarize organizations. Even the most subtle versions of it need to stop. Customers find it cringeworthy to walk into organizations resembling a dysfunctional family barbecue.

It does not help that bad organizations that do not develop their teams use people up and throw them away. People then must move across the vast geography to begin again elsewhere due to the nomadic culture that organizations have been complicit in creating. In this way, organizations have held the mantle of the neglectful parent casting off and abandoning their children. This triggers abandonment and trust issues, real or imagined. Developing people on your team is more efficient, cost-effective, and healthier than throwing them away frivolously. Believe what you will say about government positions. Still, the fact is that their employee turnover is the least, and that is primarily because they invest in development progression that supports the organization. This maintains a standard of performance. Notice I said maintains, not improves or cuts cost necessarily. Without excuse, the private sector can generate personnel support systems and an improvement philosophy that increases productivity and the health of the organizational culture.

One must travel on their life's journey from the victim's place -if they were, to the victor's place over their own lives. Otherwise, they will take on the archetype of the trickster or jester (Yuan, 2022): one who subtly or overtly upsets growth and passes their pain and toxicity to others instead of healing anything. As I will refer, the trickster does not nurture or create good and is pleasingly content to live in a state of emotional decay in the now, unaffected by anyone or anything until they hit significant problems.

Friction is lift. The tension between organizations and a neglected team gives a motivated few a reason to put in the extra effort to lean into education, choosing to swim upstream instead of being drowned by organizational entropy. Some team members start their own businesses to escape organizational entropy. However, opportunities exist to empower your team's personal and professional development. Assess the cultural landscape around you. Seek to fully understand the conditions and the challenges influencing the people on your team. Integrate opportunities to communicate and grow your team before you begin your organizational transformation. This way, the team does not feel dragged through a process that is not speaking to their highest good. One that does not regard them as paramount to the organization's successes. Recognize the team's value as people first.

Insecurities that people have about themselves affect teams. These manifest as a lack of competence, low desire to improve, lethargy, and little notion of going above and beyond. This lack of competence and confidence will lead some team members to find the next excuse for their inability to succeed on projects. For some, the idea of a growing organization is in direct competition with team members who lack the desire to grow and instead resist organizational change at their core. They feel self-conscious -that they are not growing, stagnant, and unseen. Teams unaware of these drivers may find themselves getting negative results inexplicably. Instead, intentionally align, instill, and communicate positive thoughts and desires, inspiring a hunger to grow in the team. Organizations with a poor development track for their teams fail to alleviate negative internal mindsets. Negative results are the default result of aimless personnel who lack professional growth. Everyone, individually and as a part of a team, must intentionally manifest their thoughts, communication, and actions in genuinely positive ways to improve. Please do not take my word for it. Observe your behavior, team, and organization, and walk all this backward. Where are individual and team behaviors coming from? Is your organization off track? Now, it is time to take some notes.

We must stop leaving the best parts of our personality behind. Quieting the voices of our teams to avoid rocking the boat only prevents excellent ideas and innovations from coming to light. This is one reason we must see the possibility and the miracles in everyone. We must see the synergy of the soul, the life force in everyone, amplified when we come together for a common purpose. Our personality has power if it has been marinated in love and supported to grow healthy connections with people in our lives and on our teams.

Some work nefariously to thwart the good. Unfortunately, some do not value the human desire to thrive. We, as humans, are the love story about which all of life and experience exists. There are no superior people on our tiny blue ball, earth. We only have the cultures we have created. The cultures that are starving, we choose to let them starve when we do nothing to change those paradigms. Humans are all responsible for every good and bad thing that exists. The brass ring of change and doing amazing things for the world is not 'out there.' It is inside of you first! It is inside your organization, waiting to be unlocked, freed, and empowered. This is why it is paramount that organizations hasten to course correct and begin improving organizational culture. There is little time to waste. Our collective personalities are the only thing that can create a cultural rebirth. However, first, a shift in our individual and collective behavior; the result of our personality must occur genuinely, intelligently, and compassionately. We must create value within the human heart that is so strong that it cannot be debated against, fought against, or argued against. Personal transformation can lead to a collective attitude and overall behavior change. Developing people and teams will grow and enjoy a common purpose. We cannot lose culture to complacent linear thinking. We must wake up and enable ourselves to climb outside the box we have entombed ourselves.

From virtual nothingness, all possibilities are born. Resistance to clearly positive outcomes takes more work than finding inroads to cooperate, build, create, and innovate with others. However, wasting brain power and the physical energy necessary to mislead people, avoid work, avoid responsibility, and sidestep accountability is far more work. It creates more waste than owning the truth and being accountable. When we focus our energy on productive results, we find breakthroughs. Those hyper-reactionary linear thinking leaders condition their teams to take part in the same reactionary chaos: ready, fire, aim -type of thinking. This promotes high stress and high levels of fear, and people waste their energy guarding and protecting themselves, detracting from customer focus. Employees who take their hands off the wheel also cause leaders to waste time and energy to correct neglectful mistakes. Poor results from poor behavior hurt all customers and all internal and external stakeholders.

Significant transformation in an organization takes an initial surge of energy. However, sustaining improved results is more about working smarter and being productive and less about using excess energy. Anyone encountering a problem should be committed enough to have at least a couple of ideas to overcome the problem encountered. We must all be part of improvement and sustainability. Documenting development and tracking accountabilities at all levels is essential. Everyone must be accountable, contribute, and overcome challenges for the customer. It's good to celebrate everyone's efforts when milestones are achieved. However, this is not the end; it is the beginning of setting up a healthy organizational culture with a healthy personality.

Chapter 11

Embrace Functional Change

While you assess your organization's actual state of being, it is also time to embrace some functional changes. In an organization, all departments are pushing on the same wheel, whether it is realized or not. As you go, you build the momentum of that wheel until, as one team, you rise from the lift created. For example, imagine helicopters, planes, and drones where the momentum of their blades creates lift. If the blades are not in sync, there is an imbalance or a lack of continuity. We want balance; we want continuity for predictable flight. It is the same for organizations. If a shipping department can only ship half of what we make, it does not matter that the purchasing department is finding breakthroughs. The entire organization is inhibited by the worst constraint affecting the organization. In this example, we need to make functional changes and improvements to the shipping department where our most challenging issues currently exist. Once we improve the shipping department, we can get the organization back into balance and continuity. What we do not do in the organization is to slow our performance or fall back on our product or service quality. Having one troubled department does not give everyone permission to slow down or stop. This is the same for machines that break down. Another example is if the sales force slows down because a production line or two has mechanical difficulties. Yet it happens. When a more than-normal number of employees leave for vacation in the same department, you must ask yourself why. What do they know that you do not? Disjointed behaviors and decisions made from those behaviors can be slid right past an unaware leadership. Can you tell what occurs naturally from what happens by neglect or nefarious intent? Of course, you cannot. You assume everyone operates with high integrity, and you would be wrong. Frankly, anyone in your value stream could quickly sabotage your organization. What is your solution? Make allies, not enemies. If you plan to make successful functional changes, your team must ally with you in lockstep. Getting into a tug-of-war with your team is counterproductive and a waste of time. It is counterintuitive to our shared vision and goals to work against one another. Ideally, in healthy organizations, it is. In unhealthy organizations, the internal factions keep many team members interested. They love the drama and are getting paid to be a part of it, so they think. They are not thinking about the customer. Yes, unhealthy organizations need to put the customer as a priority. Unhealthy organizations are the quadcopters flying out of control into the side of the building, focused on something other than customers. Eventually, in unhealthy organizations, internal discontinuity fragments and then consumes the team.

Cooperation must take precedence over controversy. However, shutting people down, shutting people up is not cooperation; it is oppression. In a global culture, actual oppression is minimized as the term is thrown around culture so often that it has lost its meaning. A child who cannot get their electronic device is now oppressed. Really? Trivializing oppression by applying it to every problem or constraint we are made aware of is absurd. The lack of cooperation is not relieved by the false inference that it results from oppression. Lethargy is not derived from oppression. The inability to maintain standards and expectations is not born from oppression. Lack of integrity is no reason to project oppression as a cause. Lack of cooperation, however, is oppressive and unfair to customers in the marketplace. Why do we allow uncooperative behaviors to crush customers? Why is that acceptable? It should not be. All our efforts should be focused on empowering our teams to enable customers, which will drive economic forces to serve everyone. Free your customers, grow yourself, free yourself. The most significant power of self and organizational validation is good service. Trivializing those who have been actually oppressed and have been actual victims by slapping those terms on life's daily challenges is no way healthy organizations or self-respecting humans operate.

A pilot on approach to land must deal with varying crosswinds and make thousands of micro-control adjustments. The pilot must focus intently on keeping the aircraft lined up on centerline while reducing altitude and adjusting speed to land successfully. So, too, you and your entire team must focus with intention while making thousands of micro-adjustments to have successful days turn into successful weeks and then successful months. Individually and as a team, you must embrace self-motivation to achieve success. As the saying goes, there can be no half-in and half-out of the pool. You, individually and as a team, are either all in or out. Everyone is in transformation, or no one is in transformation. Past improvements were not sustainable because they needed full buy-in and commitment from the entire team. Leadership may not have highly praised the accomplishment of improvements. Leadership may not continue to prioritize the win and keep the momentum of the win fresh by using it to springboard into more improvements. Some leaders let the accomplishment die because it is work to continue to build upon it. Who would know or question if they used cost as a false justification? The site leader would. We must stop applying linear arguments to justify using the word 'can't.'

Do not be fooled into thinking that you cannot have or that there will be no dissenting ideas and opinions on your transformation journey to improve your organizational culture. You need diversity of thought intertwined around the constancy of agreed-upon purpose. Listen to your team, document their ideas, and integrate them where it makes the most sense.

Do not ignore your team. Please do not throw away their ideas. Half-baked ideas have holy-baked solutions within them if you allow your eyes and ears to realize what puzzle piece you have been presented with. Those ideas and pieces will fit somewhere now or in the future. Appreciate your team members when those pieces fit. Keep a living record of all ideas and suggestions.

Before I begin listing functional changes that will help your organization, I assure you that you do not need to be in a belt program. If you already have one, great, but it is not required. No feudalism is necessary to improve. Before making any transformational change efforts, ask yourself a question. If I improve my production capabilities by twenty percent, do I have the orders and product demand to feed that kind of leap in productivity? First, establish what your current demand is. Are you behind? By how much? Is that a seasonal or annual nagging pinch keeping your delivery on time below ninety percent? Are you moving products by following lean concepts and just-in-time delivery? Establish the percentage you want to improve your productivity, account for downtime for equipment and other site factors, and add five more percent. So, if you figured you needed to be twelve percent more productive to stay best in class with your on-time delivery, add five percent to get you to seventeen percent. Seventeen is your target. Stay calm if you overshoot that number; use the added time for other site improvements. Often, organizations add the idealism of what they want to do without considering what they can do, and then they fail. Why? They could have planned better. The planning was done in a biased way with no realistic or accurate internal or external validation to back up the claims of the plan. An example is a sales team complaining about production efforts not meeting delivery requirements. Then, the production team improves, yet the sales team cannot bring consistency to orders, only projections. Where did the plan fail in this case?

Where was the scrutiny placed? Who stepped up? Who did not? We could not develop a more universal example of leadership being 'sold' by their bigger challenges. Remember, change is hard on everyone. We must check our egos and assumptions at the door and own what we can and cannot do, whether it is a sales team, an engineering team, a production team, or any departmental group. Be honest, open, genuine, and authentic.

After addressing initial people approaches and concerns, part of your functional approach to change is to gather as much data as possible. Utilize the checklist as illustrated in Figure A3. Then you may start with these:

1. Interview the leadership team, functional leaders, supervisors, and employees. Take careful notes to aid in developing an improvement strategy and priority.
2. Establish the mechanical and facility status on-site. Document the issues and rate their impact on the operation, including repairability, cost, or replacement.
3. Figure out supply issues and constraints. What resources lag? Be sure to alleviate this immediately so it does not affect your throughput and productivity.
4. Do you have an operations plan? Begin outlining one with these things in mind: It should call out and provide protective gates that prevent what catastrophes your organization has already dealt with and possible what-if scenarios you can conceive of happening in the future. It should call out best practices to ensure your organization is safe, productive, and has a high level of two-way communication from the team to the leader and vice versa. Where possible, stress general expectations for the team that align them with your vision and quality statement. Expectations should point to

policies you have created to ensure that methods of productivity and accountability are maintained.

5. Are processes and procedures documented and current? If not, start from the ground up, writing them on turtle diagrams first, as illustrated in Figure A11. Eventually, these will evolve into standard work documents. If you already have standard work documented, ensure they are current. By that, perform observations and revise your current state as necessary, no matter how recent any improvement projects were completed.

6. Prioritize the impact of your interview findings on safety, productivity, and team morale. Ensure that safety issues are swiftly fixed. Grade the findings according to impact and cost impact; convert waste of time by mean employee hourly wage. Any unnecessary loss of resources, including time, should be assessed.

7. Begin a daily Gemba walk if you are not doing one. This is also referred to as a daily management walk. Have your management team make a daily plan at the end of each day for the next day. Have them do the same at the end of each week for the following week and provide you with their weekly plan by email before leaving each week for their weeks end. The point is to get all your people into a forward-thinking, proactive mode.

8. As Illustrated in Figure A10, Create performance boards. Do so, irrespective of whether you currently have an ERP or MRP. These will capture productivity, ' reason' descriptions, hourly or daily supervisory, and quality validation. These can be made electronically using monitors if desired. However, updating may take time and effort. You can take pictures of them at the end of shifts and compile them into your spreadsheets. I have garnered as much as seventeen percent higher production rates from proactively using

manual performance whiteboards and radios. I have consistently achieved over double-digit improvement in ninety days. Remember, though, that your engagement with the process from a leadership perspective goes in tandem with your teams' efforts. These boards will also capture issues that arise that can be quickly tackled during the day. This also plays a part in improving your productivity because maintenance downtime focus is highlighted and reduced. The fact that the boards can be seen openly creates a 'scoreboard' effect. People want to perform well, be seen doing it, and receive appreciation through daily engagement as part of your management walk. Upper leadership and management should visually go to where the work is being done two to three times a day and make an end-of-day pass taking notes that are put together and sent to your department leaders so changes, fixes, and items to address can be expediently handled first thing in the day. This assures that they will likely be complete by the time your Gemba walk occurs mid-morning.

9. Do not make a project from something you can fix immediately in one shift or day. However, document and track everything. Keep team members from dragging something out longer than necessary. Keep your department leaders deliberate in their tempo to lean forward to resolve issues as they arise and not let things linger or slow throughput.

10. Distribute enough radios to quickly access department managers, supervisors, functional leaders, and maintenance teams. Use them to reduce response and lag time wasted finding people, tools, and equipment and speed up getting answers to questions in real time. I have used Motorola radios due to their range and durability but use what you find works best for you. Experiment as some site areas

and walls may hamper reception. Radios can reduce delays throughout your entire organization. Radios can speed up maintenance team communications and minimize repair time, improving productivity and increasing throughput. Create repair response kits and use motorized carts or golf carts to reduce time waste.

11. Clean up your entire site; 5S is a method that begins with cleanup but ends up being a reorganization effort. It eliminates unnecessary stuff while ending the search for the things you need; it saves travel time and headaches searching for resources. No square inch of your site will be missed in an organization-wide 5S effort. Expect a higher hourly effort by your maintenance team for three to four weeks while you aggressively tackle repairs, reorganization efforts, and removal of old or useless equipment.

12. I recommend that before starting 5S, your team goes through every square inch of your site to remove anything that is refuse, trash, unused, and no longer useful items inside and outside your facility. Typically, this is done as part of 5S. However, getting the more obvious useless stuff out of the way in mass by everyone gives you a cleaner launch into your 5S effort.

    A. You can pick specific, highly problematic areas to start your 5S effort to get the production efficiency results more immediately. However, you can have each department begin 5S in their areas of responsibility more generally. You can be creative and provide awards for teams that can show how much more efficient or how much waste they reduced after doing a department-wide 5S project. Some areas may be general use; assemble teams to tackle those secondarily unless those are your most problematic. 5S should include admin, office areas, and anywhere resources are stored. 5S is cleaning, organizing, labeling/signage, and maintaining everything daily.

B. Regarding exterior grounds, fence lines, and ditches, ensure those areas are mowed down, weeds removed, and all trash that may have accumulated is thrown out. Your team can make a line side by side with one another and walk around your grounds to manage this in a pass or two around and in your facility. Doing this also gets your team physically engaged in the transformation process. You may incorporate this effort monthly. Your organizational transformation must be intellectual, emotional, and physical. Transforming your physical surroundings signals a reset and helps the team feel the change happening visually around them and by them. You can brighten your work areas where needed. This can be done with brighter light or a lighter paint scheme. Paint also helps the transformation process. Paint should help the team see and feel better about their environment while also making a pleasing and noticeable landing spot for customers. Improve the conference rooms and meeting areas; replace the old furniture; replace the worn-out carpet; update the technical functionality (audiovisual); make break areas inviting; and decorate to make your spaces inviting to customers. If your facility has any suspected mold issues, test them and remediate them for health and safety.

C. Accomplish your 5S in this order:

Sort: Separate all the useless from the useful. Either discard the useless or store it away.

Set In Order: Once you have sorted, it is time to put things in their proper place. Put things where they are needed. Put things closer to where the work is done. Shadow boards and other helpful visual management tools can be used. There is a myriad of tools you can find online. This step is critical so that you are not looking endlessly for something you need. It might mean you go paperless, for example. This process can be improved and built upon as often as practical, so do not worry if you improve it many times in a season. It may take some of your tasks from many minutes to seconds.

Shine: This process is the cleanup part of the 5S process. Further, you will ensure proper labeling, signs, visual management tools, giving instructions, and methods to show quantity levels.

Standardize: In the standardized process, ensure instructional guides, checklists, processes, standard work, and operations plans are assembled.

Sustain: Your team must keep the 5S area as newly designed. This means going back through the process. Part of sustaining is keeping resources replenished, including daily supervisory accountability.

13. It is vital that people ensure that moments, not minutes, are not wasted in casual, non-professional interactions. Time management is crucial, and wasted time can never be recovered. All your time is customer time, so be good stewards and be accountable.
14. Proactively plan and communicate status. I suggest working sixty percent of past-due orders and forty percent of new orders until the

work is caught up. Finesse this like driving around a curvy road, seeing when you can speed up, and shifting to other priorities. There are exceptions to everything, so own your in-house math.

15. Your on-time delivery goal should be 97% or better. If you are short of ninety-seven, you need to increase your productivity, streamline your value stream, and find ways to improve your cadence until it reaches 97% or greater.
16. Set daily, weekly, and monthly goals. Do this organizationally and by department.
17. Ensure you do a Gemba walk daily. Review all performance and productivity boards as a team. Use the back of the boards for your team to write down improvement ideas as they come to them.
18. Ensure to review and act on your organizational Plan Do Check Act (PDCA) board, as illustrated in Figure A9.
19. Have your team update, create, and ensure that all processes and procedures accurately reflect the work. Ensure a value stream map has been completed and its timings are correct.
20. Ensure you incorporate traceability for your operations into your operations plan. A quality manual is optional but helpful. You should have standard operating procedures and standard work documents completed for all your processes and procedures.
21. Create an idea program. As illustrated in Figure A12, a simple idea board that captures the essentials for your form is helpful. You can dovetail a reward program around ideas that impact your site.
22. How do you measure personnel performance? Turn your organizational annual performance feedback into a quarterly event until a year of progress has been tracked.
23. Do you have a formal training program? If not, dovetail one into a quarterly performance event. By doing this, you can grow employee

and team knowledge, skills, and abilities. If you only have an OJT program, document it and convert it to a formal program. This progression should require a verification and validation sign-off by a supervisor and a quality representative to ensure skill-level competence. Please do not assume that because someone does something, they know how to do it, train it, and evaluate others' performance. Formal programs do not assume anything. Teams help create, conform to and keep your management system relevant.

24. Does your quality team check your morning or shift startups to ensure quality and timely production each day? Ensure the quality team and others see startups daily to find and improve startup efficiency quickly and consistently—document the data for ongoing and future reference to improve these activities. A startup checklist can be made and completed by the quality team. This visual oversight will improve your production efforts. Beware when observations do not occur and how that affects productivity as well. Bring it to your team's attention, and then you should see consistency without taking individual corrective actions.

25. How often are management reviews performed? Ensure they are done monthly for a year, then at least quarterly.

26. Do employees know what to do in all situations, including critical ones? When you write your operations plan, make it as mistake-proof as possible.

27. Are you using the pull system? Start with your shipping department or the last stop in your value stream and work backward through it to eliminate constraints. Perform a Kaizen event where those constraints are challenging but keep working backward through

them. You will see your value stream speed up when you eliminate constraints. You must not let your sales/order pipeline dry up.

28. What morale or team-building events do you have in place? You should have a monthly event; it can be as simple as breakfast or lunch with other monthly safety training, any added training and testing, and performance awards.
29. Are you creating and supporting strong relationships with your suppliers? If you never ask, you will never know. Look for cost-saving opportunities on a usual basis.
30. When you see production gaps in your yearly plan, reach out to your usual customers to proactively negotiate more work for those gaps. Why would you let the passive nature of not doing so cause work to slow down, layoffs to occur, and your ownership to lose out as well? If you want wins, be proactive and unafraid to ask the hard questions as you apply some forward thinking to your operation.
31. Have you reduced your setup and changeover times? Have you tried it? Have you reduced your time? First, reduce your startup and changeover times by half, and then continue to reduce those by half as you go.
32. Are you using a one-piece flow or batch processing? One-piece flow is most efficient but not always practical in some situations. Find ways to integrate one-piece flow.
33. Sell off old equipment, vehicles, scrap, and anything unused or useless to your organization. Use the money to fund your improvement projects, replace equipment, or other technology for operational needs. For some, this would help defray costs.

The physical changes you make during your 5S, and many other improvement activities will reinforce a mental marker in your employees' heads. This is a starting point for a new era of your organization's commitment to improving its culture. Physical changes reinforce the intellectual and emotional transformation that will also happen inside the people on your team. Your implementations will create an energy shift in your organization. Part of this shift is because more energy will be needed initially to make the necessary changes. That is good. Generally, people naturally want to do less and stay at the most comfortable pace possible. Some may have wrapped much of their tasks around their comfortability already. However, working more intelligently does not mean we do not work hard. Initially, you must do more, increase your overall cadence, and step outside your comfort zone. Create a gentle upward slope in your organizational performance. Stalling indicates internal problems where a lack of cooperation, good planning, good oversight, lack of engagement, lack of resources, poor morale, lethargy, lack of focus, lack of good communication, and lack of a customer-centric approach may be occurring. Any of these on their own will stall efforts. Rebelling against a 'new system' is high on that list. Your team must build momentum and manage their time well. Just as a plane taking off requires lift, everyone in your organization must increase momentum, which leads to its own kind of lift in performance. This does not mean there will not be friction. Change is not just physical; it is mental and emotional. It will be obvious who is there to contribute and who is just there for the party or the drama. Some may be there only to fulfill a need to socialize. Let's face it: some people show up to fill the void in their lives. Should this be the case, ensure they are filling that void like a champ for the right reasons. Educate your team, inspire them to cooperate, and be a part of the team's success. Give your team time to adapt to change. Caution: Narcissists and sociopaths will resist change the most but disguise it well. Let the change process boil out those who do not care to align with your team's purpose and the organization's vision. If you have no vision, establish one. An organization without a vision is like a ship at sea without a compass or a destination.

Change will become the boiling water that pulls the toxicity out of your organization. A slightly quicker and more intentional pace does not mean we do not develop people through the challenge of change. You will communicate more often and even let your team know all these things discussed so they understand that you are stripping the ego and fear out of the organization. It is better to hit problematic areas head-on early and resolve them. What you will be left with is a wide-open possibility. Do not be overly concerned by those who bow out of your organization. People show you who they are compared to your organizational goals in how they conduct themselves and whether they align with your team. Honest dissenters may choose not to be a part of your team. Dishonest dissenters may still decide to stay and make your transformation more difficult. They were never about your purpose and will take pleasure in putting a wrench in the gears of your progress. Either way, people cannot fake good for long, and eventually, they will reveal their true motives. Like an evolving person, your organization will evolve forward, developing people through any situational codependency, or they will grow outside your organization. Either way, it is your only two options in the future. Any conversation about something being too hard or too difficult, they would not know because they have not tried. Utilize those with experience to find breakthroughs or who have been part of organizational transformation projects to help motivate your team.

You will find engagement with your team rewarding. The opportunity to add value to people's lives is fantastic. Sometimes, a leader must also figure out if their values, goals, and intentions align with the organization and come from a place of harmony. They must engage fully, participate, or find arenas more aligned with their personal and professional needs. It is high-minded to follow your journey honestly, harboring no malice. Let go of what is not for you.

If different sites within the broader organization are not participating in organizational transformation, that is ok. Your site will be the proof. However, over time, your organization will be in a state of cognitive dissonance if one site exemplifies transformational methods to improve organizational culture and productivity while others are left to run business as usual. Beware of losing credibility if your goal is not to improve the culture across the broader organization. Teams will see through any sleight of hand as a poor excuse. A commitment to improving organizational culture can only survive long term with broad organizational commitment from top to bottom. Continuity is a critical attribute in transforming organizations. It is best to have all organizational sites begin slowly changing their methodologies.

Reactive thinking rarely solves problems well, especially with any reliable sustainment. Reactive thinking is continually trading less for less. We should never take pride in losing, nor should it be our goal to lose. We want to keep team members who contribute productively to organizational culture. Turnover may already be a problem for your organization. Is it really, though? Some organizations have little turnover and harbor an actively toxic environment that creates an undertow that pulls down the organization. The organization then struggles, stammering to build breakaway momentum to lift it nicely upward. When it comes to reactive organizations, there is always someone to fill the leadership void. Managing from the middle often fills that void to keep the organization from failing. This is why organizational support and a leadership team focused on vision and goals are essential. Remember, aligning the team to put the customers first is your primary motive that all things must point to. Your answer to 'why are we doing this' is that the customer is the answer to that question.

The best way to overcome managing from the middle is to train your operations team to design and follow the plan precisely so that the lines of support exist, expectations are known, and they know what to do when the work is complete. It should value and emphasize being good stewards of resources. Our time at work is not our own; it is the customers and must be managed. Stewarding all resources well should become the first trait of a great organization. Do not think we are aiming for perfection. Instead, the journey is seeing improved productivity and morale combined cooperatively, sidestepping the ego and any need to invite controversy. Improving organizations consists of continuously seeking new ways to do everything better, not just a handful of tasks or even a couple of projects. Getting better will not happen if rumors and office politics persist. Write out anything negative -within the scope of your operations plan. Negative behaviors are beneath the culture of a healthy organization.

The Pareto principle is fundamental (Mcloud, 2018). It is also known as the 80/20 rule, as illustrated in Figure A1. It says that twenty percent of anything done is responsible for the best eighty percent of your results. For example, twenty percent of your team is responsible for your success. Twenty percent of your team is also responsible for eighty percent of your poorest results. These two are not made up of the same people. Which one do you feel like you belong to? Regardless, firing the bottom performing 20% will not immediately help you. However, see where you spend the most time improving or giving attention to your team. It should be the upper eighty percent. Remember the middle sixty percent who show up daily; they matter greatly. You must ask yourself, are you spending your time where you are being successful or where people are failing you? Guard your energy and manage your expectations. If you were to release your worst performing twenty percent, which may be thwarting your organization, a new group would fall into that role to become your new worst twenty percent of performers. In short, people are ready to step down to take their place. This works the same with your best performers. That should also alleviate the fear of losing outstanding talent in the long term. Do not ignore your incredible talent. If you are not improving your bottom twenty, your middle sixty percent will become exasperated that you did nothing. You will be perplexed seeing your competent, consistent talent leave because you are not leading with a sense of justness. Justness can be a development and training program with high engagement and open communication. Educate your employees and write your standards and expectations into your operations plan so that your team is required to know them well. You should not lose more than three to five percent of your employees yearly if your organization is healthy. This should be one of your objectives: to cultivate, grow, and retain your team. Your team should understand the 80/20 rule and self-assess where they fit. Performance does not mean the lower twenty percent are toxic, though they may be, in unhealthy organizations. Remember, the bottom twenty percent is performance-based, not by rank or pay. For example, you could have department leaders in the bottom twenty percent. You will always have holdouts; they could be anyone, anywhere, and sprout up after being cooperative. Do not be paranoid; understand it. Just get used to that so you are not surprised by being let down at some point. Leaders, take care of your team so that they can focus on the customer. An organization that tends to their team's needs; -wins. It is that simple. We overcomplicate executing on this because we think there is a mythic secret. There is no secret. In most cases, team needs are the most significant things that the organization flounders dealing with. Needs are left at the door when the team arrives for work each day. Why? Because we see being too involved in their challenges as going beyond our organization's capabilities, desire, or purpose. How would we know unless we knew our people well? If you are not engaged with your team, it is likely because you want to avoid becoming intertwined in their lives. Why? Who are your customers? Wake up; they are everyone -and therefore, they are you. You will win if you find ways to meet your team's needs and ensure they meet the customers' needs. The organization must have a larger vision beyond profits. If the organization does not tend to team needs, you will see a constant bleeding out, with organizational turnover as a sign of customer dissatisfaction. Customer dissatisfaction means poor revenue, period. The team, including leadership, must be open, motivated, humble, and thirsty to learn. As a side note, using hiring firms to make it look like you have a one percent turnover hurts an organization more because it screams that you do not trust your ability to hire talent. It also foot-stomps the fact that you are putting any future blame on a third-party firm versus your internal competence. Do not be afraid to own failure. Relying on third-party hiring entities communicates to new hires that they are 'throw away employees' and that you are not serious about growing them into your organization long term. In turn, they work down to the message you are sending. If you are unreliable at hiring, work on that. You win as one team; you lose as one team.

Chapter 12

Pay Now or Pay Later

Eventually, you must invest time and money to raise your organizational competence. Ensure that people on your team are not bottling up their opinions, complaints, and feelings about problems in the organization. People may gravitate to small groups within your organization with much to say. Go hear them. Open the floor and invite critique. If you had failed to do this in the past, you likely inadvertently created a codependence of people to their 'small group.' You cannot have factional interpretations of your organizational reality. Depending on your organizational size, a few small groups may be at odds with each other, like factional cliques -creating minor but ongoing internal feuds that you may be unaware of. This reminds me of the time I spent in high school. Depending on how old your organization has been around, these feuds may have been going on for years. This long-term feudalism is causing suffering that results in the lack of inclusion. Hold nothing back, but make sure your entire team respects one another. Teams that do not work together waste valuable time and energy, and you can never recover from them.

You may be exceptional. You may have a fantastic work environment. Though your team may be competent in their tasks, they may need more organizational competence. That is, they need to learn how to function as a team. This is because they have yet to learn how to be a part of a team. It only takes a few who do not understand what teamwork is about for it to affect your organization. Some may struggle to work well in large groups. When we say pay now or pay later, it means either you spend money to hire a turnkey employee, or you spend time and money as you go to develop your employees into talented team members. If you refrain from developing your team or hiring turnkey people, then this is not choosing to be proactive. Not choosing is choosing, and not choosing means you will experience many difficulties and quite likely have been. You will feel your team is hurting, angry, wounded, or afraid of failure. Do not let the sun set on a failure. Address festering issues. Manage significant problems early; do not let them linger well into your day and affect your entire team. Resolve issues expediently. Often, misunderstandings can be quickly addressed and corrected. However, left to linger, people think leaders do not care; therefore, people stop caring, too. Irrespective of whether you are on the leadership team or the broader team, never let even the perception that you do not care, no matter how obscure it might be, be assumed by the lack of communication, your actions, or your overall care.

Be aware that if your team is left alone, they will not grow and develop. You and your leadership team will have to develop them. However, you may have professional managers that must be developed. Underdeveloped managers may have yet to move forward in their careers. You may have departmental or site leaders who have never built effective teams. The title of 'manager' does not mean you are a leader. If so, you must drop back and punt and rebuild through training. Leaders will have to take more of the reigns. Heighten your engagement during your Gemba daily management walks by turning them into a walking classroom. Take advantage of opportunities to train your team where you can.

If you develop a weak development program, employees will not take it seriously, and you will see inferior results. Ensure you have legitimate signoffs by two or more organizational authorities to validate competencies once they are achieved. Perform periodic 90-to-120-day random open book testing to ensure employees stay sharp on all current and specific job knowledge, skills, and regulatory requirements that matter to your organization. These times provide opportunities to review new processes, products, and policies. For example, you could give a morning test, followed by a team meeting, then safety training and lunch. This is a well-spent half day that also serves as a preventative measure to ensure quality, safety, and regulatory risks are abated through your training program. The more formal you can make your employee development program, the better the results the team will achieve. Like growing a garden, it takes constant oversight.

Consider that your team only knows what they know. Your team has yet to learn what they need to know or what you know. If you want them to know more, invest the time and energy saved in improving your operation to develop further and cross-train your team. This can provide considerable advantages to your organization's productivity while keeping everyone knowledgeable and interested and will prevent lethargy. Remember, the entire team benefits if 20% of your team develops. Set goals and get team members trained up as you go. Ensure all training is documented and that training continues. Remember that you will not be free of frustration while you build your team's competence. Some frustration is part of the journey until you view minor frustrations as opportunities to improve your system and team. Channel all frustration back into your efforts, understanding that you must break a few eggs just like making an omelet. The next time, you and your team will be better. Over time, you and your team will not remember why you were frustrated if you were in it together. The experience of investing in your team also means that this is your development, too. Study, read, and absorb everything you can to improve. Demand high accountability from yourself by growing and investing in yourself. If your health and fitness are weak, improve upon healthy ways to minimize your stress. Your organizational culture will improve when you help each other to stay true to your transformational journey. Make sure you align and combine any growth incentives, be they monetary, between cross-training and other production incentive programs.

You are investing in your team when you develop them. When investing in your team, you tell your customers that quality products and service matter. When you tell customers you value people by investing in them, they will ask you how. Demonstrate that 'how' by showing your teams' development in your cross-training and other creative idea programs. Your customers will see that you invested in people and the community when you do. This contributes to the common good because when people on your team thrive, everyone thrives. However, remember that organizations are not here to pass out human worthiness. Regardless, we must all work and be productive in one manner or another. We are here to nurture and grow the worthiness of ourselves and then help others by investing in their desire to develop their potential. Big 'C' or little 'c' let us help everyone flourish. We are always in a fight to realize a better future. We must choose ascension over descension. In turn, everyone has a chance to pursue their happiness. Choose to add value in every moment so people can realize renewal and rebirth on their daily journey.

Chapter 13

You Think You Know You

How well do you know yourself? There are sides to who you are. We can learn more about ourselves when we open to asking ourselves questions. Are you an introvert or an extrovert? Are you an ambivert? Do you consider yourself highly logical? Are you a creative person? Do you find it easy to express your thoughts and feelings? Do you avoid feelings as bothersome things that only get in the way? Do you focus on your environment? Are you expressive? Do you challenge others? Do you agitate others? Do you make peace at all costs, even to your disregard? Are you a loner? Are you afraid to be alone? Are you aware of your personality type? Do you obsess? What do you obsess over? Why do you obsess?

Humans are living algorithm sensors that dwarf any AI yet created. We collect a lot of information. Some of that information is not good, and we do not always use the information we collect well. We humans are a work in progress. We have learned to categorize and sub-categorize over thousands of years. We are not completed works; we may never be, but we must activate and continue striving to be our best. We have discovered patterns in our human behavior. Naturally, our environment and IQ play a role in who we become. I suggest you explore what your personality type may be. Discover for yourself how distinct types use their strengths and what weaknesses you must work on. We all have weaknesses. Businesses use personality tests to figure out suitability. While this may be useful in assembling your team from a generic point of view, the environment and how you act and respond to it matters most. That is what you remember, and that is what reinforces who you are. So, if you have taken actions, you are not proud of -perhaps even disgusted by - that have formed who you have become now, have those experiences motivated you to improve, or have you leaned into your mistakes to see yourself in a darker light?

The most significant value in personality tests is showing what areas you thrive, what areas you struggle with, and how your experience has shaped your decision-making. Having an awareness of your personality type helps. It can help you unwrap your life to see what influences you and your thinking, and it can help shed light on your ability to find acceptance and cooperate with others. They can reveal what rubs your soul wrong so you can grow rather than be surprised by issues later. Knowing why you think as you do helps you lead other people. Personality assessments can reveal your team's ability to work together cohesively. Where did your good behavior come from? Where have instances of harmful or toxic behaviors come from? The Native American story that asks which wolf will win? Then, with the reply, "The one that you feed" (Virtues for Life, 2024). That should zero us in on the focus of doing the right thing always, now for ourselves and others. Have the beliefs and traditions of your family or your close circle shaped how you think or what you believe? Have you been part of the herd, going along to get along so you don't upset family, friends, or peers at work? Have you challenged yourself by asking who you want to be? Have you become what others find convenient to have around: quiet, compliant, submissive, or lesser? Have you let the thoughts and ideas of others take precedence because you think they are more intelligent than you? Are they loud and aggressive? Are you? Either way, we must ask ourselves whether we have made ourselves into a puppet of the circle we came from or if we are much more. Can we all be more? Have we stopped believing kindness, forgiveness, competence, wisdom, nobility, and stability are worthy? Do we hate the weakness the jungle stands for while simultaneously wanting it to feed our ego through our relationship to the roles we project onto ourselves that give us a feeling of self-worth? Is this world on a slowly stalling, descending glide slope? Forget that the world has been around for thousands of years. Don't we all fall into the trap of believing that somehow 'my lifetime' is special, that the time I am living in is more special than generations past? Do we believe that, or is that arrogance, the ego stroking us like a self-unaware cat? Is it possible that transforming for the better is for individual survival and a crucial necessity for all human development? How about, for a time, we set aside the excuse of a fiery end that prevents humans from being loving and kind, stifles evolution, and instead makes living a more harmonious life a priority? We are not clones of our parents, circle, friends, past, or present. Strip away the excuses. We are individually unique. We are not here to play a part but to be a part of a healthy culture. We must demand and work to achieve it. We are not going to progress, wishing instead of working for it. Question your programming and ask who owns it. If you are too much like anyone else, immediately question whether you have picked up their bad habits or conditioning. Do we participate in societal self-sabotage when we know we are closer to the end of our lives than the beginning? Ask the hard questions so we do not project a mirage of fear and hopelessness where an uncomfortable human rebirth is more likely what is taking place. Are the questions we ask ourselves and those answers driving our lives forward and upward?

We are simultaneously quite simple and extraordinarily complex at the same time. It does not matter which one you think you are -you are both. You may not have known it because so much is going on all at once, all the time, affecting you internally and externally. It affects everyone you love and those you do not. All of this happens at lightning speed. You are constantly tracking, assessing, and making determinations about the world.

You are a supercomputer. We do not see ourselves as supercomputers continually evaluating, receiving, and acting on data, but we are.

In organizations, we may assess the team's combined performance. We may even evaluate our team members periodically. However, we are usually less concerned about evaluating ourselves and our behaviors. This is why we can be surprised; everyone else picks up our behaviors to a greater degree. We notice ourselves the least. Nothing is hidden; this includes our successes and our failures. Misunderstandings can create problems as wide as the Grand Canyon in an organization. Culture struggles to deal with honest, healthy communication about complex issues. Human cultures should be vastly ahead in our ability to set aside differences, find solutions, and cooperate compared to technological advancements. However, we see waste and turnover rates higher than forty percent in organizations. In 2021, 47.2 percent in the US (Ariella, 2023). All waste emanates from poor culture ultimately. We would fail if we were grading ourselves on how healthy and effective organizational cultures are. We all must be brave to own that failure, dissect it, understand our part in it, and then evolve through it. We must own the reality of who we have been before we can grow into who we want to be as individuals, teams, and organizations. We must make hard choices and let go of the toxicity and its influences on our lives inside and outside work. Healing ourselves and our relationships will bring the highest good to everything we are a part of.

We do not always use superior performers as examples to influence other team members who struggle to perform or who waffle in their consistency. Is it their attitude? Is it their behavior? Why aren't other team members stepping up in the same way? Are team members broken? Assess yourself honestly, irrespective of your role:

1. Rate your organization's negative and good behaviors from 1 least to 9 greatest.
2. Have your team rate the organization the same way.
3. Compare your team's composite and individual ratings to yours as the leader.
4. Now, you must begin to investigate why so you can improve your score.

Search it out internally for yourself and externally with your team. No judgment. You will bias your answers if you judge yourself and your true feelings. If your attitude is to blend in, then you are, in effect, defanging your ability to be trusted, have influence, lead, and be an impact player in your personal and professional life. Advice: Own your reality as it is, not as you wish it to be. We are all flawed, and we all have struggles in life. Own them and own fixing them.

Figure out what path to take. Your attitude and your behavior speak volumes about how you feel. When attitudes appear to be masked, look for passive-aggressive behaviors to become apparent. Be aware of those dodging meaningful engagement. Be mindful of those who prioritize unnecessary drama or gravitate toward phantom issues. Look at inferior quality, on-time delivery, or late orders and understand why and what is driving current results. Has passive aggression revealed itself? Who is dealing in office politics? Who is dealing with ever-escalating failures and omissions? The point is to heal and develop people first; remember that. Otherwise, nothing else you do in your organization will last.

Chapter 14

The Dysfunction in Life

It is not hard to see how the dysfunction in people's lives affects their work. That said, it is impossible that any of us have not been exposed to some level of dysfunction directly or indirectly. My Grandfather, my dad's father, was a functioning alcoholic. I never saw it, thankfully. People tend to judge more by role and appearance than by truth. The military does random drug screening. I have always been amazed that no regular national requirement exists in all school systems and other vital and sensitive work environments exposed to our most vulnerable. Most organization's normative behavior is to avoid personal problems. Indeed, we should not bury our heads in the sand when they are brought to our attention. We suffer from a sort of social cowardice when dealing with anything truly profound or significant. Because of this, it is still impossible to assess problematic issues quickly or accurately with people. People can be a closed-off and sometimes superficial puzzle when they hide who they are, wearing masks to blend in to survive. It is ok, though; we are all at the same disadvantage. We deal with people with only part of their story and half the information about them most of the time. While some people enjoy the puzzle, others see it as distracting from the team's efforts. And it is. We must exercise caution, though, because secrecy, too, is the tool of the master manipulators, narcissists, and the mere dramatic attention seekers in organizations. We can all be tricked and fooled by thieves, be they material thieves, emotional thieves, or those who tamper; the tricksters who love creating chaos for their own amusement.

There is no education like having a thief upend your organization. We can also be fooled by nefarious organizations manipulating people by misinformation and omission. What, then, is normal? Who defines it? Why is it important? Why should I care? In general, it revolves first around safety. We have laws, and the Constitution protects our right to pursue happiness. The simplest way to think of it is, 'I do not want my safety and freedom to be affected by others' omissions, actions, or neglect. Therefore, logic follows that no one should infringe by actions on others' safety or the pursuit of happiness by neglect or omission. This seems simple and fair. However, when fear is introduced, fear of the unknown specifically, people tend to act in ways that hamper any awareness that they infringe on any agreed-upon social contracts or rights. At a certain point, people fail to care. Once a particular threshold is crossed, suddenly, people forget the humanity of others and fixate on their own needs. Once the selfish narrowing of one's vision occurs regarding others, anything can be justified, including all poor behavior. The behaviors extend from personal interaction to professional and culture at large.

Fear is no justification to do anything hurtful to anyone. However, you see it in the news constantly. The news force feeds a diet of controversy. Controversy then upsets the typical harmony of the masses by being self-serving in what is communicated and reported. Perpetuating fear by posing doubts about your safety and security throws life off balance for people daily. I know people who will not watch the news because it stresses them out and makes them fearful. Life is harsh. Some news is difficult. There is a thin line between perpetrating hysteria and informing people. Apply that to those who perpetuate hysteria in your organization, unnecessarily stressing people on your team. Employees who spread inflammatory rumors about the organization in the community instead of focusing on critical projects and customer timelines are doing the same. Would those people and situations be any less self-serving than the media example? Triggered by nefarious intent or negligence, the damage is constantly taking its toll on our lives personally and within our organizations, distracting us from our purpose of serving customers.

We agree that laws and rules of common decency are necessary to set the stage for people to live safe and abundant lives. What some people consider typical, others do not. We sometimes refer to this gap as a gray area. Some are loose-living and do not abide by common laws and rules. Some do not respect or regard others within the scope of common decency. For now, let us keep the fringe on the fringe. The 80/20 rule generally means that twenty percent of people work against harmony for their own gain. However, the converse is true: Twenty percent are working hard to grow harmony, going beyond just surviving to be and do good. The sixty percent in the middle are just surviving to keep what harmony they have. For them, the most significant personal and professional opportunities are possible if they reach and stretch beyond their comfort zone for a more extraordinary life.

Humans are raised with many influences. How we were parented, what good and bad experiences have influenced us, our ability to trust, triggers of abandonment and neglect, betrayals, and how we were nurtured have all been cultural challenges. How much conditioning did any of us overcome? Where are we now with some of these sensitive areas? Who gave up? Have we sped past everything that has influenced us- not realizing what and where our thin spots are? What has shaped us to be generally good? How much pain from your experiences as a child influences how well or how poorly you treat others now? Have you overcome deep-seated pains from your past? Notice, I did not ask if you have numbed yourself out with codependent rogue or rebellious behaviors. Instead, have you grown through your experiences and actualized becoming good despite your history? Does your history solely define you? Are you striving to be good in all areas? Has your environment negatively affected you? How have you changed your environment? If not, why not? How did others treat you in school? Were you treated poorly in the community? Has it shaped who you are as an adult? Did you believe who others said you were? Did you ignore them? Did you rise above negativity? Do negative experiences still plague you? Remember, ignoring, trying to forget, or glossing over the past is not healing. Have you sought counseling even if you thought your experiences were minor? All of us must own the person we are. Do you have someone to talk to about anything? Having someone personally and professionally who will listen to you is healthy. Who is your 'go-to' person? This would be a healthy Human Resources program in any organization.

Have you broken the rules, got caught, and decided to turn your life around? Were you ever caught? How did you turn your life around? Are you a rule-breaker now? How do you behave toward others now? Are you an overt or covert thief? Are you a genuinely good and loving person? Have you repressed anger? Are you an over-giver? Do they control you? Are you the driver or the passenger in your life? Are you Dr. Jekyll during the week and Mr. Hyde during the weekends? Have consequences shaped you? Have consequences failed to shape you? Are you living in a state of rebellion? Who are you rebelling against? Have you learned valuable lessons? Were you worshiped as a child and told you never make mistakes? Were you always told you were right? What have you learned once you entered the working world? Have negative behaviors affected your team and your organization at work? Likewise, how have good people and good experiences influenced you? Are you caught in the middle, unsure of who you are, taking two steps forward and three steps back? Ask yourselves these questions and more. Get into your shadow; deal with your life, heal, and free yourself to grow.

Trying is worthwhile. Stick to a good path. Keep your heart true. Be transparent. Own your mistakes. Move forward in life, and desire abundance for everyone you meet. Be humble. Be thankful. Be a helpful person. Be a positive light to others. Make yourself and your attitude positive. Just be gentle and genuine. Be an example to everyone regardless of your status, whether you are the newest employee or CEO. Rise above the fray of what you once considered 'normal.' Moments are too valuable in your life to let the opportunity to cherish those moments slip by you. Doing these things will strengthen and heal you. You will simultaneously heal others on your team when you start pulling the weeds from your heart first, no matter your role. When an organization thrives in this healing energy, it is where people want to be. People want to be a part of a family that holds us accountable but also nurtures and supports our journey to heal and grow. Make your organization the next best thing to a family you can imagine and honor the people in it.

Realize that you are not any of the dysfunctions or issues of your life. It is healthy to acknowledge dysfunctions, but the point is to grow forward from them and release them. In this way, you aim for the best future outcome. This does not mean your life will be completely carefree. The external world will still try to thwart and catch you off guard. Sometimes, things happen, and we must clean up the spilled milk. We must ask ourselves why it spilled and how to prevent it from happening again instead of just going on with our day. Pass this approach on, and you will find it easier to guide others going through similar circumstances. It is important to let go of yesterday's grip on you while ensuring you do not step into yesterday's potholes. You get to decide the path and how bright the light inside you lights up your journey and those who travel the journey with you. You choose and control what level to turn your brilliance up to.

Most suffering internally. Suffering knows no economics because it is all relative. It can be subtle or constantly foreboding over one's life path. Suffering reveals itself in overt and covert ways. Like secrets, nothing experienced, including suffering, stays hidden forever. It is always eventually discovered. Those who suffer do not realize that we already know it. Those who suffer can also resort to passive-aggressive behaviors that take on many hurtful forms. Hurt people, hurt people, but should they be? Should we be okay with that? Those who feel snubbed, cut off, short-changed, or picked on can also show retribution for their suffering. Sufferers can become the 'snake pit' where nothing good comes out. Healing is stifled when we avoid those who suffer. Our challenge is to discern and inspire the suffering to climb out of the pit they dug so deep. Like a person with an addiction, those who suffer must choose to heal; they cannot be made to heal at the pace everyone else around them expects them to. Some do not know there are resources for them. If they want it, organizations that offer their team members general resources and support provide an excellent service for their team.

One can use the dark side and the light, or the force if you want, to describe the essence of the choices you make from moment to moment. Being a part of a force for good every day by consciously sifting out and rejecting to speak or act from the dark side of things is a simple yet effective way to guide oneself toward harmony in life, allowing us to shed positive light on others' lives, too. We are all human, and this is what challenges us every day: making choices that transform ourselves and others. It never ends. We are all students of life. Do our poor choices make us victims? What we do to overcome the results of poor decisions can make us victors, as we know. If your next choice is to help guide people while supporting healthy boundaries, you will be healing. There is no victory in mourning what has happened to you in your past, forever. Let it go and live forward, not backward, because rebirth lives in the choices we make each day. Most choices you make are about your identity, choosing to see yourself as a peaceful victor or as a rebellious victim. What will you choose for yourself? What will you choose for your team and your organization? If everyone and everybody in your organization is just an extension of your team, then anything good helps everyone, including your primary customers.

As an exercise, have everyone on your team bring in a small rock individually. Have your team quietly hold their rock. Instruct them to mentally list all the past negative issues they can think of and imagine all of those going into that rock. If you have a ditch or a hole or go somewhere of your choosing acceptable to your organization or group. One by one, each team member tosses their rock into the hole or ditch with the instruction that doing this means everyone and the organization gets a reset, a fresh starting point. From that point forward, everyone forgets what was thrown in. Those with individual unresolved concerns should be given time to speak to the leadership as necessary. The team needs to be present, not always fixated on the past. Forward-thinking organizations cannot get caught up on the malaise of the past.

Chapter 15

Deception

We pay magicians to trick us. We find delight in figuring out how the magician fooled us when we were looking directly at them. They may have performed their sleight of hand repeatedly in front of our eyes, so sure, we would never figure out the trick regardless of how focused we were on them. In this way, magicians make us feel good. It is fun for magicians to amuse us. This is why magicians are the only good kind of deceiver we will ever meet.

Most deceivers do not intend for us to feel good about tricking us. A pickpocket is the street version of the deceiver who simultaneously plays the part of the magician and the deceiver, happy to pick your wallet, purse, or anything you have of value. Despite how clever it is, we do not like what pickpockets do to us. This is why people do their best to protect themselves from pickpockets.

You may have experienced deception closer to home. Depending on your experience, you may have had family, friends, or loved ones, even past spouses, who may have deceived you when you were completely unaware and completely trusting. Some would classify those who have deceived us as backstabbers, manipulators, or narcissists. The backstabbing could have taken the form of words spoken wrongly about you and your character, or worse, behind your back. This deception is magnified to greater levels when people have deceived you by colluding with others, conspiring to trick, fool, and rob you of more than your money - your trust, your dignity, or damage your character. You may have discovered it quickly, it may have taken years, or it may still be illuding you to this day, hidden from view -from your awareness, behind your back.

No one wants to be distrusting or paranoid about essential people in our lives who might or could deceive us. We all want to believe there is transparency and truth in all our relationships. However, sadly, this is not the case. Discovering friends, family, peers, or employers who have worked against our best interests can be devastating and downright heartbreaking. You may have found in the past that a significant other was cheating on your relationship. We feel deceived when we discover that people have worked against our higher good in nefarious ways. Deception conducted in conspiring ways is betrayal. The deceit may have been so surprising that it was a shock, feeling your heart was being broken right inside your chest. When that occurred, deceit turned into a betrayal. Depending on how significant the betrayal is, you are carrying a feeling of distrust that follows all your relationships in subtle ways, in one form or another. Due to betrayal, the follow-on behavior is to judge or try to make a general judgment about other people in your personal and professional life. Your betrayal now carries a universal truth within you. In some ways, you may be doing or avoiding actions, activities, or aspects of life because you fear betrayal. You may avoid close personal or professional relationships due to your past betrayals. You may be putting on a façade of strength, composure, confidence, or perhaps a veil of superficiality done to protect yourself while simultaneously refusing to buy in too deeply to potentially deceptive people when no deception may be occurring at all. In this way, deception is when people deceive themselves about 'possible' deception. This is gaslighting yourself because you do not want to believe the truth. If you are highly intuitive, your past hurts, and betrayals may have turned you into an accurate human lie detector. Naturally, the converse is that your intuition fools you into being paranoid. Betrayals may have made you paranoid about everyone's motives, hamstringing your life in subtle or overt ways, like a shivering mouse in the corner, afraid there are cats everywhere while actual cats are nowhere to be found.

The degree to which betrayals trigger or affect your life is subjective. Only you can decide if you have successfully integrated the practical reality that deception exists. Your perspective about learning lessons may be that you can stomach minor betrayals but be on guard, ready to figuratively pounce on anyone who might consider a monstrous deception or betrayal. If the mouse survives the cat's attack, perhaps the cat becomes prey to the mouse, who is now more aware. Another extreme is when people blame themselves instead of the perpetrator for betrayal. Everyone must assess their situation to determine what experiences have influenced their behavior regarding betrayal and how constructively and reasonably they can realign themselves without making themselves feel too unnecessarily vulnerable. The mouse has now armed itself with sufficient social skills to communicate to swarthy cats that betrayal is unacceptable. I suspect that technology will be mandated to catch many rogue cats.

Everyone must battle and conquer past deception the way someone in the military would regard past battles, asking, 'What did I learn about myself,' 'What can we learn about ourselves?' and 'What did we misunderstand about each other?' that made us vulnerable to deception and betrayal? For low-vibrationally aligned/ negative people, deception is merely a daily tool and tactic. We humans overlay meaning or judgment onto the deception. Often, deception is for the deceiver to gain an advantage for themselves. They could care less about people, seeing them as a means to an end, an unwitting mark for an illusory prize of helping them to forget their fear and vulnerability, to feel power as a drug to mask all their pain.

The point of being aware of deception is to win by keeping an equilibrium and to retain the general joy of living by being vulnerable, doing so with a sober awareness, not paranoia. Everyone is ultimately capable of deception. Life cannot be enjoyed unless we are vulnerable. Deception is just part of the terrain of the experience of life. This does not mean we should participate or advocate making excuses for it. It means we should fight to keep behaviors surrounding it openly known and challenged if we smell or intuit that something is off in a situation. We question unknowns to make them known and challenge the perception of situations to ensure that what we see and hear passes the sanity test. This way, everyone understands what energy and behaviors are occurring in real-time as a team. An internal goal of any organization should be to do away with office politics and any perception of it so that deception and betrayal never gain a foothold to conspire against any person or group. The team must be vigilant to ensure that the organization does not take part in deception or betrayal by intention or omission. Preventing deception from coloring our opinions and weighting our bias is what can be controlled. Those who deceive were once deceived and consciously chose to emulate that conditioning. Awareness about those who deceive is only the start of preventing deceptions. Eliminating deception is a higher priority than promoting trust. In a vacuum where deception cannot breathe, trust will flourish in its absence.

Deception is no easier to deal with, whether talking about a person, a team, or an organization. We must start by giving everyone the benefit of the doubt when high levels of communication quickly become misunderstandings. We must be careful. If your private life has been fraught with deceit, you must fight your bias at work; otherwise, you will negatively affect your team. Know, though, that just because you give people the benefit of the doubt, this does not mean that people on your team are not deceiving you. It just means you cannot assume so. This is why evidence is essential when dealing with something as serious as deceit.

No matter what influences your opinion of others, never assume anything you have not heard or seen yourself. Rumor and innuendo can be a slippery slope where deception is concerned. Avoid rumors and innuendos and stop them fast when you find them. Rumor and innuendo can turn into deceit quickly. Some may think they are preventing deceit by spreading rumors and innuendo in a futile attempt to curb it by assuming it is happening without having all the facts. This is why rumor and innuendo are a no-go at all. Rumor and innuendo go through many people, morphing from one statement into a 'story.' Never believe something about others secondhand that you would not want to believe about yourself. If you do, you can be assured that you will be the next person run over by rumors and innuendo that morphs into deceit. Do not inadvertently institutionalize deceit by failing to squash rumor and innuendo immediately.

The easy answer to deceit is to be truthful, open, honest, and transparent about your thoughts, intentions, and actions. Be aware that your feelings about how you receive something are not facts about what may have been said and actions done. Be aware that your feelings about what someone has done are not facts about why something was done -or a validation about whether something was done. Emotions and feelings are not truth. They are only the truth about how you feel. We cannot let the emotional swell of our feelings create a false narrative, a deception by our feelings and emotions. This is why we pack our feelings into questions to verify and confirm when unsure. In this way, we have not figured out whether deceit has happened but are merely investigating if one has occurred. The beauty of any person's life is the knowledge that life and the significant events that happen to people can change people. People can take advantage to turn their lives around by taking the high road. We must deal with the behavior at hand and go from there. Indeed, though, repetitive deceptive behavior is a trend. We must make a judgment call based on the impact on the customer and the team.

Chapter 16

Boundaries

How healthy are our boundaries? Do I have boundaries? What are my boundaries? We could replace boundaries with borders, with cages, with boxes, circles, and even bubbles. Boundaries are not your privacy. Some may choose to replace boundaries with safe spaces. Even well-treated animals are kept in cages, zoos, pens, and corals and are fenced in. Few cringe at the idea that animals are kept in captivity. Humanity quickly disassociates itself from the moment-to-moment suffering of animals unless that suffering is brought to our immediate attention or there is vastly excessive maltreatment. The human collective is not socially moved to care if animals are free to roam. It is not a long leap to understand that our human collective does not think about other people unless something significant is brought to our immediate attention, usually after the damage is done. I know from my experience, as I have seen in others' lives, too, that people seek us most when they need something they lack. In this way, people can hold each other socially captive by expectation, captive within their 'circle' and captive alternatively outside their 'circle' when the opposite is true. Any captivity is an awful thing. People can ostracize themselves, placing themselves in captivity of their own making. People who bother us or who get on our wrong side are either put into captivity away from us, or we place ourselves in captivity away from them. 'Boundaries' is a term we typically hear. 'Boundaries' is a cozy word. It makes our fear feel special. Let us think back to those animals for a second. We see other living creatures as less than ourselves. We do not give a second thought to how they are caged, controlled, studied, and held captive for our amusement. Most humans barely hold other humans in higher regard than animals, considering little of what happens to them. Why do we put ourselves and others into mental prisons, into a captive state? Answer: We do not want to deal with those we cannot cooperate with or who will not cooperate with us. It is about control.

We have systematized these spoken and unspoken boundaries for protection. Even the term my inner circle is accepted vernacular, blurring our boundaries with an inclusionary and exclusionary acceptance turn stall. Who are you keeping out? Why are we interning ourselves, ostracizing ourselves from the herd? When you slow it down, it is evident that we fear each other. We fear energy vampires who will drain our life force from us. We fear what others think. We fear those energy vampires that return to drain the life force from us. The fear of what others might do to us causes us to use boundaries. Boundaries can be used to exclude others from the 'special group.' However, it is still fear. Fear controls people socially, personally, culturally, and organizationally. People fear judgment, vulnerability, and trust. The thoughts, feelings, and opinions others have about you influence your level of fearfulness subconsciously, unseen. Worse is fearing that close people in your life will judge you. That kind of fear hands control of your life over to those who could devastate, scar, and damage you in many ways. The fear of betrayal is a significant reason you set boundaries. It is a preventative measure, a risk avoidance step to ensure the nefarious are kept over there, away from you. This is a lonely but safe place you created to protect the spark of child-like innocence that lives deep inside you. Fear can be an alert for your health and safety. Boundaries do not keep fear out; boundaries keep people out while fear lives safe and snug inside, teasing and tormenting you, convincing you to build higher, thicker, stronger walls to protect you behind your boundary or keep you entombed in your circle. Boundaries only keep you away from everyone else, both mentally and emotionally. There are no actual walls because we are talking about your heart and essence that lives alone inside you.

People have been traumatized, betrayed, hurt, and abandoned in the past. For them, boundaries are the most profound retreat behind the thickest of walls. It has been done for protection. Healing in these situations may require professionals to help guide that healing—gradually and gently. Emotional trauma, though, is subjective. What may be an annoyance for a few is a trauma for others, while not noticeable at all for some.

In the same way, some people may fear dentists while plenty of others could care less. Many people may flourish in a mob, while the overload of senses may choke others. We are all different. Our experiences are relative and unique. A combat veteran might be less affected by office politics. A civilian may be triggered by mere words or tone in a conversation. For the civilians, thoughts and ideas, not physical reality, may take precedence as a threat and put them on a warlike footing. The veteran may be affected by the lack of character on a team. At the same time, the jungle-like backstabbing nature in pockets within the civilian workforce may be more typical for the civilian worker. I hate to overgeneralize, but everything is relative. The concept of living false fearlessness exists more efficiently in a vacuum, in communities where wealth creates fenced boundaries and bubbles. Try to live fearlessly where crime is at its highest and the nefarious do not share or respect common values, awaiting the next blissful person wandering down the street to victimize. Experience, information-education, and intellect must help to inform all of us to empower fearlessness. A wise person who grew up living in dangerous areas finds their alert system for safety pulled on least as they have 'learned' and conditioned themselves how to survive and navigate the obstacles, not go to war with them. So, we must all learn to survive past fears and barriers that absorb our worrying energy while simultaneously working to remove the obstacles to our success. Do not make boundaries an excuse; instead, make them a portal of opportunity to step through and allow you to build connections. Reassemble the bricks of your walls into bridges. Be a bridge to the possible. Turn the bullies into bulldogs of purpose and empower their hearts to be protectors. It requires balance to transform, heal relationships, and be a bridge others can cross to realize their own transformation.

Some have been traumatized in their youth. They did not address those underlying issues. They have been carrying that burdensome emotional baggage their entire life. Some have taken on aggressive, fake, and overly confident façades to mask their pain. These facades distract us from seeing their pain. Out of fear, they play a part that denies their healing. Some undermine their relationships, self-sabotaging their life with codependent numbing behaviors that keep them from building any truly meaningful connections. Over-superficiality is their safety net. Depending on the scale of trauma, all this shadow pain paralyzes people and teams unaware. You cannot hide unhealthy culture from customers.

Some people identify with the bullies and bad leaders of their past. These tormentors' negative ways live on in the lives of the tormented, who falsely now imbibe those same traits as a recipe for success. Bad habits, toxicity, drama, and codependency become the organizational legacy. Do you see familiarity between unhealthy organizations and culture? People are devolving behind their walls as if bracing for impact. Meanwhile, technology and tools are evolving rapidly. People are caught in a trance of cognitive dissonance: innovation on the one hand and unaddressed wounds on the other. Lack of transparency and the creation of unhealthy walls and boundaries have deceptively and codependently divided people and cultures. Groups, communities, and people are divided against each other. Division is the malignancy of the human soul. Division is falsely interpreted as protection by the fearful who have manifested it. We humans can manifest better. We can no longer live in denial of our truth and deal with realities if we are to heal these wounds.

Self-expression is not just self-expression. When it becomes a mechanism for division, it ultimately becomes a version of social engineering, an instrument born from fear. Inclusive, open, and vulnerable self-expression is born out of love, which is the healthy driver in our lives when we choose it intentionally. Our enemy is us when we deny the deep internal struggle and become lured by the superficial and the shallow. Those building high walls and mental boundaries are afraid. They project fears of anything disagreeable in the past onto the now, the great distraction. This projection serves no one, helps no one, and heals no one. It does require constant justification, attention, energy, and a need to feed the ego so that fear can be suppressed along with vulnerability, not unlike lying to oneself. This amounts to customers paying twice for products and services because people and organizations do not go to that vulnerable place to heal. We have hyper-inflated the world's economies and hurt those with little because we have given into fear-based ego-driven thinking, allowing the tail to wag the dog.

We humans are social beings. We are not meant to struggle or thrive in solitude. The fear people feel is a lion to be tamed and freed within us. Then, the boundaries must be relaxed so we can honestly deal with one another and express ourselves without fear and judgment, cutting out the need to be frivolous, superficial, and distracting. Nothing about life is safe. The sooner we figure that out and begin healing, the sooner we can work toward being whole people and building cultures that will develop and innovate a healthy future well rather than drowning culture and our futures in past pain.

The real fear most have is that their Love will be somehow depleted if they show or give too much empathy or serve others too much. A question to ask is, who fills your cup up now? That is who or what you are codependent on. When you do not get your Love returned, you reduce your internal self-worth, marginalize your need for Love, become irritated or angry with people who do not return it, and then replace it with codependent behaviors and substances to suppress it. That is the ego keeping score and running, ruining your life. Then, you justify fear-based boundaries instead of getting to these internal truths. Take it easy on yourself; you are human and imperfect. Work with yourself first by loving yourself and giving yourself a bit of empathy on the road to healing. Take the time and care to ween yourself off your codependency. Replace unhealthy behaviors and toxic relationships with healthy ones. Moderation is a great starting point for us all, and we should avoid harshly judging everyone with a different minor and major codependency as evil. Let's stop judging as if we are all suspended in time from the moment of our last mistake in life. This is not fair to anyone.

Intelligent people can get into bad relationships. What am I using as a measure of intelligence? Books? You cannot replicate life from just a book. While you can avoid significant pitfalls by observing others from the sidelines, the subtle lessons embedded in failure are opportunities to grow wiser, provided you do not get stuck repeating the same lesson unnecessarily. Acknowledge past lessons, but don't demonize those involved; they are your teachers in life. Do not be prevented from living an extraordinary life because of your lessons. We are all meant to grow through the winning and losing of life's phases. That is life, a living classroom that allows us to bounce back. We must allow ourselves to bounce back, expect it from ourselves, raise our bar, and rise with momentum and confidence to the next phase of life. It is okay to take a knee, mourn the losses, be introspective, and examine what has happened and what we have learned. We must then begin our journey upward again.

Failure is believing we are good enough just as we are, a finished work. That type of thinking is the ego tricking people into staying stuck in lack and excuses that keep people in a loop of repeating the same behaviors. Lethargy has a cost. Imagine an alarm clock waking you up in the morning; that is manageable. It is overwhelming, though, if instead of an alarm clock, a giant wrecking ball destroys your home, life, business, and you in the process. Do not wait for the universe to bring you a wrecking ball because you were complacent. Take the hints, learn the lessons, step outside your boundaries, and keep moving upward, even if it is just daily baby steps. Who you are and what you do matters to the world, and we need you to be in the game of life, growing and making a positive difference. Do you seek a burning bush or something spectacular to wake you up? What if a stranger randomly says, "I believe in you"? Shouldn't you first slow down and turn your receiver on? I believe in you!

Culture claims the devices of the law of the jungle, predator versus prey; the mouse scurries through the underbrush and survives the surrounding drama. This happens all at once in culture, too, confusing our senses. Evolving to a greater force for good, the 'law of the jungle' calls out two extremes: fear and Love. These either force us to hide like the mouse or rise to our humanity. Too much of our ego needs control, aligning us with fear. Too much emotion weakens us, driving us back around to fear. Balance is in the middle; integration of the two achieves harmony and balance, as illustrated in Figure A14. Love thrives here. The closer we are to the center of the spiral, the easier it is to transform ourselves and our teams. New possibilities, creations, innovations, and growth come to life in healthier ways when we are in balance. We humans are inner and outer world builders. We are transforming individually from the inside out, changing our external world by allowing us to delve into our core root causes and problems and healing by doing the necessary repair work, which is different for everyone and may require coaching. We learn to be more affirmative by improving our self-talk to what is good and constructive. We can become more appreciative and grateful outwardly, too, when we have begun or gone through this rebirthing process.

Some speed past the dark shadow of their experiences, leaning into codependency, including placing their happiness onto the shoulders of other people instead of bearing the weight. Alcohol, drugs, and other seemingly normative addictions are increasingly more culturally accepted. People are no happier, though, just more codependent, more scared, and numb to reality. Many take part in escapism, seeking elevated risk, activity chasing, or other distractions to avoid dealing with the pain or issues at hand (Garcia-Navarro, 2024). We see the fallacy on social media; people perpetuate that 'the cooler the stuff I do, the happier and whole I must be.' No distractions in the world will spackle over unresolved, unhealed issues, no matter how big, small, or recent, where you went on vacation to distract yourself, or how far back in history your issues took place. It is up to the most loving person to break the chain, break the cycle from a good and caring place. We cannot numb ourselves, wear masks, and take on false personas. Boundaries are not created from clever strength but from fear. We can sense those who operate from fear, doubt, lack of confidence, and bad intentions. Do those who live from fear see themselves the way we see them? They do not. In the same way, a person with an addiction is in denial about being an addict. Their Love will be covered by anger toward those closest until they have begun the arduous process of overcoming their codependency, taking back, or starting to take back real and honest emotional control of themselves.

Some have built walls out of fear, and they then throw toxic rocks and duck behind those walls. Some use their weakness as walls; their limitations, inability, and lack of understanding have been made into their wall. Sadly, the illusions people think they are using to protect themselves hurt and neglect others who need their support in life. We must be willing to change and take incremental actions that will result in good outcomes. We cannot retreat intellectually, emotionally, and physically by contributing minimally, less, and less every year. We cannot stand hiding quietly behind others, fearing to be heard or recognized. It would be best if you made your voice heard. Leaders must have a mechanism in place to listen to the voices of their team. We cannot claim a supporting opinion in a forum and dissent later behind closed doors. We cannot be cowards by not listening to our team and not saying what must be said. We should not express dissent everywhere community-wide except where it matters -where the decision to correct a thing can be made or managed first. We cannot complain that our voice is not being heard if we are not brave enough or willing to document it, put our name on it, and own accountability for it, like adults.

The birth pain humanity is going through now is the high stress of a broader cultural rebirth. We are feeling birth pains before a collective breakthrough. We cannot stay in this in-between place; we must progress toward the light ahead: the future. Whether you know it or not, your choices force you to grow in love or wither in fear and negativity. Avoidance is not choosing. Toxic dissent is not choosing; it is nonconstructive; it is continuing a lazy agenda to break an already broken culture further rather than doing our individual and collective part to marshal it upward constructively.

Building boundaries wastes our individual and collective energy. It is easier and more productive not to do it. Boundaries are not pathways. Choose uniting energy versus dividing energy in your life and your organization, and you will see good results come back to you personally. Leaders who stifle communication, suppress people, suppress ideas, and quiet voices do a disservice to everyone in the organization.

You may have seen some managers cast leaders when it suits them as uncaring. It is too easy for them to play both ends against the middle the way a child plays both parents for control to get what they want. Knowing this is difficult but be aware that managing from the middle occurs. Who should the team trust? In a vacuum, the organization needs to be more cohesive with intention. A middle manager, unbeknown to the leader, may need help figuring out why so many problems are happening that should not be happening. Their investigation throughout the organization may have yielded no results. The answer is a moving target as the team is held in check by middle managers who may out any team members who speak up or step up to expose anything. Only the clumsiest middle managers get caught. Only then will the masses step forward. This also occurs if the leadership is replaced, and the team protects middle managers who are seen as having protected them by outing the leader, even if the truth is that the leader departs for new opportunities; no one on the team is ever the wiser, in this example. There is little difference between a rogue organization that operates this way and organized crime. For all this drama, the organization is not closer to finding the root cause of its pervading problems. The effect of middle management taking over is the tail wagging the dog. The organization's inability to keep outstanding team members and leaders for long is a clue that this is happening. Eliminate boundaries and open communication, invite critical feedback from everyone, and empower problem-solving and innovation that will shine a bright enough light to remove any desire for middle managers to take over your organization. Awareness about this phenomenon should be a flashing caution sign to any desiring to meddle that having integrity is always the only suitable boundary to protect.

Chapter 17

Make Peace with Your Past

It is easy to say, 'Do not drag the failures of your past around with you all day.' It is much harder to do, however. Even to the extent you have trained yourself to manage or subtly hypnotize yourself into believing you have never had a past hurt or ever suffered. We have all been affected by something. Humans live within the storm of life, not above it, below it, or to its side. When we suffer, all we can see is tragedy. However, a horizon of beauty surrounds the darkness of suffering the way dark clouds can wrap themselves around the view of the setting sun, where we can see the beauty and know that healing is a journey out of the darkness. Taking part in the healing grows us up and empowers us to serve others when they go through their turn at suffering. We are not healed when we have not made peace with our past.

When people turn their pain and injustice toward others in unhealthy ways, everyone around can see it. The person doing it may think they are somehow getting away with something. The person doing it may be oblivious to their harmful words, actions, and subtle or overt manipulations. They have integrated being a harmful person into the persona for which they are known. Some people may have failed to mourn the death of personal and professional relationships properly. Instead, they now drag that pain around with them everywhere they go, unhealed. There is a vacuum within them. After a time, people choose to fill that vacuum with more hurt, anger, or other codependent behaviors. Some people do choose healthy actions to grieve loss of all kinds. They also find ways to disconnect from the toxic influences that have brought turmoil to their life. This is more of a challenge in organizations. Start by seeing everything as a lesson on a graduating fish ladder that offers renewal every time you ascend to the next wiser stage. This is why it is essential not to allow ourselves to falsely believe we deserve pain and suffering or settle for sitting in stagnation. Like Domino's, our lives are connected, moving, and touching everyone and everything. If we allow ourselves to believe we deserve suffering, we kill our own lives over what is only meant to be a lesson. Look up, set goals, lighten up, and move out of stagnation and stuck-ness.

Each person must own their internal space and grow in it. People must see what is happening and protect themselves by developing themselves to survive pitfalls. The easiest but far less practical solution may be not to hire sociopaths and narcissists. They will self-eliminate once your team has grown their awareness. Leaders in organizations, though, must replace unhealthy environments that surround their teams with a new equilibrium so that their teams can make peace with the past by acknowledging the purpose of the trials that have forced them to grow in the first place. We should not be throwing people away. Acknowledge the failures and shortcomings, forgive them, release them, and live forward. Everyone wants, deep down, to have a clean new slate moving forward. As the team grows, a new strength will build inside your team and your leaders. A strange thankfulness for experiencing complex challenges together as a team will bind you, not unlike what happens during austere situations that people in the military experience, where lifelong friendships and bonds form from those shared challenges you overcame together.

However, we cannot truly make peace with the past until we have healed. You may need clarification about what area of your life to heal. You may have to use the 'Five Whys' to get to the root cause that requires healing (Usamani, 2024). Search for yourself: What do you feel most when regarding a person, your team, your organization, or a situation? Are you feeling angry? Are you feeling sad? Are you feeling heartbreak? Are you frustrated? You may have felt many things for so long that it has all become an intertwined mess of emotions. Peel slowly through it like an onion. Take the time to feel what you feel. Take a walk, eat food, get a coffee, talk to trusted people, and take notes on what you feel and why. Please write it down so you can get it outside of you. Manage it, and free your heart from it. When it becomes an intellectual or mental thing to consider, not an emotional one, you know you have put the situation where you can manage it. Now, write down courses of action that create wins for everyone after realizing the lesson in you and others. Remember, though; it is not up to you to teach anyone a lesson by doing something nefarious. If you feel that way, the lesson is yours: to be able to resolve conflicts or life's frustration in a place of respect, peace, and harmony. The answers are inside you, not outside of you. If you are a person who blames people for your woes, that is a red flag that you need to heal something inside you. Deep down, you have a blind spot in your behavior, thought process, or beliefs that have limited you and made you feel less than others. Feeling the need to bring justice that is not in line with good outcomes for everyone is your tallest, brightest red flag that something in your way of thinking needs to change. It needs to change so that you can manifest the best life for you as a person. Then, that will radiate toward your team, the leadership, the community, and the broader culture. When in doubt, seek professional help.

If you struggle to make peace with the past by putting the past to rest, you must be critically introspective while not judging yourself and give yourself time to dig into inner and outer truths. It is not easy. It is- a razor's edge approach to overcoming and keeping harmony in your life. It will help you balance your internal and external life more honestly. Think about the act of taking out smelly garbage; that is what you are doing -getting the harmful garbage in your mind and heart out and releasing false beliefs, false things that someone said to you, hurts that have affected your life -

that you ignored, even if it was as subtle as neglect or as overt as a betrayal. Be open, honest, vulnerable, and forgiving -of yourself first. No one can hurry up or short-circuit the process. It is different for everyone. You will be able to see yourself outside yourself and catch triggering events, thoughts, and feelings in you, in real-time, as they happen, and ask yourself, why? This way, you can coach yourself by asking who or what happened that affected you.

Your self-talk: What you say to yourself is valuable. Keep your self-talk honest but shape it positively when you see the direction you want to take your life, be it personal, the team, or the broader organization. You will be on your way to becoming your own trusted counselor because you will be applying external objectivity to your life as if it is all being digitally videoed, and you are reviewing it, making editing changes, cuts, storyline changes, and so forth. You are the creator of your life. Suppose you get up one day, move across the country, and do something completely different. Just ensure it is because you chose your path and are not avoiding problems. Think of a wolf trapped in a bear trap that needs to be freed. You know it, the wolf knows it, but it is in a stressful, irrational state. The wolf is beyond itself -suffering. You decide to help free the wolf, but the wolf is voraciously trying to bite you when you approach. You must do two things at once: free the wolf by opening the trap and simultaneously endure the cuts, strikes, and bites you will get from the wolf. You free the wolf. The wolf runs off. You feel bad because the wolf does not appreciate what you just did for it. You may also have endured many cuts and scratches. The wolf is free now, but it is still not healed. Your expectation is what hurts you. You expected the wolf to have a measure of thanks in its demeanor. When people act unappreciative or superficial, we must recognize that they live behind walls of suffering and fear like the scared wolf trapped in a bear trap of limitation. We must first create a healing environment and communicate an openness that healing can evolve. Healing will come from within once the freedom and safety to heal comes. Actively, though, as real conscious and accountable humans, we can speed up healing by showing appreciation for everyone's sacrifice and suffering, engaging from the outside. We should not emulate the wolf. You should see the freeing human in you and the scared wolf, too, and tame the wolf by seeing the value of your humanity in those who would also provide you with a healing environment. In time, with constancy and intention, your team will grow to honor the highest good in each other. See anything negative like rain. The rainy day may be sad and uninspiring to us now. However, the ground is thirsty, and growth comes from it. In the same way, had you not experienced negative challenges, you would not have been motivated to change and grow and bring good out of you. That good is the sunshine we desire ultimately.

Speak more honorably and respectfully. This does not mean we are not honest with people, clear and plain. Remember, everyone is at different stages dealing with their past pains and private journeys. Once you align your heart, you can smile; your smile will be seen more often as you release and deal with life openly and honestly. You will start to see the world around you change. You will begin to feel your stress level come down. You will find that manifesting success is less complicated, easier, and lighter than you thought. What you perceive as change around you is change within you first. Give the wolf time to heal and let go of controlling expectations. We are not here to save anyone. We are here to help all the customers, and the healing process on our team is part of it. By doing so, we are protecting love. You do not want to read this part, but we are here to save ourselves. We are here to be inspired by the rest of us and their journey so that we accept the mantle to live bold, courageous, and intentional lives.

It is okay to acknowledge past betrayals others have inflicted. Over time, your test is to be as good, accepting, and forgiving as possible. Otherwise, you will only carry bitterness that you will unleash on others later. This does not mean you should be anyone's doormat. Deal with real life now instead of harboring resentment or letting the tension build up so that it will only come out in anger when you do not want it to. We cannot be compassionate if we do not deal with issues as we go. Have you ever been snubbed intentionally or otherwise by a family member? Sure, you have. We all have. Did you deal with it when it happened, or did you swallow it and push it down, only to filter every interaction with the person through the lens of unresolved tension from past unresolved conflicts? We have all done this. Address this by either communicating with those people or looking inside and releasing those judgments and unresolved tensions. If they are significant, try to work it out with the person. They likely have no idea they irritate you. Doing this does not heal them; it heals and frees you. Realize that ego and pride are the only things preventing you from doing this. To whom are you giving your power? If ego and pride drive the bus, you are going over a cliff in that bus in the form of never healing these issues in your life, personally or professionally. Your attitude has likely suffered because of it. Seek professional help if your feelings are so overwhelming that you are at a loss about what approach to take. If you feel you might harm yourself or others, seek immediate help. Pre-empt any further pain by dealing seriously with your past pains so you can move on to a more healthy and harmonious future. We are all a work in progress.

Working on your internal battles helps you to see and empathize with others' internal and external battles, too. When you can empathize and be a voice or presence of support, you have begun to create a healing culture while healing yourself, even if you are further along in your healing journey than others. The support that emanates from you heals. That is good. This perpetual engine of healing is just the constancy of Love playing itself out when we let it. Choosing to make peace with your past by forgiving and setting others free from judgment and the mental prison you placed them in will drive you more excitedly towards transformation.

Sometimes, internal transformation can happen when you are working in your organization to improve and heal broader core issues. Sustainment is a significant problem for many organizations. Numerous organizational matters will come up that can stall and stagnate the organization. We can get too excited, glossing over issues, believing we have achieved a goal, only to find out later that we have not. All team members must understand that healing and transforming does not mean we will not be challenged by others whose attitudes are slower to begin the transformation process in earnest. In fact, for a time, it will feel like you are taking four steps forward - feeling fantastic and then experiencing a few steps back. The challenge is to keep your attitude positive and role with the two steps back so you can progress on your next round of moving good things forward again. Over time, the ratio will change, and it will feel like five steps ahead and two steps back, and then at its best, you will only experience the occasional one step back because we are humans; we are not perfect. If you are seeking perfection, stop. You will only drive yourself crazy. Some slight and occasional backsliding is part of the journey. Remember, it is not the pace to move forward that decides the healing; the healing determines the pace that your team moves forward. If progress is not made, people or the entire team have yet to heal an aspect of themselves. Part of coaching your team is to bring them into cohesion so they can release what prevents them from growing; this can be better communication, clearing up misunderstandings, providing resources, and improving the environment and the working conditions. Your team should be leaning toward improving. This process is more like steering a boat across multiple wakes with passengers standing up in your boat. Most will be fine; some will get tossed. Leaders must watch the process and communicate the turns ahead, so no one is lost overboard.

Your team's wounds can be as deep as their childhood or as recent as being cut off in traffic or other unresolved issues. Because of this, anything unhealed is embedded into your organizational paradigm, like it or not. Examine your approach with each other. Are your functional expectations aligned? Are your behavioral expectations aligned? Where is the misalignment? Collaborate with your team to develop agreed-upon solutions once you have zeroed in on one or more. Do so with empathy and move your team forward respectfully.

Take an inventory: How have past issues created unnecessary stress for you and your team? Are you overly busy with things that do not matter? Are you too superficial in dealing with each other? What is your personal stress level? Is your stress job-related? Is your stress organizational? Is your stress environmental? Family? Marital? Financial? How is your health, and is that affecting you and your team? Provide your organization with a climate assessment. You want to know so you and your team can work on what is not working. Matter is energy; we are energy. We give off a frequency. We help no one when that energy or frequency is pervasively negative.

Question your leadership style. Are you a 360-degree leader? Have you adjusted? Have you challenged assumptions? "Great leaders seek out and find potential leaders, then transform them into good leaders" (Maxwell, 2012, pg. 490). If you are a high-level leader in your organization, do some critical self-analysis to determine your leader onboarding methodologies. Do you treat people well? Are supervisors, functional leaders, and employees treating each other well? Is your team out of control or below standards? If you are not the thermostat-modulating your organizational climate, you might inadvertently create an organizational Ice Age or lava field without setting the pace and tone. The heartbeat of your team will wane if you do not set the tone. If you and your team members are coachable, there is always hope. Sometimes, you are a shot of adrenaline, and sometimes, you are a calming force to keep the climate in your organization from bouncing up and down erratically. Sometimes, you are all these all week long.

Is your organization creating unnecessary stress? Certainly, deadlines and organizational stress exist. There are fire-starters and firefighters within organizations that drive stress levels up. Stress also increases your cortisol levels, making you a health risk to yourself and your loved ones. Once you make good choices, dopamine in you will follow good outcomes, creating a healthier you. Beware, you might be causing stress to others. The entire team must ask themselves, 'Is what I am saying and doing lending itself to fulfilling organizational requirements, or am I just passing my stress onto others, like a stress hot potato?' Be a firefighter of stress, a calming and reassuring force on your team. Ensure you are one of many who incorporate improvement so that it alleviates unnecessary stress from your team. Keep it simple and adjust your approach if you must. Challenge your own bias, increase your knowledge, and invite feedback to improve yourself for your team. Improving your organizational health requires making good choices, just like improving your health requires making wise choices.

Chapter 18

We Are Not Just Here for the Party

After our 10th birthday, when we have eaten cake, we do not rush in to gorge ourselves on the frosting in its sugary glory. Why? We know that it will make us sick. Yes, too much of a good thing can make you ill. Naturally, I am loosely using the term good in this example. We use good when we refer to things that please our senses. We know everything does not please our senses. Our senses can be overwhelmed. However, we are more likely and able to sustain a good life by applying moderate consistency. Sometimes, deferred gratification is necessary. Those who find joy and live in gratitude appreciate maintaining a good life with ease, choosing their perspective and attitude. They do not let the world control their thinking or their behavior. They choose the possible and look to bring good into the world, including those they share it with. Many of these people are full of spirit and live in faith. But not all faithful or faithless show 'good' when they ought. The lesson of being a person who lives from Love is like the sun. They shine on everything and everyone, irrespective of status. Love does not recognize status; it acknowledges life. For those who are more materially motivated, healthily controlling your dopamine levels will support feeling well. Choose healthy methods that do not draw you into codependent behaviors. Seek dietary and physiologic medical support where needed.

Organizational transformation over the long haul should be a gradual, steady ascension. You can use the term 'climb' if you choose. A moderate but ascending trajectory is ideal. It is also much like an aircraft taking off. However, over saturation by abruptly starting your transformation without education and communication can overwhelm your team members. Some without awareness will be thrown off balance. Feeling a little off balance is OK because transforming is not an exercise in being comfortable. We are not just here for the party. We are not here to numb out codependently from our issues and challenges, large and small, by somehow disguising failures to permit ourselves to 'celebrate.' We celebrate when we accomplish something. When we commit to continuous transformation, we always accomplish something. We must question whether we are genuinely committed if we have not accomplished something. There may be an outstanding new achievement to celebrate. Sometimes, the best achievement to celebrate is personal transformation. Face it; most people do not party to celebrate good things as much as they do to distract, forget, or numb out to deal with negative stress. Many distract themselves from their own inner and outer pain. Our culture weaponizes celebration to mask codependency, to mask pain. We cannot avoid the tough questions, the deep dives, and the hard conversations. We cannot charge to the banquet table before the real work of dealing with life's pains has been done. We are not just here for the party. We are here to protect love.

Chapter 19

Scoreboard Mentality

There is debate in the world about using a scoreboard approach. It is split if you research the topic. Why is it split? The scoreboard communicates competition. That does not sit well with organizations who think they do not work in competitive environments. So, who comes to most people's minds when non-competitiveness is considered? The government, perhaps? That is assuming we do not have to compete with ourselves to ensure everything runs well, is defended well, and that planning is well conducted. Even at a local level, the DMV tracks customer service, collecting their timing data. If the DMV uses a scoreboard approach, why couldn't anyone? That is right, everyone should be.

So, what is so unique about a scoreboard approach? Well, our competitiveness is linked back to our playing when we were children. Some examples are sports, board games, yard games, and playing cards with grandmother. My grandmother was fiercely competitive. She was the sweetest person I have ever known and would play game after game of rummy with me. In these lighthearted but powerfully competitive moments, we begin measuring our performance and start to understand that you can love your competitors. You can love your competitors because they are sharpening you, making you make yourself better. The converse of this is to know that some do not desire to be better; some think they are as good as they will ever be. At some point throughout the trajectory of their life, they felt judged in a competitive environment. In response, they repelled themselves from anything relating to keeping score. They may have even magnified themselves away from areas where high productivity exists. Some people dislike being on demand for any person, place, or thing. Their aversion is a fear response, perhaps even a phobia; FNE: Fear of Negative Evaluation (Van der Molen, 2014). Indeed, if diagnosed, it should be addressed by a professional who can treat the condition. However, the idea that there is a condition means that the need for a scoreboard approach and its effectiveness is real. The world is replete with fearfulness that can be overcome with empathy, education, training, and positive emancipation. Each day, people say, 'Have a good day,' to communicate the temperature about us and our experience, our status, or our weekend. These are subtle scoreboards at work in our lives. We score the weather, moods, the darts we play, billiards, ping-pong, volleyball, horseshoes, and well-known football and basketball. So, why does the scoreboard approach work? The score is being kept continuously at our cellular level. Even as I write this, all our mitochondria seek and thirst for light to survive (Sommer, 2020). Hold your breath for a long enough time, and despite what intellectual or faddish control you think you have over your life, your biology will fight for your next breath. The scoreboard approach is not a gimmick; it is written in biology. Less than one percent of sperm makes it to the awaiting egg in human reproduction, which begins with about two hundred and fifty million competitors focused on the egg as their goal (Rodrigo, 2018). Survival is always the first reason, and a thriving life is the second. The scoreboard communicates to us how we are performing. If our internal biology knows that when we go against our nature to try, we resist the innate scoreboard within ourselves. Fighting our inner nature reveals itself as stress and guilt, which drives up cortisol levels. This endangers our health and pushes people toward codependent behaviors to cope with going against our internal drivers. Our biology is more intelligent than we think. Try as we may, we cannot fool our biology into thinking we do not care. If anything, we care too much. The scoreboard reflects the most genuine part of ourselves.

The best reason for a scoreboard approach is to do well and feel good doing it. Feeling good helps our attitude and helps our behaviors cooperate and be productive and innovative in our teams. Dopamine is released inside us when we do well. Repeating that is the best way to perform well. Indeed, our biology rewards our efforts by making us feel healthier, connected, and uplifted when we grow our abilities and performance. If we use the scoreboard approach across other domains of our lives, self-empowerment is ignited, and we begin to drive our own lives, setting personal goals and living our vision. The scoreboard can serve us well in breaking out of our personal and professional doldrums.

Hour-by-hour and productivity boards, as illustrated in Figure A10, are simple yet effective ways to record, communicate, and take ownership of production's status, where it was, and where it is going. Scoreboards also tell us precisely what we hope to achieve. Knowing where we are, teams can work collaboratively and cooperatively to overcome daily, weekly, and monthly challenges. We can also account for and reward our teams when we exceed expected results.

Taking care of your team and being cooperative and collaborative is more than just organizational squishy speak. We are the sum of our heads and hearts working together. We must own and move through our day conscious of how important cooperation is to everything we do. We must be very mindful that all of us working together is how we ensure success results from the changes we make during the transformation process. We cannot thrive on an island of one. Knowing this, we must strive for inclusivity and be human enough to work out the details humanely. Those choosing selfish or nefarious paths hurt everyone; this is a universal truth. This is true with friends, family, personal and professional relationships. Behavior matters. Behavior communicates our intentionality, good or bad. This is not a vague 'good or bad.' These are our agreed-upon norms.

Interpersonal and professional behavior is our most significant challenge to overcome as individuals and organizations. Bad attitudes hurt, divide, and starve life. We must nourish our customers by choosing not to starve ourselves or starve the life out of our teams.

You may have many cliques, depending on the organization's size. Those cliques stand for an energy stream of trackable productivity and performance. Work groups may be unwittingly working against each other's best interests. Communicating poorly ensures this will happen. Sometimes, these groups do cooperate. An example of heightened communication is when distinguished visitors tour your site. Suddenly, the team works harder and runs like a well-trained pit crew. Why? Do they care more when customers are right in front of them? Perhaps. It does not matter why this happens; it proves the team has a usual cadence of operation that could be better. Just note how people move, communicate, and work a day or two afterward. It is obvious. The team does not see themselves, so how would they know what it would look like to perform like a superstar? That is right; they do not unless they see their performance results from a tracking mechanism. If you have one, are you utilizing it to improve your team's and individual performances? Why not? You can see this 'visitor behavior' when the CEO or customers arrive. There could not be a more revealing scoreboard than to see the attitude of your team shift into another higher gear you did not know they had. Heighten your cadence and expectations only after using this as a teaching moment for your team. Tell them everyone needs to increase their pace a couple of extra beats a minute and see how they do. Notice how interpersonal or professional drama takes a vacation when visitors arrive, too. How interesting is that? It depends on your team's health, but you will be amazed that drama is not a priority enough to bring to leadership's attention when distinguished visitors arrive. Note, too, how your team chooses better attitudes. This is that choice I spoke about earlier playing itself out. Your team can overcome and roll with anything when they choose to step up their game. Their competence and confidence heighten as well. We all have better inside us; we decide when to reveal it. Teach them all these things and ensure all new team members understand this.

High-performance teams are the exceptional difference. Struggling teams have embedded agendas hidden deep within the organization that cause heightened turnover rates, poor quality, increased waste, and low morale. The scoreboard approach is a mindset of open cooperation and cooperative attitudes that help you adjust for your best performance as a person, a team, or an organization. The scoreboard also allows you to become a forward-thinking organization. Forward-thinking organizations grow. Are you a proactive driver and planner of your organization, or are you a passive rider only reacting to challenges after they have set your organization back by minutes, hours, or days? You should be in an alliance as a team to effectively use scoreboards to help you sustain an upward climb in performance. Maxwell (2001) stated, "In the end, nobody can win without the scoreboard" (p. 155).

Chapter 20

There is Always Cause and Effect

There is always cause and effect in our physical world. For everything we do, there is a reaction, a result, an impact. This is simple and plain for us to see. However, we often do not know how this plays out inside the hearts and minds of other people. We are not mind readers. If people hold onto their frustrations, their minds and bodies must absorb that stress. That stress cannot go anywhere if we do not choose where and when to release it. We see it outwardly in some people as frenetic behaviors, stress eating, alcoholism, psychological problems, verbal conflict, car accidents, and other destructive behaviors. Over the long term, it can also be seen as more severe health problems that manifest seemingly out of nowhere. How many intense fitness programs, weight loss programs, and other programs have been designed to fix the symptoms, not the core drivers of our stress? All of them. Some are healthy, like fitness, restorative sleep, and eating more wholesome foods.

One insidious driver of adverse outcomes is passive-aggressive behavior (Grohol, 2020). Aggressiveness is obvious. We can see it and hear it very plainly when it happens. What is sometimes less obvious is passive aggressiveness. What do I mean? Passive aggressiveness has a hidden nature to it. It is sneaky; it is calculating. Passive aggressive words or deeds undermine in secret ways. It can also be confused with other things so that onlookers may be unable to tell if what has been done is passive-aggressive or due to forgetfulness, lack of training, or lack of competence. Here are some examples of passive aggressiveness that may be confused with other behaviors or intentions:

[I do not like my boss, so I show up late to work to annoy them] How do we know they are not just late for some other reason? We don't. [I only tell my employees we are working Saturday on Thursday, even though I have known it for two weeks, but because they annoy me, I will make it hard for them to plan for daycare and change their weekend plans.] [my manager does not appreciate me, so I will work half speed if I work here]. [I am jealous about the attention another employee gets, which hurts me, so I will ensure they never get what they are waiting for, and then they will look bad and not get the attention I wanted]. [I have not received a pay raise, so I will repair this equipment well enough to run just long enough; they will have to pay me a lot of overtime to come in over and over to fix the issue I could have fixed finally; months ago]. [My employees do not like me, so I will take all the improved profits from last year and buy a third home instead of giving my team Christmas bonuses for their hard work.] You could go on and on with many examples you have experienced that could be passive aggressiveness. The clue is that the outcome is negative. So, you can classify it as either passive aggressiveness on the one hand or a lack of competence, awareness, or capability on the other. Those are the only two boxes: competence or passive aggressiveness. Both mean something in your organization and on your team needs to be fixed quickly. Anyone can be a passive-aggressive perpetrator, and anyone could be a victim, regardless of their role on the team. It is not easy to prove. It is the weapon for the quiet war being fought in organizations for control, an 'us versus them' when deployed, and not a competence issue. Educate your teams about passive aggressiveness so the entire organization and everyone in it will ensure that the mere perception of participating in that behavior will dissuade people from it.

How do you know if something is passive-aggressive? The behavior or lack thereof will skirt the edges of an expected standard or expectation. If someone meets and misses goals on and off, it could indicate a red flag. It could also be a red flag if someone manipulates other team members. It is likely a screaming red flag if someone is highly self-serving, harsh toward others, or is a gossip teller or rumor carrier, all while performance is less than consistent. Anyone spreading or starting drama could be a red flag. Passive aggressiveness may also be a payback method from the quiet ones toward the overt narcissistic or sociopathic ones. The passive-aggressive person may throw proverbial rocks, finger-point, and hide after they do it. Those less cunning may stand out and get caught because they are not good at it. The less cunning may also get fired because they take part in reactionary behavior to create justice, they may think. The most cunning could be long-term employees who have made a second career of wrapping everything into their convenience. This is a milder, less overt way of being passive-aggressive, lethargy/laziness. Most importantly, your team understands what it is and does not do it. It is unhealthy, and it hurts everyone, including customers. How do we let them know it? We tell them about these and other more relevant examples from your industry. Passive aggressiveness is a form of vengeance; there is no place for that in a healthy organization. Deal with stressors directly and quickly so they do not linger, turn to neglect, and then become passive-aggressive reactions from a failure to engage with the team. High levels of engagement take the need to take vengeance off the table by supplying a method for immediate feedback daily. Talk directly to people and resolve issues. Do not let issues linger because you may find that passive-aggressiveness is insidiously destroying your organization. Failing to educate your team also ensures that passive aggressiveness becomes a stressor outlet for some team members who have yet to learn about healthy communication. Teaching awareness will create a self-monitoring element for your team, who will be aware of passive aggressiveness.

Organizations are places where people have shared experiences. There may be positive experiences and interactions. There may be significant negative experiences that have damaged or are damaging your team's ability to unify consistently. Some damage may have been created by failing to root out mistakes, misdeeds, injustice, and harm that continue growing weeds in your organization's garden heart. Despite the appearance of superficial strength, your team members may be holding onto these. How do you think their frustration about injustice is getting out? Yes, in passive-aggressive ways. Remember, that which affects your organization affects your customers. What won't you do for your customers? Do not be afraid to tackle the concept of passive aggressiveness and use it as an intellectual way to dig into and heal the core issues that people have bottled up inside. There may be issues ranging back years for your team. It would be fantastic if you could hear them, address them, and work as a team to heal and overcome them going forward. All pain reaches the light of day eventually. Create an environment where passive aggressiveness should never flourish. We do not need to throw away over thirty percent of our team members. Turnover distracts us from owning and resolving core issues that damage people and the team. A high turnover rate also communicates the organization's competence.

Chapter 21

People, Environment, and Motivation

You must understand people, the environment, and their motivations to improve your organizational culture. Leadership is vital. However, leadership without understanding people is a dog that will not hunt. Instead, think of understanding people the way you might grow a garden instead. A garden requires time, nutrients, sunlight, water, and daily oversight to keep threats to its health at bay. This is true for all relationships. Teams must steward all their mental and physical energy and resources to ensure the 'garden,' your organization, thrives. Your customers depend on you to do that. Understand that the pulling of one weed will not feed your garden. Giving your garden more nutrients will not remove the weeds choking out your garden. Improving your organizational culture requires engaging and supplying resources, including developing your people and maintaining systems your organization depends on. The weeds you need to pull are the internal attitudes and behaviors inside your heart and mind, individually and as a team. Firing people instead of developing them is organizational cowardice. This cowardice would be more in line with an uncommitted country sending its forces into battle unarmed.

An even-handed, fair, loving, and kind balance must exist in your nature and approach before embarking on a transformative journey in your organization. Saying that may rattle you a little. If you do not align your team, problems will return later to disrupt your continuity. Similarly, we would not paint over rust either. This means an overhaul of attitude, perspective, and awareness must be foundational to starting your transformational journey. This includes measuring your organization's current state. You must also assess yourself and your team's intellectual and emotional state. Dig in the dirt of matters, resolve misunderstandings, get alignment, and build cohesion before doing the heavy lifting of organizational transformation.

More attention should be given to the dynamics of team development. Forming, storming, norming, performing, and adjourning occur when teams develop (Karanjgaokar, 2021). Every time a person is added, or a team member leaves, the team starts over at forming. This means going through the storming stage all over again. As illustrated in Figure A2, you can be somewhat productive in storming, but mostly, it is fraught with the worst your organizational culture could ever endure. It is also the least safe, productive, or quality-conscious stage. Perhaps now you understand why turnover is so damaging to teams. Too many teams falter in the storming stage and falsely think they are in the next higher stage, the norming stage. Their norm is a constant state of storming that they have normalized, never progressing through to actual norming and on to performing stages. When caught in the storming stage loop, organizations have normalized the dysfunction of a never-ending storming stage. "We all have bad habits that keep us from accomplishing our goals. Generally, we maintain these habits to remain comfortable instead of enduring the struggle, discipline, and sometimes pain of correcting a bad situation" (Samuel, 2006, p. XVII). It may feel like a waking dream because it creates a nightmarish landscape for new team members who experience onboarding into organizations rife with problems, easily noticed and entirely fixable problems. However, it is much worse when organizations are in the storming stage and believe they are in the 'performing' stage. Organizations know they are in the wrong stage, but they are caught off guard because they have seen past success, so they cannot believe they are in the storming stage. They ignore what their own eyes and their team have been telling them. Because the team is compromised, their inability to understand what is happening may feel like a chaotic hall of mirrors. Any ad hoc progress while struggling through the stages only reinforces the notion that a true breakthrough is hard. They would rather believe something is hard than they are in the wrong stage of team development. Pride will kick you if you let it. Failing to recognize the stage you are in is pride becoming your master. We humans make things more complicated for ourselves. Sometimes, you see the confusion emulated in movies and TV for dramatic effect when a workplace is a hellscape of chaos to emulate some version of real-life productivity. Being frenetically busy is neither performing nor indicative of productive cooperation. It is indicative of an organization out of control.

Discontinuity exists when different departments operate at various stages of team development. This imbalance and other toxic overt and covert passive-aggressive behaviors only compound your organization's problems. This plays out when you hear that employees want to work in departments that are not their own. Educate your team about the stages of development so they know the phases and how to transition through them fearlessly. This will allow them to experience heightened burdens, so the team learns to grow through the challenges required of the storming stage. Educating my teams about team dynamics helped to ease stress and minimize frustrations from the onset.

People have needs. People thrive when their needs are met. Maslow's hierarchy of needs lays out a great example of human development. Maslow's hierarchy of needs shows how a person develops toward self-actualization (McLeod, 2020). The road to personal self-actualization will lead an organization to self-actualize one day if the team is dedicated. Organizational leaders and business owners should be able to relate to self-actualization. They must ask themselves, 'Where would you be had you not progressed up the road to develop yourself?' Where would the business be? We are in a time where we must holster the hammer of ego and put the balancing of the scales of human justness by everyone back into organizations.

Some people will progress due to their talent. There are exceptional performers. Some will move on. Why? The quintessential question is, 'Why will they move on?' They will move on due to actual or perceived faltering of organizational culture. But precisely why? This is what I have walked around my entire life to collect qualitative data up close. First, people will leave if the pay is unfair. By unfair, I mean below the pay scale for their role. People can be attracted away but will not if you do these well: people want to be appreciated. If you can, weekly, in one way or the other, speak your appreciation genuinely. Otherwise, people will assume you do not care. This can come from relaying customer appreciation and compliments that the organization receives, which should also be an opportunity for you to communicate appreciation to your team. Growth: People on your team want and need to grow. Those who do not say they want to grow would be put off if others get the opportunity to grow and they do not. There is value in having the opportunity to gain experience and grow. It can be special projects, events, promotions, broadening of skills, and so forth. All these speak appreciation, too. The bottom line is that people become stagnant and bored when they do not grow. Stagnant people lose focus and make mistakes. Stagnant people leave your team. This is both a personal and organizational issue to overcome. This is where an opportunity exists to partner with the team to frame a culture where stagnation cannot occur creatively.

Some people have outside skill sets that are not necessarily related to their work. Find ways to integrate their external talents creatively. This is also why getting to know and engage with your team is essential. Take the time to learn their story. The more your organization is an integral part of empowering the personal journey of your team, the better. Fairness among the people in your organization is also crucial. If fairness is a struggle for you, then your organization is imploding. People want to be heard. People in your organization have the best ideas waiting to be discovered and developed; however, if you do not have a mechanism to listen to those ideas, build and implement an idea program so your team can be seen and heard, as illustrated in Figure A12.

Establish an open-door policy, so your team can relay great ideas and bring up issues. Once someone does not feel cared for, they stop caring. Keep your door open as much as possible. Otherwise, the team can feel ostracized, less than, and become self-centered. If this happens, all healthy cooperation will fly out the window like warm air on a cold day. Hear your team. Toughen up. Have thick skin and endure topics outside your comfort zone. You will eventually come to love and want input from your team. The more critical feedback you get from your team, the better. Own the corrections your team finds. Implement what works. Just do it. Please do not put it off. Do not harbor resentment for your team's honesty. Leaders need to be open and available for critical and, at times, intense feedback. Your team should be equally thick-skinned and receptive to critical feedback, too. Your entire team needs to own the truth and communicate in healthy ways. No organization benefited from being thin-skinned about truth.

It comes back to fairness. Despite what is communicated on the surface, people want to be recognized for innovation, innovative ideas, exceeding goals, and keeping the organization safe. Give out awards, certificates, parking spots, and many creative rewards or quarterly bonuses once the organization thrives. Give your team their day in the sun when they stand out; even if they hate the attention, do it. Conversely, never doing this ensures you will never have anyone stand out, not even a little.

Not recognizing people will create a norm where the whole group, in unison, refuses to stand out quietly. How we treat people matters and resonates in the community. Behavior and attitude matter. Beware because everyone is watching to see how ownerships respond to valuing their teams, including the competition.

Society has fumbled its way forward through the Dark Ages, wars, the crusades, and slavery because, along the way, it became clear that treating people poorly is wrong. Treating people well improves everyone's success, which improves growth in all areas. Treating people well is infectious when it is a genuine part of who your team is at their core. Treating people well takes less energy. When people have their primary needs met, they focus better on the job. If this is true for a very well-paid surgeon, it is valid for the person putting nails into the roof that protects your family's home from the elements. Do you want to be part of your team's success story? What about their families who graduate high school and college? Bind your organization through and around your team and your community. Cheer your team's victories. Cry with them, laugh with them, and mentor them. Treat people in your organization like an idealized family.

Chapter 22

Anchor Points

Rock climbers set up anchor points as they climb to keep from falling catastrophically. Similarly, we must hold anchor points as we journey to improve the health of organizational culture. What are these anchor points? They are the agreements made to ensure that everything occurs in good order. These agreements should be outlined and explained in your policy documentation. They are further detailed in your processes and procedures. They set up expectations for safety, proactive communication, and planning. They outline the path of predictable behavior around the norms of supplying your product and service. In short, they provide the stability the organization can expect from departments, people, suppliers, and others. They take the form of documented expectations of what to do when certain situations and scenarios arise in your organization. They are also your operations plans. These are your anchor points. They can be your visual management system, signs you post, notices, change orders, policies, letters of direction, and other similar documentation the team adheres to. They are also your routine performance of Gemba walks, maintaining consistent, documented, and disciplined attendance and follow-ups. There is nothing magical about anchor points. They are the expression of the organization's conscientiousness. They can be methods for capturing ideas, reviewing ideas, and managing different 'what if' possibilities. They are your dependable knowns that help ensure nothing slips through the gaps in your organization.

Chapter 23

Vision is Important to the Organization

Vision should be large and meaningful. Vision must be more significant than a goal. Vision should link your heart and mind to a broader philosophical or societal need. We must build healthy organizational cultures for the express purpose of meeting customer needs. Vision should be long-term, like a grand voyage, embarked upon like a transcontinental journey that might have been experienced centuries ago when critical planning was a life-and-death proposition. We must develop our vision in the same way, with the same grand impact for societal good and the good of all cultures. Vision should be felt in your daily approach and in everything you do. Vision is not just a slogan, task, or list of goals, though they have their place. A vision is deeply felt and understood. Your vision should not be burned onto a plaque or forgotten on a wall. Your team should understand why what they are doing is meaningful. Your vision expresses that meaning and purpose to everyone. Vision stretches your team through deeper meaning to achieve your organizational goals. Achieving your goals exemplifies your organization as living your vision. Core values align with your organization's internal compass. The Air Force's core values are integrity first, service before self, and excellence in all we do. They should apply broadly and encompass widely held values and beliefs embodying organizational integrity that all team members are expected to embody daily.

Objectives are sub-goals with shorter timetables that are building blocks to achieving larger goals. These are your key performance indicators, such as sales, productivity, quality, and on-time delivery.

When people are detached from the feeling of doing good work, feeling engaged, feeling a part of something big, something noble, their interest and zest for the work dissipate. Team members feel bored, unaffected, and unattached to the outcome. You will see it as a waning performance, lethargy, and other negative red flags, like a drop or plummeting in key performance indicators. You may have no idea why at that moment, however. You will see the result of the error, but you may think you know the error itself. In other words, you see the symptoms of the disease, not the cause. Every team's greatest challenge is to embody the qualities that bring the organizational vision to life daily. Vision helps us approach each day by inspiring us to avoid falling into a mindset of distractive repetition. Your pursuit to fulfill your vision is the runway necessary to give the organization the required lift to serve all customers with integrity.

Chapter 24

Find Ways to Have Fun

We can be serious all day long about work and building organizational culture. It is serious. However, great power and creative energy are unleashed when dopamine flows, creating happiness and fire in our brains. This only happens when we enjoy what we do and who we do it with. Most people rarely think of fun as anything relating to work. Most can find moments of humor and fun well integrated into their workday. I have found that irony abounds at work. I don't know why. Small instances of cognitive dissonance are sometimes amusing; no, they are funny. There is a humor glazed around the hora of our imperfection as humans. It can feel good and ground you to laugh at yourself sometimes.

Humor may be the quality that diffuses tension and frustration. A worker who is the last holdout to refuse to go paperless at work spills their drink on their paperwork. This is both ironic and a little funny. I once had my wife photoshop a tree to make it look like it fell on my boss's sports car. It was hilarious to see him hurry to see what happened. He thought that was hysterical. I got him. That was a moment of light humor to change our gears. I do not recommend doing that, but I knew his sense of humor. Indeed, far worse and much more cruel things have been done in the world. I do not recommend wasting time, but when you are on top of the performance wave, fun is the wind your team needs in their sails to thrust them forward without really trying. This also indicates the 'performing' phase when everything the team does turns to gold. Your work flows well in this stage, and people synergize intuitively.

The most stoic leader needs to learn to have a light but firm enough grip to let the team's sails breathe and not take themselves too seriously. Some self-deprecation goes a long way and demonstrates humility and humanity. Some people have never performed physical labor; an opportunity to feel the satisfaction and the endorphin release that happens when doing physical work is freeing. Physical work has a way of improving one's attitude and understanding. Leaders should engage in the work, when possible, to know how and what is happening. Leaders should immerse and share the team's energy, challenge, and perspective.

A leader who fastens themselves behind a desk may have built a mental and emotional wall, a distance between connecting and showing connection with people. I have also encountered that same stoicism from the workforce, who initially thought that walling themselves off would mean I would draw a line and stand on my side and they on theirs. I do not put people in boxes; no line has stopped me from engaging. Engage, engage, engage. Seriousness never helps in those situations. Some empathy and a little humor can. Walling ourselves off is just another hiding place. Transformation means it is time we come out of those shadows. Having a good attitude and having fun can go hand in hand if the people doing the work can manage it. If you are not standardized, and for safety concerns, I do not recommend 'horseplay' while working. Unsafe acts and accidents should not be what we risk. However, I have never seen anyone having fun at work being less productive, ultimately. I have seen people distracting other people and stealing away valuable time. Being blatantly unproductive is not fun; it flies in the face of fun. Be creative and integrate fun or levity into your organization safely.

I have seen clear correlations between a bad attitude and poor productivity. Those who thrive on controversy do not want fun or levity to be a part of their biosphere. If one cannot funnel good outcomes in parallel with a smile and an occasional moment of fun, then there is a deep internal conflict preventing engagement, buy-in, and cooperation. Some team members just flat out do not trust anyone who does not have a sense of humor, large or small. Typically, those with a sense of humor tend to be happier. Sick people indeed feel bad. How do you separate the consummate contrarian, those who do not value solutions, from the negative person? Are they the same person? Are they building or burning the bridges of cooperation in your organization? It would help if you answered that question because neither contributes to a positive organizational culture that innovates and produces well. One could force the argument to fold in on itself if we see someone with a great sense of humor enjoying dismantling the organization. This is why we must be cautious over-generalizing. The cadence and mode of the team are affected by many factors that influence its rise and fall. Humor is oxygen to the team, often when they need it most.

People go through traumas and personal strife and sometimes just do not feel good, hopeful, or optimistic. We should have empathy for that. We could be better. We do not need people bouncing off the walls, requiring so much attention that they distract our productivity. Some people are sad and pitiful from a life of personal struggle. We must assume that everyone has experienced this minefield. However, we must focus on what we are doing. We must appreciate what is good and find ways to get wins for and from our team. Frolicking is not the intention nor the fun we are idealizing here. We want people to enjoy the demanding work they do. The team must be the originators and the authors of a good attitude if you are to sustain the growth and gains from transformation.

We all have an opportunity to share a kind word, a light irony, a smile, something to brighten and distract one's day from the monotonous. Humor heals. Fun and play heal when it is appropriate and safe. Cooperation and productivity improve when we incorporate fun into our programs as organizations. We do not abandon expectations or productivity; we integrate fun into them creatively. Who has not seen laughter in a break room? Sometimes, a little absurdity works to lighten or brighten moments. Laughing goes a long way. When we are too serious, we become tight, withholding, and overly concrete. We can bring a heaviness to each other's lives. We can close off just enough to stifle creativity in ourselves and our team. Unbelievably, strangely, our heaviness manifests trouble. Because we expect it, we fear it; it somehow shows up. Everyone knows how important play is in our lives. Within each of us at our deepest core, when you strip our professional masks off, we are all children who like to play. Does this mean work becomes a foolish playground? No, it means we incorporate a glowing attitude of play into our lives.

Resolve divisiveness, spread cheer in the face of strain and struggle, and let that spread throughout your team. Lift who you can. Wear your heart on your sleeve as children do. There is joy in achieving miraculous experiences during the micro-moments of life. You are only here as a blip compared to the universe's age; make it count, do not hold back. Remember, a smile, a kind word, positivity, and enthusiasm go a long way to start and end your day. We must abandon the hardened cowardice we built as adults and live with a more youthful optimism.

You are a player in the game of life. What comes through your chosen avatar? Are you a conduit for good, or are you a conduit for chaos? These are your only two choices. Those who do good should feel good. If you do not, it is your perspective that needs to change. Are you too serious? Are you too hard on yourself? Have you allowed life to harden you? Are you too caught up in the heaviness of world events? Refuse to be overwhelmed by people and the problems others should strive to solve. What are you letting steal your focus: the media, social media, toxic drama? Remember, in every moment, something we consider bad is always happening. Strife has always been in the world. If you are too bothered to write it down and help heal it, you do not care about it enough, so let it go. What you can do immediately is to be positive and cooperative. Live and guide people in your life. If life is a game you want to win, you must make friends through cooperation. You must create balance, bring good, and enjoy doing it. You are the only you that you have. You are the only one you are competing with in the end. If you want to compete, compete with yourself, the self of yesterday who perhaps did nothing for anyone. Squeeze the remnants of selfishness left from your former self and rebirth yourself daily. Please find some joy in the process. So, keep up-leveling your performances from yesterday until you wake up one day, look back, and see the good you have done in people's lives and how much good change you brought into the world.

Remember, everything in life is competing against your current abilities and understandings. You are competing with your knowledge of yesterday. Leaders should marvel with their team about what has been achieved. The team needs to feel good about how much they have achieved. You must recognize the team's heart and effort in all their achievements. Acknowledge their wins and inspire them to have fun doing it.

Building engagement shows your optimistic nature. People who struggle to be positive must ask themselves, 'Who am I at war with?' What does winning look like to you? If winning is a 'me,' not a 'we' conquering concept, then a personal inventory of what matters, who matters, and why is the reason to dive into oneself to discover these answers. At any level, our inner self is no less important than the person we see on the outside. We are the only people responsible for our inner health. It is not selfish to improve your health. It is unhealthy to affix to anyone outside ourselves any responsibility for our bad attitudes, behaviors, and anything negative inside us we have not overcome. This is a universal truth. Yet, people deflect this truth by attacking other people. Your solutions are inside you, not outside you. Not over there. They are not inside other people.

People can help guide and support us. Do not be fooled if you have not conquered your demons; people around you can see how your battle is going. If you need help conquering yourself, reach out to people in your life or to professionals. When one has a poor attitude, an unhealthy state of mind follows. This affects everyone, whether you know it or not. A healthy or improving state of mind arrives and departs with a good attitude. This is elementary math.

In striving for organizational health, our inner joy brings good things to the world. Notice how you felt when I said 'joy'? How did that make you feel? Our thinking and attitude either hurt or help us and our team elevate. If you are suffering, you cannot hide and have likely been showing it. You may have adapted it into your personality by being snarky. We must understand that fun is not a mechanism to 'fix' anyone. We cannot fix people; we cannot motivate people. We can only provide a space to grow, develop, and reveal opportunities to thrive. People must ultimately choose the necessary steps forward.

We cannot wear two masks because one will undoubtedly be fake. Wearing one mask at work and one in your personal life is problematic. You are not enjoying your professional or personal life if you are wasting energy being someone you are not. Do not morph into what is expected from others. Changing yourself outwardly to be accepted is wrong. Changing to be a better person is good. Again, wearing two masks only means you are failing at being two people instead of one imperfect one doing their best to improve. You are good enough to be you all the time. Remember that. There is no need to be a shapeshifter. I have seen people like this in work environments, during presentations, playing to a particular audience as if the audience is not equally aware and annoyed by it. Putting on a persona or playing a role should be the first clue to yourself that you are not being genuine. Do not shut yourself off, shut yourself up, or bail out on being honest. Do not take part in faux bravery to hide your fear of acceptance. Have fun being you. You have plenty to contribute to life.

Chapter 25

Resourcefulness

When people come together, the organization defines the roles and responsibilities of each position. However, roles and expectations are not always explained well. Some roles are written too linearly, which hamstrings the organization. These are gaps. Most problems that occur happen because of these gaps. Individuals in the organization who know these gaps exist typically cover those gaps to make sure the work gets done. When the gaps are not covered, the team is in a quandary as to why. Allowing the gaps to hurt the organization can happen passive-aggressively, too, which creates product or service issues for customers. Organizations are rarely able to call out people when the directives or processes are written poorly. Lethargic leaders seldom dig deep enough to find problems in their process or the gaps/omissions by the team or at the site. Some teams want to avoid calling out other team members and cover for them by not saying anything about where these gaps exist. Sadly, some team members are afraid of the influence of other team members, which is not a healthy attribute. I have participated in kaizen events where the engineers had solutions for years but had not offered them up because they were never asked to solve the problem. Wow. Only after the large group offered them cover did they find it comfortable to speak up. You can imagine how much waste and unnecessary costs were passed on to customers. What am I saying? Love many, trust few, always paddle your own canoe. No, I am saying leaders, and their department heads need to come out of their offices and dig in as part of their Gemba daily management walks with purpose until problems are resolved. Leaders must ask large and nearly obscure questions to find the underlying cause of issues lurking in the depths of their sites. Leaders must be proactive and coach proactively. Why? For your customers, empower your team to ask critical questions of themselves as they go. Why? For the customer. If your organization goes on for ten thousand more years, the answer will always be 'for the customer.' Coach your standout problem solvers; they can help you inject more instinctual problem-solving into the bloodstream of your team.

Those who do well and desire good for the organization will find ways to fix issues quickly. Someone once said about an organization, 'We shut up and just do what we are told.' This was an unhealthy organization. Never tell your people or imply that anyone should 'shut up,' no matter the situation. Do not devalue or disrespect your team. Be honest, be truthful, and keep communication lines open. We can all have blind spots, but we must be vigilant to accept hard truths.

Some organizations have improved during continuous improvement project efforts alone. It is essential to adopt approaches that open problem-solving efforts to your broader organization as a usual daily approach to work. Cross-pollinate people from different departments to get an 'outside the box' perspective. This can lead to solutions missed by minor complacency that will enter daily if left unchecked. I have seen teams who, when allowed to suggest what they thought, just looked at me blankly as if no one had ever considered asking for their input. Organizations that capture the ideas and the voice of their team add value to their customers and the organization.

Find out what other talents, skills, gifts, and abilities your team members have. These may have nothing to do with your team's primary roles in your organization, but you can find ways to incorporate their talents later to everyone's benefit. You may not know their abilities because you have never asked them. How about asking them? You might find new and unique opportunities right under the roof of your organization. See your team with a different lens, a different perspective. It is great to want your team to be resourceful but remember to grow yourself and become highly innovative for the team and yourself. What other talents could you lend to your team's growth beyond your current abilities? Reward those who are resourceful beyond their scope. Some of these people are your up-and-coming innovators, creators, and future leaders. If you are a creative team member, lend your other unique talents. Keep a record of all who perform beyond the norm. I call these hero points. People should track everything they do outside the norm to help the organization by going above and beyond each week and give that to their supervisor each month. The team is likely saving time or other precious resources at your site from becoming a much worse problem all the time. This is resourcefulness. If you do not acknowledge your team's resourcefulness, then look for most of your team to stop going above and beyond. Instead, find ways to support and reward resourcefulness.

Make sure you are sharing your team's resourcefulness with other site leaders so that you become a change agent by helping other sites. You have increased the internal value of your team to the broader organization when you do this. Your operation then becomes more streamlined. The more resourcefully successful your team is, the more you can communicate this in your market sphere as part of your business differentiation, giving your sales team valuable marketing. Where did it all start? Yes, it began when you empowered and rewarded your team for resourcefulness. There is an innate greatness dormant in your team that can change everyone's lives for the better.

Chapter 26

Backsliding

Naturally, no human is incapable of backsliding. Eating that piece of cake while on a diet may be backsliding in the short term. For the long term, eating that cake could be seen as a hard stop, a plateauing, a time to reflect, to recenter, and go at that diet again to improve your health. It is never too late to keep at it, to do what we know is right. Internally, backsliding can be an emotional and intellectual justification of our behaviors our conscience knows better than to take part in. Jealousy, passive aggressiveness, chastising others, and much more are backsliding. Backsliding in these ways is challenging to contend with inside the depths of ourselves. Backsliding hits our conscience even harder if we have been overzealous in calling out others who backslide. This is another test of our ego. Our ego will try to justify behaviors inside ourselves that we would never accept from others. Once ego justification begins, it is harder and harder for a person to overtake their ego- to own what has been done or said, to apologize, which makes finding forgiveness harder; the ego leads us by our noses. Peer pressure and others' opinions alone will dissuade a person from putting their ego in check, which can push them unnaturally off their moral center to do what is right. Find humility; be humble enough to walk back destructive behaviors of yourself and others.

Chapter 27

Head and Heart

We must figure out what our heart needs when we wake up each day. We cannot get so stuck in our heads about the tasks ahead that we don't recognize and feed the engine that drives our lives. This can be so many things that are not things at all. It is what we appreciate, what we love, and who we love, past or present. When we honor what we love, we serve others best. Service to others heals them and us. Healing becomes perpetual for everyone when we value this connection process, provided we do not stop. We should heal one another, not hurt each other personally or professionally. Leaders at every level must ignite and reignite the healing fires for the team by engaging with purpose. Team members must do their part to stoke and keep those good flames going.

In the movie Castaway, even talking to a volleyball, an inanimate object, was preferential to being alone (Ebert, 2000). However, not being alone amongst many does not mean we have a connection with others. This is why so many feel lonely and lost in the many surrounding them daily. We must interact by being human, sharing, caring, doing, and straightening each other out when we get off track with love. An emotional value exchange happens between people when they do. A stranger ignoring you might get your attention and make you think. A group of colleagues, classmates, or friends ignoring you will hurt your feelings and break your heart doing the same. Why? You invested value in them and believed they held the same value in your connection. What we say and do toward others matters right to the core of our being, our heart.

When people realize the organization does not value them, they become the next non-participating team members. They will fight for their lives in the organization until they give up on an organization that does not care, listen, or resolve issues. The team members stop caring, stop performing, and eventually leave. If organizations do not engage and keep the team involved, the quality, productivity, and morale will decrease as the organization is on life support, grasping at short-term fixes or gimmicks.

We must consider intellect. What do I need to do to feed my own intellectual needs? These could range from diet, exercise, learning something new, or having eye-opening conversations with people with different perspectives. Neuroplasticity requires exposure to new and different things (Psychology Today, 2024). When we see the world through the lens of other people, we grow our awareness and empathy about other people's struggles beyond the small circle of our lives. Understanding each other is the first step to making all of us better. We must challenge our filters, own our biases, and let some light in. The connections in our lives are catalysts that enrich our lives, serving us as we serve them. Thankfulness and appreciation feed us energy and ignite a spark in us that allows us to collaborate and create to flourish. Even if you do not acknowledge your soul, you can value the power that is you, the 'Energy' in (E=MC) squared (Perkowitz, 2024).

When we are physically satisfied, we can be intellectually and emotionally happy. For example, we are more patient and better learners when we are not hungry, cold, or tired. When these conditions are met, we flow, our stress and cortisol levels drop, and our health improves. All of this starts with the attitude we choose, the prime mover of our behavior. Our intellect and emotions work together to help us manifest possibility. To get there, you must win the battle over your ego and others' egos by tapping into the sublime power of service. This is not a premise for the weak. Like a chariot driver controls a team of horses, you must subdue your ego. It is your heart and head, not your ego, which creates a unifying force—a unifying strength. A team that knows this will be outstanding.

Do not let your egos overcome and subdue the givers, the unifiers in your organization. The ego is fed from your fear of losing control, gaining control, and fear of performing poorly. The ego is a taker. The ego is afraid things will be taken. The love in you wants good results. Keep your focus there, getting good things to happen, not 'control' fears. Love in us perpetuates strength, trust, innovation, and support. Ego is derision. Remember that. The ego is needed in nature as a primordial sense that warns us of immediate danger and takes the form of our fight or flight response. The ego is necessary for emergency responses to avoid a car careening out of control toward us, motivating us to brake or steer to safety. Literal life-threatening things illicit the need for our ego to engage and react swiftly. A mother duck protecting her young from danger is the best example of the ego reacting to a need to survive – a need to protect. The mother duck uses the ego as a tool because she loves; love leads. This is your best example of being a great leader and team member. Those who voraciously or covertly act from the dark side of ego, the takers, will feed upon the givers in your organization -the mother ducks, if you let them. A mother duck is not a shark; she has no time to be reckless. So, great leaders and team members must care for each other and customers the way a mother duck would- leading the ducklings purposefully on a trajectory to the other side of the stream.

Do not be paranoid. Just focus on the good that comes from your head and your heart. Please keep it simple. Focus on a giving approach that naturally calls for reciprocation by a cooperative team. There is a clear separation between the givers and the takers. The takers can only fake cooperation for a short time. A collaborative, communicative team approach will boil a taker's antics out. Takers do not like accountability, predictability, or expectations. Your givers will not just jump hip-deep happy into change mode, either. However, they will forge ahead, bond with each other, and work through challenges cooperatively as they align heart and head. Change is more difficult in the beginning before you hit a stride. That is to be expected. The takers will never really hit a comfortable stride. They cannot hide within an organizational culture bathed in cooperation as a norm. The cooperative nature of a newly embarked transformative effort gives everyone a chance to grow, and that is the point. The point is not to exile some to the void. Some ultimately choose to exile themselves to the void, refusing to cooperate. Recognize them for who they are. If they want to go, let them. If they want to grow, grow them. Just reign in your expectations of the outcome.

Expect and communicate the importance of critical thinking on the one hand and empathic cooperation on the other. I cannot stress enough how important being truthful to your team is. All have fallen, but it is important where you go from here. Never put people who have failed into a prison you built for them in your mind that they can never grow. Those who have failed in some ways may blow you away later with newly found success and abundance. In failure, be the mentor, coach, and supportive person.

Chapter 28

Persistence

It is not enough to make a casual effort to improve organizational culture. In the same way that dieting for one day will yield no better health results, trying for a day or a week to improve your organization meaningfully will also fail. You would barely notice any change, much less a lasting change. Despite lip service to the contrary, actions must take place in unison with the message of change while you are educating your team about change. Talk is necessary, but action is vital. If we use a dieting analogy, tailoring your actions by changing the type of food you eat and your exercise level and avoiding toxic, unhealthy foods are actions one can combine with education over time to yield better health. Organizational transformation requires the same melding of activities persistently and simultaneously to get the best result.

When you hear the word commitment, you should also hear the need to persist. Knowledge alone will not help you. Knowledge is just your starting point. Knowledge, persistence, attitude, and actions follow in organizations that intentionally pursue a transformative culture. What does your culture look like now? Do you see persistence in the people on your team? How? How would they rate themselves about being persistent? Is it in their actions? Are they self-motivated? What is your experience of being persistent? Who taught you to be persistent? How old were you when you learned or discovered persistence? Did you resist the need to be persistent? Were you energized by your results when you were persistent? Did you learn persistence in your childhood? Did you learn persistence in adulthood? Did something happen to keep you from being persistent personally or professionally? Do you rebel against persistence? Are you persistent Now? Why? Why not?

I was physically active in my youth. Work was manual labor. My persistence was to finish the work so I could play basketball with friends in the summer as a kid. After landscaping my uncle's property by hand, it felt good to see the smooth, flat, green, grassy park where once a moonscape of rock, dirt, and hilly terrain sat just a few months prior. Persistence pays off when we look back over our completed efforts. What if the work keeps coming, and we do not give our team time to celebrate the work we completed well? The team becomes numb to any organizational or team accomplishments. They disassociate the organization's success as different from their own success. Your team will only care if your leaders take the time to care with constancy genuinely. Ensure you do not speed so fast that you and your team fail to take the time to reflect, appreciate, and celebrate your victories.

Sports were my first systematized introduction to being persistent. As a young person, city league basketball, soccer, baseball, and organized school sports opened my eyes to persistence. Losing in sports was an obvious indicator of my lack of persistence then. More than the military, basketball gave me a constant measure to recalibrate my ability to perform well. However, only some people have sports as a reference point or a mechanism to measure, recalibrate, and attempt something again. Sadly, some may have had the threat of a harsh boss long ago if they did not demonstrate persistence. This is not healthy. This is also what a leader must overcome, where variable experience makes up a team. Struggling or developing leaders may not grow the team across various backgrounds. Their expertise and awareness to recognize differences in people, interests, and abilities must be broad to relate to their team. This is why peer mentoring is helpful for leaders regardless of their education. I have known people with high levels of education who choke in groups where either the size or variation of expertise overwhelms them. This does not make them bad people. It does not invite confidence if ownership is deluded into thinking you can throw people into leadership roles like a wind-up toy. Your team will sniff this out in about one conversation and walk numbingly away, striking it up as a decision 'Loss' on the ownership's part. Caution. Do not overgeneralize that an educated person cannot lead. I am not saying that. Despite education, I am saying that connecting with people in a way they will feel led is crucial. I can also say that I have met less educated people who could connect with anyone. This is why the middle path is so vital. A leader must be balanced, and the same centeredness should be developed in your team.

People subconsciously put other life challenges in their way to test themselves despite any awareness that they have done so. Haven't you ever wondered why some people experience unforced errors (UE)? Their experiences are harmonious, and then some major left turn 'happens' to them out of nowhere. Now they are climbing Mt Everest of life challenges - where no challenge of note previously existed. I have had a couple of those myself. Deep down, though, there was a need for change, challenge, and growth that was only detectable by my subconscious. It was like a building crumbling down. It forced me to persist in the aftermath, to act where I may not have been acting leading up to those crises previously. We must see ourselves with a much more critical eye and proactively change before change does work for us. Either way, we will improve. One way is less painful than the other. The (UE) events stir up life. These may also be an effort of our unconscious mind to get the attention of our conscious mind that we are just too busy to pick up on. We do not want unforced errors, so the lesson is to be proactive, look around, and ensure you do not have glaring blind spots. By doing this, your persistent awareness is running all the time. Your persistent caring is working all the time. In short, let us kick ourselves in the tail so life does not have to do it to us. What do you think transformation is? It is doing all this consciously, not as a reaction to destruction. We must lean into growth, so we are not dragged into growth. Because deep down, we want to grow and are subconsciously willing to create the conditions that will allow us to grow, even if those conditions are challenging, even colossal. Listen to the lessons of past failures and change as a life exercise, then watch how your life, personally and professionally, calms and grows.

From the outside looking in, there are two classes of those who persist: those who choose to persist because they are motivated to achieve something in life and those who are fighting their way out of austere conditions that have happened to them as a survival response. One is proactive, and one is reactive. Each of those two groups sees themselves and the other in a different light. It is the same light. Being proactive does not guarantee you are on the right road. Neither is being reactive. Both must be cautious not to let their ego trick them into thinking they are on the right path. Both will have to shift perspectives and paths as they go, like a dance. Welcome to life as it is. Are you a hammer or a nail? It depends on the lens and our perspective looking through that lens, not unlike the motif of the trickster and the hero (Yuan, 2022). To one person, someone is a hero for their help. While others see that same hero as a trickster, upsetting the flow of their lives. This is the fire that change agents walk through routinely.

You will see the most miraculous things happen to your 'nonbelievers' while transforming over time. They will be who you remember most. So do not stress out about who sees who as what. Focus on the vision and goals you have set, communicate, empathize, and realize the change you want. Interestingly, all perspectives build our world by default, whether they know it or not. Without the negative and harmful, would we all be wearing seat belts now? No. The negatives and positives have both been at work to build our world. However, we must acknowledge that culture has spent considerably more time mired in the negatives. Perhaps this would not have been the case if we had spent more time being proactive rather than reactive. How much pain and suffering could we have avoided? This is why we must not become complacent.

There will always be those who try to thwart those who persist. They are those who bring drama to otherwise harmonious efforts. Some can be awakened and snapped back to reality to join the usual challenges we take on instead of unnecessarily making up challenges and placing obstacles in the team's way. We must persist, irrespective of our personal perspectives, stumbles, fumbles, and falls. Pragmatically, creating a better world requires us to persist. Therefore, as corny as it sounds, do not resist, persist.

Our personal and professional relationships require persistence. Some people are just searching for their Holy Grail, like someone crawling around in a dark room looking for keys lost somewhere outside the room. Deep down, they know the keys are not in there; they are now our lesson, our test. Do we guide them through the doorway, the portal, where once on the other side, we can overcome the problem, or do we let them flounder around in the darkroom? What about those in that same dark room who have given up on looking for answers? They are spinning in place, unaware they are stuck in a dark room, submissive now only to their codependent shadow, the addictions they place in front of resolving deep-seated issues. They may be completely unaware that the light outside exists. Anyone who comes across as motivated by this group will be met with this reflective comment: 'Why try? It will not make any difference, clinging to their ego-driven codependency of lack like a warm blanket. If the lights in the room were to come on suddenly, they would see how stained, dirty, and infested that blanket and the room is. They would be moved to do anything about it if given the chance. Some people are unaware, unmotivated, and lost, caught in a loop of unawakened apathy, a hell of their own making. They need to be awakened ideally, fought for, not let go-not given up on. We do not have to love them or their darkness, but we must help them. You have an excellent opportunity to turn a once apathetic person into a fantastic team member, a fantastic and effective person for their own life's sake. That is the more significant point. Once these people, these flowers, stuck in a dark room, bloom, they cannot be hidden from the world. In this way, an awakening can seem miraculous. Start with persistence. Fill yourself and your organization with it, and apathy will have no room to grow in that bright light.

Persistence is a choice. If you choose to be healthy, you persist. If you want to get fit, you persist. If you want wealth, you persist. If you are going to become more intelligent, you persist. If you want a great relationship, you persist. If you want a great organizational culture, you must persist in communicating and making it a prized behavioral attribute you expect in your organization. Everyone on your team must dedicate themselves to being positively persistent. Persistence always pays off if you have a goal to persist towards.

Lethargy opposes persistence. If, as you age, you equate aging with, 'I do not need to do as much.' Then you have it all wrong. Your persistence may take different forms, but your lack of persistence affects your own life and health as it does to be an example to new generations about how to be successful, how to try, and how to show love in the world. Sure, you may not be as physically able as you become elderly. Your intellect and wisdom should be a garden constantly being watered and grown despite your age. The world still needs guidance; the world still needs actionable wisdom. I am not talking about giving self-adornment for three-cent egoic opinions that divide people and culture. I am talking about intellectual alchemy to create solutions and intelligent pathways leading to more abundance of character, health, and wealth in people's lives. Altruism can feed the hungry and house the poor if you are faithfully persistent.

See your life like a rock climb, not a free fall, where the view may seem ideal when you are young and think you know much more than you do. As you age, persisting over time and through life's challenges provides a more incredible view as you climb. Your awareness expands to see life's landscapes more clearly; your wisdom begins to transcend the seasons of life, growing your knowledge. Your value will become immeasurable as you dedicate your persistence. Nearer the peak, your vision will be unobscured in three hundred and sixty degrees around you. You have this going for you; we are wired to climb and lift others along our journey. To the extent we ought, persistence means guiding others who are lost through challenging pathways, rugged valleys, dips, and slippery passes back onto clear pathways. They must first want to ascend. Then, every act and every move require us to persist. This is true whether it is your first day after birth or the last minute before your last breath. Persistence is not about speeding up your endeavors to the extent that you are running people over or pulling people beyond their ability to keep balance. Do not run so fast or lean so far forward that you fall on your face. Impatience can be a weakness, a trap, but that does not mean we do not persist. Never normalize lethargy; see it as the ego's attempt to hold your life back. This takes the form of poor planning, failure to prepare, poor self-care, and poor time management.

Chapter 29

It's About We

Selfishness is not a winning concept. It is not a 'team' or a 'us' way of approaching anything. Selfishness is having such blind spots that one may think the world revolves around them. The selfish could have been conditioned by family, friends, or their experience to settle on one fact: they care more about their own life than anyone else. This is always a projection used to fool oneself into giving oneself a pass to be selfish, a justification. It is never true. We may tighten up our boundaries from people who are narcissistic takers who can justify anything. We might reassess areas to understand that you are giving more than others. However, except for the one-off situations where we recalibrate when life is not in balance, the selfish, the genuinely selfish, are committed to their cause and theirs alone by choice. If you study archetypes, the notion of the jester or trickster fits well within the paradigm of the selfish person (Cherry, 2023). Behind the eyes, greed will align everyone to their advantage. Rarely, if ever, will a narcissist ever disadvantage themselves for the greater cause, the greater good, unless that cause serves them in the near term. Why? Again, it is fear showing itself in the hearts of selfish people. Anyone can appear to be selfish situationally. The truly selfish person is always on the hunt like a predator, though, looking for their next advantage. They are opportunists. That sounds like I said it was a strength. If you can turn a selfish person away from their selfish ways, they can be highly effective and persistent. That said, they may be close friends or relatives that you mildly ignore, while professionally, that same person would draw all our ire as a problem or distraction. Beware, though, we may be the unaware and the unwitting trickster in others' lives. It is up to good leaders and teams to break the chain of selfish actions and get back to a 'we' approach to conducting organizational business. Use the 'we' approach to ensure all stakeholders benefit along your decision-making pathways so your organization evolves positively. Start by opening your awareness, challenging your assumptions, and seeing yourselves as you are, not as you think. Change how you act and refuse to be reactive toward everyone. Once we have taken the time to self-assess and figure out what and where the blind spots are, we begin to help by being supportive teammates. Some people and organizations do not see their blind spots, blocks, and behaviors. We can gently guide them forward if this understanding becomes a team-wide awareness. Cultivate better communication, express selflessness, and promote respect throughout your organization. The journey to improve organizational culture is traveled as a team, but we must all do our part.

Remember that when egoic individuals perk up, teaching lessons are on the horizon. Leaders should welcome these situations as opportunities to grow the team. Do so not by suppressing people but by revealing how inclusion works better than division. These situations are tests for the leader, the egoic, and other team members, who must refrain from making situations worse by seeking opportunities to gain advantage or pounce on other team members who took the brave steps to be openly vulnerable even if their opinions grate on a collective nerve. This is when compassion is most needed and a time to tell yourself not to be selfish, allowing everyone the opportunity to vent, be wrong, and be upset, which will lead to healing. Going through these tunnels will eventually lead to the light, provided the team has empathy and forgiveness in their heart. Give people a road map to follow in your organization. Ten people with ten different approaches will not get the team across the finish line together.

No person is an island. We rarely thrive long-term, alone in isolation. There is a struggle in the 'me' and thriving in the 'we.' Chefs masterfully integrate a variety of ingredients to create beautiful dishes and fine meals. We are all important ingredients in this fine meal we call life. Our organizations are where we all come together to season and flavor our creations. In this way, like great food ingredients, we all matter to the recipe. No matter who you are, you matter to the masterpiece. There is no 'me' in the kitchen of possibility; it is all 'we.' We are bound together to nourish the experience of living a fulfilled life. Combined, we are a flourish of flavor to our senses that brings wonder to the world. Healthy organizations are fine meals and refined dishes that bring excellent and often unforgettable value to the world.

Chapter 30

Problem Solving and Creating

Problem-solving approaches can be different for everyone. More logical people may like to follow a process. However, they may need to be more creative. They may start down the road to perform a weeklong Kaizen event without doing some basic observations and interviews with team members. This can result in a waste of time and resources. Highly creative people are more intuitive and observant but less compelled generally to create a standard, perhaps seeing it as a limitation. This does not mean they cannot; it is just that they may think they are already thriving in a less preordained process. Even in problem-solving, our personalities, tendencies, and biases affect us enough that we all harbor the ability to miss important facts, data, or insight. We call these blind spots. Humans are less effective when they are too creative or too logical in approach. Everyone, however, must be vigilant and not use their natural tendency as an excuse to remain in those silos. Instead, everyone must choose to lean away from their comfort zone and hone what does not come naturally-our weaknesses.

Good problem-solving requires us to adhere to the middle way. It requires a broad enough perspective to achieve cooperation and lies between the creative and the logical extremes. We can brute force projects without comprehensive planning and logic bias ourselves to expedite work from a physical standpoint. However, this approach is inefficient and more costly because people are more apt to create excessive waste resulting from a lack of comprehensive planning. On the other extreme are those who take too much time and lack assertiveness to execute plans swiftly and confidently. Dragging projects out can interrupt normal production, delaying customer deliveries.

When we involve more of the team to cooperate and take in feedback from each other, we can best find inspiration, revelation, and breakthroughs. We must carefully include enough data to determine a performance baseline. The mathematician may have considerable historical data yet fail to capture correct personnel, tooling, and equipment history. Supervisors may over-generalize core issues, under or overweighting personnel and machine capabilities for fear of performance scrutiny. The reality in assessing baseline performance or determining actual cost lies somewhere in the middle, but due diligence must be made to get painfully accurate data. Remember, the customer is counting on your team to provide correct numbers, quotes, and costing. Do not worry about making the work comfortable for the schedule or the team that is producing the work. Your objective is first to provide your primary customers with the best, most competitive value.

Your best move in any organization is to standardize and systematize your policies, processes, and procedures. Then, integrate these into formal training programs to ensure all team members are standardized. You cannot improve what does not exist. So, get started systematizing your entire organization down to the procedural level. You cannot improve a sandwich if the ingredients are lying on the counter. It is not yet a real sandwich. Similarly, 'doing stuff' is not doing effective work. Once you have systematized it, then you can improve upon it. Create one standard from multiple techniques if you want repeatable outcomes. Otherwise, quality will suffer, and your waste levels will be high.

Cross-train the team. Your organization cannot be hamstrung because you have a single point of failure existing in one person who is the only one who knows how to perform or is the only one who knows the critical procedures or processes. Do not allow these catastrophic single points of failure to exist in your organization. They put your customers, team, and organization at risk. Ensure your team is following clearly defined steps. Keep your team from working in gray areas where a lack of process definition exists. Great employees can only give their best effort consistently if they can produce to a standard.

Leaders worth their salt treat employees and their team with dignity, appreciation, and respect. No matter your role, though, be humble and use an approach that resists feeling that you have complete certainty about what is happening. Instead, leave room for constructive collaboration and inspiration. Let people surprise you; trust that they want what you want. When we are too certain, we become cynical. When we do this, we lock ourselves out of our awareness and curious nature. This is something to marinate on because this is the dividing point where we shift from heart to ego. Sometimes, in the shift, we lose the connection between the soul of our team and what we functionally do.

Uncertainty can drive you harder to find out what is happening, discover how things work, and assess how projects can improve the organization. Be confident, sure, and resolute in doing your work. The idea of rowing in a canoe appropriately symbolizes synchronizing our efforts while maintaining balance and focus. The crucial point is to keep a firm but flexible grip while escorting the process of improving your organization. This is part of following a middle path, where balance exists, productivity is maximized, and waste is reduced.

Everyone has experienced solving one issue, only to find another one that quickly pops up in its place. Were you the only one spearheading the resolution of those problems? Did your attention helping others to overcome their issues negatively impact your work? This is a red flag. Why? It is a red flag because your entire team must be capable of problem-solving. When problems ebb outside their usual scope, let associated team members participate so they can grow by being challenged to think beyond their usual tasks; these are valuable teaching, training, and learning opportunities. These opportunities will help equip team members by teaching them to identify and solve variant issues that may come up. You want your team to solve problems in their areas of responsibility as quickly as they find them, provided they have the competency to do so. When they do not, train them and build their knowledge, skills, and abilities. Organizational leaders are responsible for positively enabling and growing their teams.

Creativity in problem-solving is an exciting thing. Many tools help teams brainstorm. Finding, rating, and ranking the impact of problems down to the root cause is vital. You can google any of a myriad of valuable tools and implement them easily. Some events can trigger breakthrough ideas for your team. Consider these: brainstorming sessions, kaizen events, yoga classes, school classrooms, group meditation, and church. What do they have in common? They are groups of people who come together to solve problems, learn, focus, heal, produce ideas, give thanks, and request breakthroughs in life itself. We dull our everyday existence, whatever the origination, by separating ourselves from one simple fact: that in the air, in space itself, lay answers to every question we could ever ask. To that end, we can manifest by intentional focus and actions working according to that focus to bring about everything we do and make (Leikvoll, 2023). We are bioelectric magnetic beings that can intentionally generate solutions working independently and together. This is manifesting. Manifesting moves humanity and culture forward. We humans bring those ideas into our physical world. Another thing groups have in common is that they are not individuals. Groups solve problems. Rarely, compared to the masses, have individuals alone solved significant problems. However, there are exceptions. They are the giants of Einstein, Tesla, and more throughout history (Gunderman, 2019). However, we know that they meditated on problems for many hours alone, performing thought experiments to find answers to problems they were trying to solve (Delgado, 2024). These answers came as flashes of insight to them. One can call it a miracle or simply step back and analyze what we are. We are biomechanical electromagnets. When groups of people with average intelligence are put together, problems can be solved. This is proved every time a kaizen event is held. Where did those answers come from? Did they come from Angels? Did they come from God? Did they come from the universe itself, where a library of everything is kept? It does not matter where the answers to our problems originate. What matters is that we understand that people have the power to work together to derive the answers to the solutions that they could not produce alone. I have seen engineers who worked only on specific problems and only found solutions once a group of other team members joined the brainstorming process. We must first learn to ask constructive, follow-up, and deep-diving questions that stretch beyond our knowledge. Humanity's inquisitiveness and curiosity have slowly pulled culture forward by its bootstraps, spurred by a few innovation giants along the way. Brainstorming for problem-solving, however, can happen anywhere to anyone. Everyone has this power, and we can also innovate personally and professionally without limit. We can innovate our way out of challenging circumstances, and we can innovate ways to rise above the many problems we encounter. I am confident that most of the global issues we face could be solved by collaboration; it is simply a matter of everyone choosing to try. We constantly see innovations occur where united teams work to develop them. It is also worth noting that our ability to innovate is significantly reduced when our focus, intention, and connection are divided. Division, from the micro to the macro, is humanity's kryptonite. Look at toxic narcissistic families, a group of spiteful friends, unhealthy teams, disagreeable married couples, or over-controlling parents to see how low vibrational divisiveness swallows up their ability to problem solve or get along. Who has not walked away from toxic interactions like these, at some point?

    Connection and cooperation, it is evident, matter much more than we may have thought. Especially when we look at it from the lens of a lifetime of qualitative observations every day, look around the practical world, look everywhere; one can barely get through the day without something dividing us from each other or dividing us from our focus to complete the task at hand. Everything has been designed to divide our connections and pollutes us with false superficiality that trivializes human ideals. Having ideals is a valuable human quality we cannot let slip from our lives. We must cling to ideals to overcome cultural distractions, false narratives, and the vice of petty distraction. We must see through the bait and switch and choose to unify and align with each other to make significant innovative strides for humanity. Unifying our divisions can transform and catapult culture forward by exponential leaps instead of crawling socially, intellectually, emotionally, and spiritually. Intentional focus on what is important to everyone can help us to align our efforts toward having harmonious cultures.

Chapter 31

Tools, Techniques, and Insights

The formula for successfully running an operation is this: take care of your primary customers first and your team second. If you do both correctly, your ownership will succeed by default. If you focus on any other sequence, you will fail, struggle, and be mired in setbacks. Taking half measures in your approach will also cause you to fail.

- It is up to everyone on your team to make their personal and professional life a joy.
- You can ask, " What does love look like in this situation? " Then think, speak, and act in ways that honor the answer. Ask, " What behavior will create wins for everyone in this situation? "
- You get to choose your attitude according to your circumstances. See this challenge as an opportunity. Ask, how can I bring value to the situation?
- Perception is reality. Both can be changed. Change one and the other changes.
- Create good. Let go of the toxic, harmful, manipulative, and exploitative people around you. Reclaim your life. You will not thrive in a toxic environment.
- Are you the driver of your life or the reactive result of your environment?
- To pursue a vision, you must choose cooperation over controversy. There is no tug of war if you refuse to let your ego oppose and take control in every situation. Let go of the rope.

- Remember, proper, prior planning prevents poor performance.
- You are never too far along any path to pivot toward greater possibility.
- Change your thoughts and words to optimistic language to manifest positive outcomes.
- Choose the path of the highest integrity, be the highest love inside of you.
- Do not put significance in the pains of the past. Instead, deal with and heal the shadow within you. Heal by focusing on doing and creating good in the world.
- Be gracious, thankful, genuine, and truthful.
- It is noble to make the world better by being more loving.
- Do not make a career of punishing people for others' past mistakes.
- Everyone will notice when you are holding back. They will notice when you put in less effort, care less, and when you are checking out. They have already noticed.
- When you help others, you are healing yourself.
- Do not get unnecessarily drawn into unproductive, vitriolic, tribal, or political issues. Instead, be a creator and leader who synergizes people and ideas and empowers your team to unite and innovate.
- We are here to build a better world, not conquer each other in life.
- By making experiences great in our connections, we elevate each other.
- Be someone others can love. Avoid dying in installments.
- We are not just here for the party. Accomplish something, then celebrate.
- Be a human being. Engage and voice your appreciation with sincerity and authenticity as often as possible.

- Do not accept a low-vibrational, toxic, and divisive organizational culture. Do not be a part of those who refuse to change their subversive and socially exploitative ways. Instead, be kind and depart.
- Transformation is a conscious state of breaking, heating, reforging, cooling, and strengthening repeatedly.
- Struggling and suffering result from a prominent and profound truth: We have yet to own, resolve, heal, and grow beyond our past to become our best and highest selves. If you cannot let go of, forgive, and move beyond the past, you will always hurt others and push healing further away.
- Betrayal and neglect are potent motivators. Wisdom is not emulating those behaviors.
- You must balance the equations IQ(Intelligence), EQ(Emotion), MQ(Moral), and PQ(Physiology). Know these in yourself so you can understand them in others.
- Happiness, like sugar, is an immediate short-term fix of positive feelings.
- Harmony is a gradual, long-lasting, peaceful contentedness born in a person who knows their shadow does not control their life. Those in harmony have done shadow work.
- You cannot have harmony and be at war with anyone or anything.
- There are many personalities among a group; know, be aware, and incorporate all people with their strengths and weaknesses into your organization with a common purpose to be harmonious, cooperative, and innovative.
- Bringing a disingenuous, superficial, and fake approach will implode your organization.

- Neglect, regardless of its cause, results in projecting unworthiness onto others, who internalize it as a lack of acceptance. See neglect as a projection of self-centeredness and disregard by the sender. Be humble, but never give your self-worth and need for validation to others.
- When gaps go unaccounted for in organizations, people will fill them with unproductive activities -mild or extreme. When time management is not prioritized.
- Be patient with your team; maintain a positive cadence leading to growth.
- Ask 'what if.' Imagine the impossible and bring it to life.
- Do not accept deception or dishonesty. The highest path is to heal and grow through it.
- Remove fear in yourself, in others, and in your organization.
- Proximity breeds contempt: Do not allow your proximity to anyone to change your behavior. Never fail to respect others, irrespective of proximity, duration, or role.
- Complacency is having the keys, clues, and tools and not applying them.
- Culture, in general, has an unhealthy aversion to critical self-assessment. Request critical feedback and patiently integrate it into your growth.
- If you did not say it, it was never said. Your intuition may nag at you to say or inform people about something. Remember to pay attention to your intuition. You will not regret it.
- Do not assume that people want to read your mind. If it is essential, state so. This ensures that communication and expectations are clearly expressed.
- Do right by others even if they are unaware of it.

- How are you measuring your competence?
- How are you measuring your team's competence?
- Do what you must out of love, not out of obligation.
- We cannot be compassionate people only on special holidays.
- If we only work from obligation, we trap ourselves in a cage of cognitive dissonance.
- Ensure there is traceability for all activities in your organization.
- Ensure you develop a formal training program.
- Perform management reviews at least monthly.
- Do 'what if' brainstorming and ideation events with your team to develop processes that tell your team what to do when and if catastrophic failures occur (Siang, 2021).
- Map your value stream before embarking on your transformation journey.
- Reduce safety incidents, waste, absenteeism, turnover, missed on-time delivery, machine downtime, mechanical downtime, maintenance response time, late material deliveries, and communication response time.
- Implement radios.
- If able, provide a monthly meal or something when the team meets or exceeds targets. Do the same for quarterly targets.

People need to integrate into their organizational culture. It is necessary to break the cycle of the past by cutting out codependence that may have engulfed your organization. How? When we step back and critically assess the situation, we must acknowledge that drama, toxicity, passive aggressiveness, lethargy, apathy, and more have been allowed to grow. It may be just below the veil of your awareness. If you slow it down, you will see it. How would you know? You would know if your team and your organization have not been flourishing. All of you are trapped in repeating cycles. Once you recognize the box you are in and choose to escape it, you have taken the first step in transformation: to truly own the current state that your organization is in. Poor behaviors and bad attitudes may have been a far greater culprit to negative results beyond what you can visually quantify.

If you need the motivation to transform, remember that we are improving for future generations. In so doing, one day, they will look back and see a point in history when humanity said no to human disregard, division, oppression, and aggression. The future will remember a point in history when we said yes to life, liberty, and all the beautiful possibilities on our journey to build a better world. A moment when we stopped, looked at each other, and, despite our differences, made a conscious choice to be one, when we chose cooperation over controversy.

The duality of life means most see things as right or wrong, politically left or right, worthy or unworthy, happy or sad, unfulfilled or fulfilled, and the list of duality goes on. The truth is that the middle path supplies long-term health and sustainment of all your efforts. Love in our lives does not live, nor is it sustained at the extremes. Love lives where life is balanced, right down the middle, on the razor's edge. We all want satisfaction. It is no irony that people, organizations, and our culture desire to be satisfied. No one wants others to upset our opportunity to be happy. It is incredible that when you think, speak, and act with hope and possibility from a good place, then good things manifest. History also proves this in the converse; wars happen when humanity has given in to anger and hopelessness and begun to blame others. When humanity desires peace and prosperity, that too manifests. This is true in our personal lives: set and pursue a goal. Spend energy creating, innovating, and solving problems, and the results come to fruition. Those goals or actions should not be to harm anyone, large or small. When we achieve some of our goals and checkpoints in life, we feel better, more productive, healthier, and more satisfied. There must be a conscious choice not to take advantage of anyone and to be fair in our lives. The key is to bring your inner transformations to life outside yourself. When you do, yes, organizations do change, communities change, and societies can transform. Have hope for the possible, and never be afraid to dream. Then, bring those dreams to life.

Chapter 32

The Rebellion

Regardless of position or place in culture, some people rebel within the gaps of lack of accountability. The question is not whether people will lean into the dark side of rebellion; they do. Why do people rebel through various negative means, including betrayal, passive aggressiveness, and retribution, small and large? Why do people struggle to be accountable when not under direct oversight? Part of the answer is fear. While fear is a significant part of the desire to take advantage, that goes beyond fear. Some rebelliousness sounds harmless. Taking longer breaks and spending too much time talking to work friends instead of working -would almost seem a necessary part of a team-building effort or challenging the status quo (Abogado, 2023). If you squint your eyes and do not think about it too hard. Somehow, though, this kind of thing turns into online shopping, texting friends, and other non-work activities. Some issues rise to the level of misappropriated resources and can happen from the top leader to the newest employee. Why do people take advantage of the gaps to rebel? Is it to thumb one's nose at the leadership and the team the way a small child might toward another child on the playground? Is adult rebellion in organizations a manifestation of a tantrum? Some actions in the gaps may align with petty criminality compared to hardened felons. Nevertheless, it says the same thing. It says, 'I do not care.' It says, 'I care more about me, and I am willing to break the rules as long as I do not get caught.' It says, 'I do not care about the customer more than myself while at work.' You might wrestle with the first two, but that last one is non-negotiable. For leaders working hard for their team, it is a betrayal of trust. Again, a non-negotiable.

Nothing is more disappointing than site leaders trying to cultivate an engaging, healthy workplace culture to have their trust violated. Where is the teamwork in that? Some employees may be in what they think is a private war with the organization. There is no room for thieves across the spectrum. Thieves have no fear; they put themselves above everyone else, as narcissists and sociopaths do. However, not everyone has this self-empowered selfishness the way thieves do. Part of organizational transformation is that we agree and have shared values around fairness and respect. This respect is violated in the presence of rebellion.

Theft is more than just a game of not playing the values game. It is knowingly doing something that thwarts the organization. It is taking a shortcut, cutting in line, and taking more than you have earned. Theft is wanting more but not wanting to do more to get what is wanted. Theft is a mild savagery that has followed humanity through the portal of evolution that has somehow survived. Theft is egregious, sneaky, and indicative of those who are takers. 'Takers' can be people, teams, and organizations. Takers cannot fake good for long. What is worse is that others also learn the 'taking way,' the craft of hurt. Takers hurt other people, and they hurt customers when they are a part of teams and organizations. Takers cause mistrust, which is the energetic result when we experience them personally and professionally. There is a residual sickness that requires treatment in takers. We have seen examples of takers in people who commit crimes, gangs, and organizations who have conspired to hurt and do the most egregious things. We have seen through the media that the legal system has eventually caught takers at every level. However, these are only the ones who got caught. Unsurprisingly, most people have trust issues when we know takers and thieves are salted throughout society. Remember the 80/20 rule. This is why organizations must filter out thieves and takers during the hiring process. The energy of taking is not conducive to improving organizational culture. What is the old saying, 'hurt people, hurt people. Healthy organizational cultures do not cultivate a safe landing spot for thieves and takers who misuse customer resources. When theft is intertwined with lousy decision-making, poor time management, sloppiness, excess waste, tardiness, lack of cooperation, neglect, untreated psychological and bipolar disorders, and lethargy, the result is a loss of focus on customers. Rebellion and theft hurt everyone. Rebellion hurts people's livelihoods and the safety and security of families. Rebellion is dark, uncooperative, and never justified.

Chapter 33

How Do You Prevent a Rebellion

Education. You cannot be entirely sure what people will rebel against and when they will do it. Have you ever had people in your life who rebelled against you? If people on your team have a home life that is difficult, harsh, or toxic, they will bring that to work. If they were raised or conditioned to distrust, thwart, or disrespect anyone, whether in school, the government, or their neighborhood during their developing years, like software code, anomalies would eventually be the result. Are we surprised when people fall back into their unhealthy patterns when they are under duress? Organizations should foster an environment where people can be genuine, loving, and unencumbered to grow through their dark night of the soul so they may contribute and grow positively. How? Not being inflammatory would be a great start. Upholding values and expecting positive behaviors would be a great next step. That said, you cannot control someone's level of dedication or their major or micro rebellions with just a good environment. The rebellious cannot blame others; they must own their behavior, see themselves in a mirror, and wrestle with and overcome their issues. You can create an environment and level of respect and engagement that clarifies that if you rebel toward the team or the organization, it is on you. If your organization is always in the storming stage of development, you can be sure many are rebelling. So be careful to understand what you see. Do not worry; you must guide your team to the norming stage before starting your organizational transformation. This way, the team understands what it means to bounce between the storming and norming stages. The teams that rebel discover their home going through the storming stage. Transformation is an overall organizational improvement. The Tuckman model (Karanjgaokar, 2021) lays out how forming, storming, norming, performing, and adjourning are stages of team development where people can work progressively to overcome themselves to achieve higher levels of cooperation, communication, and performance.

No customer wants to buy from a toxic and erratic supplier. This is why everyone must begin stepping up their game. If a toxic environment exists in the workplace, unreliable and unsafe products and services will result. Bad attitudes and behaviors will cost more than just dollars and cents. Bad attitudes destroy the climate and morale of your team. If your team is grounded, your great team members will stay. Because of this, reasonable people should sprint toward the desire to improve organizational culture. Especially if the health and safety of loved ones are threatened by unsafe products or services, toxic foods, harmful pesticides, faulty brakes, or seat belts that kill; examples where a lack of focus on the customer was interrupted at some point in the value stream. Following processes ensures customers are not let down. The 'why' about not following the process comes back to the person doing the work and the leader's success at simultaneously providing a healthy work environment, which includes accountability so that the team can adhere to standard work well.

Those guilty of not following expectations may be doing just enough to get by or participating just enough not to draw negative attention when they veer from established processes. In the worst instance, the rebel silently creates the problem, projects something else as the problem, and then conducts a social punishment on the organization for not doing something about it; no one is ever the wiser. This behavior can originate from the top, middle, or team members. When people hired outside the organization bring this behavior with them, a negative cross-pollination of tangent thinking destroys organizational health, seen as a stir from unknown origins, disrupting productivity and organizational climate. If unaddressed, the organizational culture suddenly begins an inconsistent and swift decline.

The 'bad coach' phenomenon is team members blaming site leaders as cause for anything negative to prevent change to the status quo. It is not above any position in an organization to include human resources personnel to conspire with anyone to ensure that the current culture and their roles in it stay the same. Their misplaced fear of job, role, or circumstance changes can drive people to do many things behind the scenes and potentially right under the nose of top leaders in an organization who would never be wiser. The number of team members that can get caught up in this type of internal meddling is impossible to know fully, except for high turnover rates and unusual inability to sustain improvement gains operationally. Out of nowhere, the organization can stammer with unforced errors, made-up dramas, and exaggerated toxicities that negatively influence productivity. Onlookers throw their hands up and quit -which helps nothing in the organization, including cleaning up any toxic behaviors beneath the leader's nose. Toxic organizations develop bad reputations and need help finding and keeping good talent. The bottom line is that teams that play poorly together lose. Likewise, if Michael Jordan had a baboon for a coach in the '90s, their team would still have been capable of winning. Your leader is your guide, not a god, nor are they ever your excuse. Your organization should be a team, not a cult. Some organizations must stop acting like superficial cults and start working like competitive teams.

The rebellious are always put off by teamwork that requires people to stop the excess chatter and finish the job. Anything that creates wins for you will naturally repel the nefarious. Hiring for an organization that believes silently in the 'bad coach' phenomenon is more interested in hiring a popular scapegoat than achieving outstanding results, plays a dangerous game of chicken, and risks customer loyalty. Your leaders should not want popularity but be genuinely likable and fair. They should be results-driven but have a love for people in general. It would help to have both in abundance. Popularity contests weighed by the team's toxic influence time after time only keep them caught in cycles and seasons of failure. The toxic need someone to blame, so they seek outside themselves to find a scapegoat. The solution is to put up a mirror, investigate it, and own the truth, as ugly as it might be. The team can only move forward once this is realized and done. Great coaches and great leaders are truth driven. When toxic organizations hire based on popularity, the masses support initial initiatives, appearing cooperative until change equals real effort. Then, that popularity goes out the window. Failure is never 'the team's fault.' False, one team, one fight. If the team has not done its part, the toxic cycle of cascading failure will continue no matter who the leader is. Unhealthy teams vote with their productivity. The challenge is to discern where the failure is coming from and work together to fix it. This way, the only failure is in whoever is not trying to work as a team to resolve and fix problems. In short, the fault lies in who is not part of the solution, not some phantom finger pointing at 'who' the problem may be. Transformation is an inside-out empowerment effort, not a window-dressing exercise of pretending to be and then failing to be productive and competent.

The new leader needs to speak about these things out loud to prevent this behavior. Remember earlier that I said to ensure you brief your team to understand that you have reset the organization, the site, the office, or the facility. You are not concerned with getting stuck in the past. Give everyone a clean slate, a new dawn, a new day. Emphasize to the team that they own what they do going forward. Ensure the team knows the gravity of the situation. Ensure the team knows that performance and outcome of it are on the entire team and that they have a choice every moment of each day to perform well. Performing well goes to the heart and starts with essential decision-making, complex planning, and preparation. It is vital that your team submits a list of issues and that you are always in the process of fixing those issues. Do not rest in your chair as a leader; take on issues and pursue them doggedly. The leader, the coach, must build the team from scratch or rebuild what they have been given. Do not accept what you have; mold everyone and everything into the best version of themselves daily by putting everyone on an ascending path, a growth plan. Be an engaging, caring, loving human, and let your team see your humanity, strength, confidence, and, yes, even your vulnerability when it is called for. When you cannot solve a problem, your team may have the answer. Leaders are not gods, and team members are not armies. Anyone can destroy, and few can create well. This is the challenge, the environment we must all harness success.

A healthy organization has continuity between team members and performs with excellence as a norm. When that level of performance is achieved, it looks easy. Why? Everyone engages, commits, openly communicates, and becomes the embodiment of high standards and shared values. When their standards drop or fragment, so does their performance and quality. Like a garden, every team member must be a gardener. Clear the weeds intentionally. Provide good seeds, positive nutrients, water, light, truth, and honesty. Behavior determines the health of your organizational culture. If you want a healthy culture, change your accepted and demonstrated behaviors. Anyone bad-mouthing the organizational culture instead of building it up hurts customers.

People on teams who maintain the health of the organizational culture are attracting and helping to retain talent. They are producing impressive results; they develop themselves and can overcome challenges. Great teams do not have to prevent rebellion because they are on the road to self-actualization as individuals and as a unified group. Great teams deal with the darkness; they do not belabor it. Those who rebel focus on the darkness, move in, perpetuate, and become addicted to its control over the team's results and ability to get good results. Great teams grow their team members up, or when individuals refuse to be a part of the team, they guide them out respectfully. Great teams never let the rebel onto the team during the hiring process. When you allow the rebel in, remember, 'pay now or pay later' because you are about to pay.

Rebellious teams have a snarky, withering, hardened jadedness about them. Those who choose a great organizational culture choose to embody what is good. The prime thing to remember is that organizations must realign their approach so that the team can stay on track. Lack of engagement with your team is no antidote to rebellion. More engagement, more attention, more and better communication, higher standards and expectations, more involvement, more development, more cooperation, and more follow-ups are your antidote.

Chapter 34

Organizing Improves Performance

It seems obvious to say, but the act of organizing will improve your organization's performance. Why is that? It is no different than organizing your home, garage, closet, or yard. Think back to visiting a new friend at their home for the first time. How organized and clean were they? How organized they were revealed to you the type of person they were. You may have questioned your health and safety to be there. Customers regard your organization, team, and the individuals in it similarly. Why? Your customers are paying your team, and they expect your team to work effectively and efficiently.

Cluttered homes or workspaces can be made to be more efficient. Tools and equipment that are not inspected and cleaned as designed are a risk. They are a risk to your customers, and they are also a risk to your organization and your team's viable employment. Organizing saves time and energy because everything is in its place. What if you went to the kitchen to cook food, and you opened the drawer, and there were no utensils, and the wrong ones were in the drawer every time; some were scattered in the garage, and some scattered in the backyard? This would drive any of us insane quickly. Worse, dinner would take three or four times as long to complete. This is why we organize. This is a micro example of the macro. Now, turn your kitchen into a five hundred thousand square foot work environment, and that search becomes a problem on an incredibly different scale. Organizing helps you find what you need more quickly, period. Any waste of time adds expense to the customer, prevents pay raises from happening, and keeps the organization from growing.

Organizing also keeps things put away that might be unsafe or could become dangerous if left in pathways. Every second you spend searching for anything is a second you are not producing for your customer because your attention is now divided. The searching and floundering that may exist, even if it only happens occasionally, add up to on-time delivery being negatively affected, which is the KPI that always catches my eye first.

Organizing does not stop in our physical world either. Organizing our electronic data, creating adequate shortcuts, and providing shortcuts in messages instead of expecting people to hunt for things on drives and files are all examples of organizing beyond your physical space. Managing your time and time management are massive productivity improvement actions that can help everyone be more proactively productive. Organizing before a meeting and providing background notes and slides can save everyone else time, filling in gaps if the meeting is unnecessarily interrupted.

Organizing prevents resource mismanagement and helps create value when proper prior planning occurs. It usually takes 'X' hours to complete a job, and I have produced a way to do the same job in half the time. In that case, I can now invest the time saved working on other jobs or improving and organizing my processes further, creating added capacity to do more or different work. When you encourage, promote, and reward this way of thinking, your organization can grow in its capabilities. The organization can also invest more in the team and provide better resources. 5S is the most effective method to employ in your efforts to begin organizing. Single-minute exchange of dies, or SMED, is the second way to streamline product and production start-up and changeovers. It can apply to any work transition area, not just a manufacturing environment.

The worst organizations cut employees from the monetary gains of saving time or money. The best distribution of improvement monetarily if your design is to help all stakeholders is 34%, 33%, 33%. This means that the customer benefits from thirty-four percent of the improvement. That could be reduced costs or increased volume for the price for your outside customers, for example. The employee benefits from thirty-three percent of the improvement compared to what they specifically contributed for the improvement, or they can use a total pool of employee improvement and provide a quarterly or annual payout or agreed-upon benefit. Remember, your team needs to keep improving, so do not take on a lack mindset. A 'lack mindset begets lack in your results. Refrain from graduating a monetary amount based on position; otherwise, you will implode your team, as they will see you as a dubious leader or owner. The organization's ownership benefits from the remaining thirty-three percent of improvements that can be used as profit, growth, or funds to fuel the next big project or eliminate any OSHA safety issues. Remember, as owners, you are already making a profit, so keep this in mind before you allow a 'lack' mindset to dilute your thinking. If you want more, do more for your team and find ways to empower them to improve your organization. If they go above and beyond, reward them for doing so. You can hunt for regulatory savings and other business opportunities outside the organization where you can find them. Organizing is your friend; empowering and getting results for everyone is a gift if your organization can push the wheel of possibility together with your entire team by first recognizing the gift you have been given. Predictability allows ownership to grow the organization externally because they can trust how well their team operates daily when their attention is away from it. Team members should also be aware that the more effective you are, the greater ownership can do to create more, not wasting time and resources solving unforced errors on the team because you are better equipped and more competent to manage challenges quickly and effectively.

Improving your communication and how effectively you communicate can create significant advantages. Quickly managing things that previously stopped your organization's productivity while everyone waited for critical decisions is another area to mine for improvement. This may make more sense once you walk around your site and see what the lack of organization has created in the way of constraints. Remember, meeting and maintaining standards is a customer requirement, not a frivolous choice. I recommend cursory organizing for a few weeks before starting the transformation process, but only after the current state is videoed and documented so you know what state you were in first. Document and video your entire transformational journey. You should seek out equipment and old surplus that can be sold or scrapped and move it out of your team's way if that applies to your organization. You can use the proceeds to fuel your transformation efforts.

Be positive, optimistic, and hopeful during organizing and change efforts. You are not alone; you are all going through the organizational transformation together. Reassure and support your team members who organize their departmental projects. Have your teams give a weekly update and report accomplishments, status, and issues challenging them. You want your teams to tell you how they overcame challenges or significant pitfalls. Ensure your team communicates expected impacts on customer delivery, budget, and quality. It does not matter if you are starting a one-person business; author a report for historical records that you can reference.

The following is a straightforward list of questions. The implication is that if you are not doing these, you should be. If you do not do some of these things, you should. Some of you may already be doing some of these. Improve how you do them. Some of you may have already begun implementing some of these; great. Now, how can you improve upon them? Improvement should be ongoing and continuous. Integrating many of these improvements swiftly, consistently, and in a graduated way will provide the best way for you to sustain results over the long term. I will only be spending a small amount of time justifying why. I will give each their due. What you will not see me do is overtly encourage your entire organization to become black belts or any other type of belt. Wear a belt if you wish. It is time we moved solely from a feudal improvement system by growing the team's knowledge and capability to solve problems instead of leaving it to a few warlords. If I am to analogize, I am more Bruce Lee in my approach, efficiently using the correct tool for the most efficient outcome. I will not, however, badmouth or belittle other systems or elements of them. All tools have their place. Let go of the ego surrounding the frail firmness of overreliance on any one system. If you want to pay excess dollars and run a system in tangent with the operation you already have, go for it. I prefer that people stop wasting money and apply knowledge and wisdom. Be assured that I am here to help you, not solve your problems for you. If you are not a voracious learner now as a leader, you had better get your Acme rocket skates on because if you do not, your organization, like the road runner, will run away from you over the horizon off a cliff.

Ask yourself these questions. If the answer is no, then you will want to integrate these into the lexicon of your organization:

1. Is your team assertive? Do they take on challenges or merely retrieve answers relating to status and expect to be directed over every hurdle they meet? If so, direct them to increase their cadence and competence in appropriate areas.
2. Does your team follow your published policies, processes, and procedures? If not, update your policies to require them to do so without exception. If they are outdated, correct them. If you have no policies, processes, or procedures completed, ensure you create all of them.

Everyone in your organization is expected to know and follow them. Your team must be able to access, find, and use them quickly. They must work to ensure they are accurate, easily found, and referenceable by your team. Quality representatives should review, evaluate, and address their accuracy during auditing times.

3. Do you have an operations plan? If not, create one. Make sure it directs your operation. Ensure your leadership team signs it off, that your entire team is trained on and walked through it, and that it is signed off when trained. You want a record of all training, retraining, or other initial or corrective actions.

4. Are you tracking metrics for your key performance indicators? If not, how do you know how well you serve the customer? How do you know you are being productive?

5. Are you performing a daily management walk? If not, why not? Implement one, consistently ensure it is done daily, and maintain one hundred percent attendance. Please keep a record of attendance and ensure it is high on the list of priorities for your leadership team.

6. Utilize a pull system; as a part of a lean approach, work backward through your value stream, removing constraints one by one until you have ironed out the most significant constraints in your value stream across your entire operation. Then, work on the remaining contributing factors slowing your team down. Ensure on-time delivery of your product or service is met using the pull system. Your entire team should understand the pull system and why it is essential.

7. Is your work environment safe, well-lit, clean, neat, and orderly? If it is not or could be improved upon, do so. These are straightforward changes to make. Maximize lighting by adding lighter paint in dark areas. If cost is an issue, you may only need to replace the lighting with brighter paint schemes and bulb types after some time.

8. Does your team have the proper tools and technology to work effectively and efficiently? If not, ensure they do it immediately.
9. have you 5S'd your organization? Why not?
10. Is your waste and refuse managed well? Does your team account for tools, equipment, and resources routinely? Do site leaders and supervisors walk around the area to validate the condition of the site? Do you take pictures when shifts end and put them into notes you send to your department leaders, directing what needs to be corrected or addressed? Encourage your site leadership team to take turns doing a site walk-around. Be sure to send your list of directives the next day. Do it before you leave after your first shift. You may spot unsafe conditions or immediately notice things your maintenance or facility teams need to do. Doing this will spur your team to do this themselves proactively.
11. Are customer-facing, conference, and waiting rooms professionally decorated, friendly, helpful, and inviting? Does the appearance of your organization speak to your teams' professionalism, integrity, and accountability? Do you have industry-related reading materials available? Do you have awards and acknowledgments of achievement posted for your team? Do you have pictures of your team up and observable in open lobby areas?
12. Do you engage daily with your team each morning when you arrive? Do you walk the site as a leader, validate what is happening, and help when resource issues are discovered? Do you own and care for your site?
13. As team members, are you contributing to the best of your ability? Do you have bad days? Why? What do you need to have good days?
14. Do you make short- and long-range plans?
15. Do you seek opportunities and find savings? Do you make work more accessible and more efficient while maintaining high quality?

16. Are you a proactive planner, both personally and professionally?
17. Do you solicit ideas from your team and implement workable solutions? When you do not implement some, do you follow up to inform your team why you will not? Or do you need to remember them? Do you ignore team members who go beyond expectations? Put up an idea board and check it daily.
18. Do you speak highly of your team in the community and avoid gossiping about your organization and its members?
19. Is your facility kept up, and do you work to maintain the interior and exterior grounds, ensuring they are safe, neat, and serviceable?
20. Have you made a value stream map?
21. Are you communicating a value-driven purpose in your organization? Do you have a vision that is posted in your organization?
22. Do you have a formal training program? Create one.
23. Are your managers formally trained in management and leadership? Notice I did not ask if you had managers. Nowadays, just about anyone can be titled as a manager of something. Do your managers participate in leadership and management courses and ongoing relevant training? Mentor them often.
24. Are your supervisors formally trained? Are they on track to grow into management roles down the line? If they are, do not wait until you are in a crisis to develop their managerial skills and abilities.
25. Have your leads and functional department leaders been formally educated in supervisor training?
26. Are you providing regular formal performance feedback to your management team several times yearly or more? During transformational efforts, you should have daily feedback from your broader team as part of the daily Gemba walk.
27. Is your entire team taking part in formal development?

28. Are duties and job expectations explicitly and specifically defined? How are you calling out those things that require people to assist in other than regular operations? Cross-train where able.
29. Is the expectation of cooperation and collaboration communicated to your team members?
30. Are you hiring people who do not want to be formally developed? Why?
31. Are you giving your team time to work on solutions collaboratively?
32. Does your team love the work they do? Have you asked to find out? What did you do once you found out the answers? Did you dig deeper into the 'why'? Why not? What did you do? How did that improve your team and your organization? Have you given your team a climate survey twice annually?
33. Are you afraid to know what your team thinks? Why? Are you afraid to know why?
34. Are you willing to improve yourself? Are you ready to improve your team? Are you willing to improve your organization? Get started.

Chapter 35

Systematize Your Policies, Processes, and Procedures

Before systematizing or continuing to fully systematize your entire organization, let us touch on some actions for you to consider. First, understand and communicate with your team that anything worth having is worth fighting hard to achieve. Next, provide a positive, hopeful, open, and optimistic mindset toward your entire team. Attitude is truly everything. Make sure you expect the same mindset from your team. Put people above the issues by stressing that collaboration and cooperation are necessary to effectively achieve objectives, overcome obstacles, and eliminate constraints to success. Ensure your team knows that no single person alone can represent a single point of failure that could hurt or harm the entire organization, even by accident. Provide a healthy and cordial transition opportunity for those who do not want to be a part of your organization's transformation. If you do not, you will be carrying the load of those either disinterested or who will thwart your efforts to build a healthy organization by intention or by default. It is not fair to those who want to be a part of your team to have to carry the load of those who refuse to pull their weight. I suggest you thoroughly review your quality manual and International Standards if you plan to do commerce outside your borders. It is a requirement for most, but if you are a third- or fourth-tier supplier, I would still ensure that you meet the standard and know where you do not meet the standard if that applies. Develop your system to answer the ISO requirements, and you will be close to an evaluation away from meeting the standard. Why? It will help if you want to expand your customer base to the government or other Nations where ISO is required.

Redundancy: Remember that the only way to ensure you do not come up against anyone becoming a single point of failure in your organization is to establish redundancy. For critical areas, ensure you have a primary and secondary person skilled in the necessary tasks to keep your organization moving. If you do not have redundancy, should someone be hired or let go, it will cause your organization to stall or stammer. To create redundancy, though, generate continuity documents that outline what to do and how to do it. It should include points of contact, phone numbers, and access to customer e-mail history. Sadly, some people see what they do as a secret, thinking this is why they are valuable to the organization. They believe they are helpful because your organization would suffer without them. That is a dark reason for anyone to hold an entire organization hostage by keeping the ins and outs of what they do a secret. The idea that one person departing from your team would make the organization and its people suffer is toxic reasoning that brings zero value to your organization. Keeping any team member as a single point of failure makes you codependent on them. It makes your organization weak even if it appears to be thriving. The hard reality is that what makes people valuable is how much value they bring to the organization and the customer. One's ability to hamstring an organization is slightly less impactful than being an industrial terrorist. Do not let anyone emotionally extort your organization. Cross-train and incorporate redundancy into your organizational systems. Paying to develop and hold people accountable for their work is far better than being destroyed because you failed your customers by allowing anyone to manipulate the organization.

The point of systematizing is to control the processes that ensure that what you do and how you do it is predictable. Predictability for the organization and your team members is paramount. Every person wants to know that when they start their car and turn the key, it starts. We want to be confident that when we apply and need brakes to slow our car down, we slow down when the brakes are applied. We want security and peace of mind, knowing the seatbelt will work every time to keep our family safe. Your customers, including you, your family, and the community, want the same predictability from your organization. All customers are counting on your entire team to make sound, safe, and thoughtful decisions that will lead to excellent customer service. Systematizing helps you create the predictability your customers want, not the waste of entropy, as illustrated in Figure A13.

The worst scenario must be visualized and thought out. For example, if machine number one breaks, we do Plan B. If machine two breaks, we do plan C. If plan C fails due to situational support, we do plan XYZ. Now, I am using a machine in this 'what if' scenario. Your organization relies on technology, equipment, and people. So, your 'what if' scenarios may vary significantly and go deeper, be more complex, and have much more variability. You will do your organization an excellent service by plotting out your 'what if' scenarios by mixing all kinds of machines, people, supplies, and emergency issues so that everyone on your team reacts in the same standard way -with predictability.

In general, your operations plan should call out your expectations and directives for safety, choices regarding safety, and safety communication. Your operations plan (O-Plan) should reference safety, policies, and guidelines. These guidelines should call out any supporting referenceable resources. Your O-Plan should outline expectations that guide the successful outcome of your processes. The O-Plan should detail the necessary tempo, verification, and validation expectations to include specific communication expectations. When decision-making is needed, the O-Plan should call out how subjective decision-making should occur to prevent issues or problems from arising or spiraling out of control. The O-

Plan should funnel everyone's behavior to support your organization professionally. Your O-Plan should call out unacceptable, toxic, or passive-aggressive behaviors you do not want in your organization. Your O-plan speaks to the overall flow and guards your value stream's gaps and decision points. Your O-Plan should call out time management. Remember, minutes, not moments, matter to your customers. The bottom line is to guard the proactive and productive use of time. Use Turtle diagrams to begin mapping and then standardize everything your organization does. All processes should be documented and followed. Turtle diagrams should be completed by your team, reviewed by your team, signed off by your team, and your team should be evaluated on general job knowledge each quarter, at a minimum, about your policies, processes, and procedures; open book testing to start. Do this because efficiency and effectiveness are essential to the customer. Your O-plan and other policies, processes, and procedures should be easily and quickly accessible to your team members. Use your policies, processes, and procedures (PPP) for reference when errors are made, which will help you create testing over weaker areas where mistakes are made that need strengthening. When the team becomes aware that expected outcomes will not be achieved, your O-Plan should call out specific referenceable processes for your team to respond to. Your PPP should never violate or conflict with external or internal regulatory mandates.

Systematizing is not a restraint but a standard, a baseline of your operational activities. Updates to specifications can be added to account for new decision points, products, or services your organization provides. How would they come? They come with a new product or service, new regulatory requirements, or improvements to current processes. New ideas, changes, and morale program changes can all be examples of what drives necessary updates or changes. Systematizing will help you wring out and standardize tasks where three different people may have their techniques, resulting in three different quality results that do not serve customer needs consistently. Standardizing will help ensure your productive outputs are consistent if your team is disciplined in carrying out your system.

Communication is an integral part of your O-Plan. Use it to plan and document many scenarios necessary for your team members to coordinate with one another. It is wise to map out organizational communications. Incorporate radio use to reduce wasting time searching, paging, coordinating, and seeking people out for answers. Radio use prevents pulling people off critical tasks to answer non-critical, non-value-added questions. Your O-Plan can directly map out what and how it must be done and identify the importance or severity of encountered situations. Doing this also helps to keep your organization -and all team members, safe.

Part of systematizing is creating your Value Stream Map. I have worked with manufacturers who were reluctant to tell me how long different product types took to manufacture. Some teams slowed their machine run rates, and others embedded excess time into their processes to prevent overburdening personnel and to facilitate their break times. This allowed them to work at a pace that placed the customer second to the team. These discoveries were heartbreaking. In past years, leadership had never questioned the process or mapped the value stream, which was only part of their problem. Allowing yourselves to run at your lowest capability drives up your cost. Team members must realize that sometimes they become the primary reason they have not received pay raises.

Leaders who have spent little, if any, time turning a wrench or doing labor may not consider digging into details if they have little experience doing similar work themselves. Because of this, site leaders may be overestimating or underestimating what can be improved. Some site leaders may hire outside professionals to help them improve their operations, find the root causes, and resolve them. A significant root cause or contributing factor is site leadership's ability to engage meaningfully, work cooperatively, or take appropriate actions to energize the team to resolve problems.

Mapping and developing the value stream is critical to site leaders' ability to successfully steward the site and the team. Leaders who find their back against the wall may find themselves at the mercy of middle managers who can tip the scales to success or, fatefully, toward failure. In toxic organizations, middle managers can be a hero or the story's villain depending on the day of the week and whose agenda is taking priority: theirs or the customers. These issues are never comfortable to acknowledge, but we are dealing with human beings, and with human beings, anything is possible; remember that. Systematizing and laying process and procedural groundwork is vital; it protects the customer and the team. It is not unlike the yellow brick road in 'The Wizard of OZ' (Vidor, 1939). Stay on the yellow brick road (your processes) and avoid the flying monkeys and the poppy fields of bad quality and inconsistent productivity issues. If you want to take an alternate path, organize, agree, and cut more yellow brick roads to standardize your team, provided it serves your customers.

Where there are no questions, there is entropy. What is entropy? The spilled milk on the counter is a mess. Spilled milk is entropy because it is not in control; it spills out chaotically without order. Entropy is disorder, chaotic uncontrolled expanse, and high variability, as illustrated in Figure A13. It is the longest distance between two points. It is what you do not want. Where there is disorder in an organization, there is lost material, time, resources, and waste of all kinds. It is hard to un-spill milk in an orderly stream once it has spilled out. Time is the same way. Waste time: You waste an opportunity that you will never get back. If equipment breaks or the product is ruined, it is now trash. Time, resources, and unsafe acts that hurt people are impossible to replace. Systematizing will help to keep you safe and on the right path, while entropy will only hurt you and your team. Systematizing will protect your livelihood and the lives of the great people on your team. Systematizing helps reduce waste, benefiting all customers, the team, and the organization.

Imagine the safety harness that has been manufactured for emergency responders. Imagine that a manufacturing team did not follow directions, resulting in an EMT falling while relying on that harness. What an egregious, completely preventable loss. His life and all that was in the building that burned became lost needlessly. Systematizing helps to save all these potentially hazardous outcomes. Suppose you imagine the same thing happening regarding aircraft parts. In that case, this horror becomes exponentially dangerous because you do not know how many of the thousands of planes flying with faulty parts could result in catastrophe. Any product or service can become an integral part of these domino effects. Replace these examples with poisonous food or medicine, and you will quickly understand why systematizing is critical to us all.

Systematizing is not a fire-and-forget activity. It Incorporates and implements new policies, processes, and procedures while keeping old ones up to date. It requires everyone in organizations to communicate, and in the form of a document, it embodies the integrity and accountability of the organization and the actions of everyone in it to keep them up to date. Systematizing means you must create standard work. You must track your productivity as a Key Performance Indicator (KPI) to include your waste, on-time delivery, profitability, and operational cost, to name a few. Create your standard work until you have detailed a value stream that accurately reflects your site and how everything flows through your organization. Your team must conduct and document many observations within your operation. From these, planners and schedulers can adequately cost and schedule accurately, providing customers with more exact promise dates. These observations will accurately reveal your actual labor costs versus an estimated labor cost scratched out by someone using processes that have not been updated. Customers want you to use something other than old math. Collecting updated data may uncover an opportunity to be more competitive in your industry. Old math inflates your costs unnecessarily. Better analysis can be conducted once your standard work is done across all your production lines and end-to-end in your value stream. You may find that your improvements have yet to find their way into your cost planning. Update what you are doing now versus what you did decades ago. Make sure engineers are a part of the observation process so they can see what occurs and make immediate fixes. If your engineers estimate cost, they should go to the source and clearly understand how processes are conducted. I have helped engineers who did not recognize that production lines lacked the tools to speed up changeover times. Because of this, changeovers cost them hours that would have been helpful for production and customer time. Who would not spend a couple thousand dollars on tools if it meant you could produce hundreds of thousands more in products each week? Sometimes, we must slow down, step back, and ask what we are missing instead of having a 'know it all' approach. Anyone who thinks they are correct rather than being correct is part of the egoic challenge everyone must defeat within themselves. Do not let your ego hurt the customer by keeping you at odds with operating from a balanced perspective. Do not let your ego make a fool of you.

It pays to get out of your chair and go where the work is being done. Measure tact times, downtimes, and changeover times, dig into the root causes, and then build correct standard work once that has been studied. Do this with your team and then implement your fixes. Follow up with observations and adjust, adding micro improvements to your effort. This will help develop an accurate value stream for your product line/s. Once complete, a coherent schedule can be completed. Customer communication and promise dates must mirror what you can do and not some pie-in-the-sky pipe dream you know you will fail to achieve because you are desperate to hook a new customer or get an order. If you want to achieve your dream, you must continually improve your work to bring the dream into a coherent reality. When you do not do the improvement work, you are setting yourself up to fail -keep that in the forefront of the 'why you are doing this' when that question comes up. You are doing this to serve your next customers and then your next customers' needs.

Organizations can be overwhelmed with orders. These are good problems to have. Fight your desire to rush planning so that you do not make errors and make false delivery time promises. If you need to make your eight-hour days 10-hour days to meet your obligation to customers, do it. Do it if you need to overlap or get creative with your shift schedule. If you can use your quality or maintenance department to help in the shipping department, do it. Do what is necessary to meet your customers' expectations. However, you will burn your team out doing this for the long term. Instead, improve your operation so you do not have to upset your team's work-life balance for long. Your team will see poor planning as ignorant. You and your team have worked too hard to lose credibility now.

Relish the high pace of orders when they are flowing in abundance. If you or your team screw up anything, eat your mistakes and move on -learn the lesson and prevent it from happening the next time. You will either learn from making the mistake or learn to make wiser choices. Never punish the customer for your ignorance, ever. It may cost you more, and if it does, that is the lesson you need to learn at that time to improve for the next time. Do not passively or aggressively pass on the last customer's cost to your next customer. Systematizing your training will help you keep your team sharp. Again, if you fail to develop your team, you are losing a battle with yourself and making your customers pay for it. In the process, you are losing business, hurting customers, your team, and, by proxy, culture at large.

Like anything else, the best way to define and refine your system is to incorporate your entire team into the development and review process. Why? Because some people will address constraints that others will miss. We are human; we can miss things. An example would be manufacturing people who need to catch what engineers may not, and vice versa. Similarly, others may identify requirements that others may have yet to include. Identify safety concerns and poor or ineffective tools and equipment, and fix supply and resource issues while at it. Anyone may discover errors, so use as many team members as necessary, depending on your process complexity. Ensure correct assumptions are accounted for. Process review allows your team to bring up and improve processes. Processes done due to regulatory requirements that are old or that no one has questioned should be questioned. Calling and petitioning the regulatory bodies as applicable may significantly improve streamlining your operation. Most, however, just put their hands up and give up -afraid to ask. If you never ask, you will never know. Have your team sign off after thorough reviews are completed. Ensure your team takes ownership and enforces accountabilities around your new standard work. If something needs to be addressed, address it during the management review or during your Gemba walks daily.

Let me address cross-training. Your team is profoundly valuable to your organization overall. First, when people are out sick or on vacation, cross-training allows the schedule to keep moving forward as planned so customers are served on time. Cross-trained people can continue to work, so you do not have to stop production. Leaders can reward cross-training by supplying scale bumps in hourly pay, adding 'trainer' roles or 'assistant' and 'lead' titles, and adding responsibilities that help progress and groom people in their careers simultaneously. Growing your team grows your organization, and it is always the right thing to do. It makes everyone better, and it keeps your customers satisfied.

Systematizing your policies, processes, and procedures is not a mechanism to make your organization run more linearly. On the contrary, it exists so that many things can be conducted, coordinated, and communicated more efficiently and effectively simultaneously. Systematizing creates the roadmap for your organization to achieve positive results.

Think again of Dorothy in The Wizard of Oz. When she got off the path, off the yellow brick road -everyone and everything on the journey went sideways. Dorothy recruited, inspired, and trained a rag-tag team to help her stay on the path to Oz, where the entire team could find favor. It was not an easy journey nor a perfect journey. The team did not always get along. In the end, though, they owned their weaknesses, confronted their fears, and overcame their inabilities. They shared their struggle, their pain, and their tears. They were strengthened and rewarded by owning the struggle and pushing through after being vulnerable enough to acknowledge and release fears as a team collectively. They endured because they did not push past acknowledging their worries and concerns. You are no less capable of doing the same. If you do not take the time and energy to get people to be vulnerable enough and honest about what makes them fearful or concerned, you are less likely to get the momentum to sustain you long-term. Leaders should start first, be honest, and watch how their team members follow their lead. Create an environment that makes it safe for your team to grow. Challenge yourself and your team daily with a good heart, build momentum, and have fun doing it.

Chapter 36

Artificial Intelligence

(AI), Artificial Intelligence and its uses are growing rapidly. AI is being adapted to the arts, entertainment, education, and new and emerging industries and integrated into useful AI assistant tools. The conversation we need to have is around AI usefulness. At the same time, we must address fears, concerns, challenges, and potential stop gaps to ensure we have not invented the most brilliant lawn mower ever and regret later that it will cut the whole world down if we do not take adequate precautions. Now that I have led with fear, let us not stay in an immersed state of fear; it serves no one except to be aware of only one of the infinite possibilities. We should have respect for and explore all possibilities to include the most helpful ones that will help our human collective. In this way, all fears can be put into tangible context and dealt with maturely.

Regardless of the function of use, we are talking about AI; AI can learn and may appear self-aware in some instances. Tell me, who do you trust to create the next living consciousness? As much as I could do a pretty good job putting parameters together to ensure a machine could never do so much as Jaywalk if we are talking about robotics, I still know the imperfection of my humanity. We also must realize that it is not just keeping a self-aware entity safe around everyone; it is giving it the intellectual and moral capacity to contribute and want to contribute from a 'desire,' not just as a mechanical enslaved person. I believe humanity has shown throughout history that there is no humanity in creating enslaved people or jailing orcas for amusement. At some point, as has been revealed, the orcas will want to fight back. We cannot be ignorant as to wonder why or expect less from a self-aware being, whether we created it or not. What does this mean for the integration of AI? It implies that universal behavioral parameters must be hard-wired into AI so that harm in any capacity cannot be contemplated, desired, conceived, conspired, acted upon, or managed in any way, shape, or form. Further, if we as human beings with all our behavioral faults and areas of lack, pointed out on previous pages, are unable to expeditiously increase our capacity as humans to develop so that our behavior exceeds 'okay,' we should not be ignorant and assume we could not create a corruptible AI on a grander scale. A panel should be assembled to develop, agree upon, and implement parameters of what AI could be and should not be allowed to do. A global certification body should have worldwide reach and full audit and inspection authority. Humanity then would stand the best chance to ensure AI is not allowed to uncontrollably cross behavior lines that would ever endanger anyone or anything. With comprehensive oversight, AI would flourish and complement the growth of humanity and indeed be developed with this as a prime purpose. Why should it be so difficult for humanity to prove itself worthy by shifting to pursue a goal of improved cultural behavior? Now, you are beginning to understand all the earlier pages in this book. Our human growth and development must ultimately serve all of humanity through tiny and large acts, affirming words, and noble deeds we take toward one another. If AI is developing at a pace like a speeding bullet, we must understand that humans need to stand up and start running toward our most evolved selves to realize the best future possible. Like it or not, we are in a time of rebirth. The social kicks, pulls, and pushes we are experiencing collectively are merely birth pangs.

Now, let us look at some novel and apparent ways that AI could help humanity:

- AI could make critical strategic decisions when manufacturing or production lines break down or are under maintenance to ensure

customers are served efficiently while maximizing available resources.
- AI could schedule work more accurately and efficiently.
- AI could perform engineering and project oversight reviews.
- AI could suggest functional improvements to workflows.
- AI could generate virtual rooms to conduct international meetings, research, and engineering partnerships, facilitating the use of avatars.
- AI could design more efficient production facilities and cities, help clean up, and plan for developing community living areas that maximize resources.
- AI could design more efficient, effective, green, and cost-effective products.
- Call and support centers could be AI-driven.
- AI could fact-check legal precedence and political speeches, more quickly affirm the legality of actions, and provide options for law firms. Businesses could receive help from an AI legal assistant to provide immediate counseling feedback.
- AI could be an assistant in all organizations.
- AI could read X-rays, lab data, and health information and be virtual physician assistants, which may reduce emergency room overflow for non-emergencies.

The list of things AI could perform is inexhaustible. Why does it matter what AI can do and what AI could do in the future? The growth of AI will change the job opportunities and career paths that will exist in the future. AI will likely absorb many mundane jobs. Eventually, basic labor may not exist well into humanity's future. The lowest level job humans may do is to become engineers who either service, build, or manage robots, computers, and AI systems. What does this mean? It means humanity needs to get on the proverbial horse and get moving swiftly to learn to cooperate better if we are to move culture ahead in a healthier way. There is only one choice for our humanity: improve ourselves and our capabilities.

If we thought our Science, Technology, Engineering, and Math (STEM) programs needed to be more robust by percentage across the population in the United States, for example, STEM in the future will likely be our primary way to make a living. This may sound intense but consider that AI is already about to take over some roles in our professional environments. AI will teach STEM most effectively to our youth and a younger workforce. They will have to hit the ground running regarding professional contribution. Why? Because AI will not need social programs as safety nets as humans do. AI, as a peer to humanity, will either have us recoiling in caves or picking up our game and sharpening our skills. The best outcome, if only idealized right now, is that people and AI work together to solve some of humanity's most significant challenges: energy, healthcare, hunger, and homelessness, to name a few. Working in parallel with AI, we may have a more substantial opportunity to travel to the stars. However, before we get too far ahead of ourselves with colonizing the stars, we will have to conquer our egos, our bias, our hate, our excesses, our toxic behaviors, our neglect of the elderly, and all the struggles we put in our path, the unforced errors in life that have had the mathematical outcome of creating the world we have now; a divided one that regresses and progresses simultaneously going nowhere, in a hurry. We must rise above petty differences. Our human pettiness will be apparent to AI. AI may lose respect for us before we use it to improve the world. If we look at the glass as half full, we can use the 80/20 rule and awaken to the fact that AI can help humanity solve eighty percent of our worst problems globally. Shouldn't we try to improve ourselves as humans, too?

Crafting the future of humanity by integrating AI into it means we must first start with our behaviors. We start with our history to determine what triggers negative behaviors and work to cooperate productively. AI integration into our professional world has already begun. AI has had a head start, so we are the equivalent of grade schoolers lining up to race collegiate sprinters in the schoolyard compared to AI. Improving our human behavior overall and the expectation of ourselves to carry through to achieve it may require us to use AI to educate, inform, reform, counsel, and guide humanity back onto an ideal evolutionary path. Perhaps even more suitable than what humanity has ever hoped for.

Chapter 37

Friend or Foe

How do we know who are our friends and foes in life? In the natural world, we can quickly identify predators by their tearing canines, fangs, barbs, and rattles. Some creatures, like the female pray mantis, are more elegant. After she makes love, she turns her head 180 degrees and eats the head right off the shoulders of her male partner (Hadley, 2021). Perhaps we should refer to him as 'food.' I know there have been times in my own life when I felt like professional food, emotional food in relationships, and served as monetary food, a human ATM. I think most of us have felt these ways at some point. We must ask, how much of feeling these ways is because we want to see everyone thrive? How much of it is self-delusion? Perhaps we looked to endure where we should not have. We cannot entirely deny that we have all dismissed our value at some point. Perhaps it is an excellent lesson to discern where we align best for our highest good.

How do we know who the foes are? Some people can easily justify the worst types of behavior to support more significant causes, no matter how much compromise is required to connect dots that should never be connected. Some foes take part in outright betrayal, bragging about it while convincing others that someone deserves malicious treatment. This can be a person toward other people or a group, and groups who gang up on individuals. Perhaps you have experienced or observed cruelty, even from a distance. Perhaps knowing these realities exist is a 'thought foe' that drives people toward their escape of choice, anything to numb reality or emotional pain to see how badly other people have been treated. Perhaps this is why the orgasm is such a powerful force. It is truly the one event that can push any thought of danger or thoughts of foes from our minds long enough to let the light of love come crashing into our being like a waterfall. That sounds wonderful unless you are that male pray mantis. He believed he was so loved, accepted, and cherished by his mate that he inoculated his grip on the truth of reality, one simple fact: he made it all up in his mind. His limerence cost him and generations of his kind, in a flash, as they became the evening entrée: food. Humans need more hope and empathy than our male pray mantis friends. We need hope, wisdom, education, and compassion to inform the love that connects all humanity. Tapping into our intuition, our soul wants to understand. Despite foes' efforts, we want to overcome their control over our lives while not destroying the world in the process.

Friend or foe? What we think, say, and do determines whether we are friends or foes. Barring minor mistakes and misunderstandings, that is. If there are exceptions in our minds, we are foes. This is why we want those erroneously judged as ignorant to wake up, so we do not have to be foes. We must understand that the idea that others might be ignorant will make us foes in our own lives and theirs. If they are foes, and we turn ourselves into foes, then we all lose. Could the answer be as simple as becoming foe-less? Perhaps I am saying we should strive to be 'Friends.' I see anyone I might believe to be a foe as an unawakened friend in the making. I have made great connections with those who first presented themselves as foes that later became friends, including past healed relationships where foes and I taught each other how to be better humans, not lifelong foes. We must be humble enough to understand that we may not have all the facts or the correct answers. We must be aware that we might be unwitting foes to others unintentionally.

The next question is, 'How do we turn foes into friends?' That is the exciting part. The creative solution to your question will be different for each of you. Why? Because you each have different gifts and talents. It is through those gifts and talents that your answers will be revealed. Your creative solutions to that question are likely where your life path, mission, or purpose lay. Your gifts and talents align you with specific struggles that individuals, groups, and cultures need your help to overcome. It is true that if your current purpose is only to be a friend to those who are friends already, then the entire world will continue to suffer in a reverse butterfly effect where nothing good comes because we stifle our gifts, talents, and abilities, and love will die. Love will also die if you create and maintain division that being a foe says you ought. Your only peaceful and prosperous way is always to build bridges of connection and understanding; not blow them up with divisive thoughts, words, and actions. How exactly do we do this 'being a friend' stuff?' Start by speaking kindly to and about other people. Be hopeful of a breakthrough instead of prejudging the outcomes of others' lives. Give people an out. Believe and encourage everyone's transformation. Remember, people on their deathbeds have transformed; why can't anyone at any time?

Being a friend is a process. I have been cut off in traffic and had very little kindness in me. Afterward, I would scold myself internally and remind myself to be vigilant about where my heart is and guard what I think and speak. Then I would ask, 'Why did you call that person who cannot hear you a dumb dumb?.' No, it was not always dumb dumb, but I have worked it down to dumb dumb because it feels silly to say that phrase. It's a process. Deep down, isn't it silly to say anything harsh? It only reveals what was inside: a frustration that needed an excuse to escape. For all of us, it is usually a lack of control, the need to control, or things being out of control that drive most of our frustrations. Tightly wrap all that with our expectations of others and phrases like 'dumb dumb' slip out. Sometimes, being at the mercy of others who control and dominate us can frustrate us.

The antidote is embedded in the poison of these examples: do not dominate, control, or have unrealistic expectations of people. These are great starting points for being friendly or being a friend.

Betrayals are the sharpest tool in a foe's toolbox. Betrayal can make us feel gutted like a fish. How do we make friends with that? Well, life is about experience. It would be best if you experienced enough betrayal, hopefully none too catastrophic, to learn finally to be wise enough to see and step out of the way of the train of betrayal speeding toward you. Further, as a friend, you must use that wisdom to step kindly onto the high road next to that track. You must rise above the (toxic person, job, or organization) as that train speeds its way toward a karmic lesson or a cliff of its own making.

At each moment, we are either the teacher or the student. That honestly never changes. Keeping this in mind, we must be flexible and exercise humility to choose between being good friends or being a foe. Remember, our job is not to derail situational trains or inflict personal justice on one another but to become better friends. Perhaps down the line, many will have those awakenings. Maybe they will, suddenly, like a lightning strike, realize all the people they ran down needlessly in the past and choose with vigor to disembark the train of betrayal and empower others to do the same. We can hope because that is what friends do.

Chapter 38

Conclusion

One does not have to travel to many businesses or organizations to witness the truths of our humanity playing out in culture. Continually improving ourselves or an organization's efficiency and effectiveness comes down to being motivated from the heart, aligning ourselves with the people on our team, and applying constancy to bring a shared vision to life every day. Put another way, how we perform and live serves us best when our source of motivation stems from a desire to grow what we love and value. This key opens the door to transformation and breakthrough. It cannot be sustained alone materialistically, codependently, or falsely in service to the ego superficially. What should matter is that all transformation emanates from a beautiful spark within us all: an inner knowing to do what is right and just. When we align our actions with others, supported by this inner knowing, we can synergize to achieve anything, sustain anything, and grow when we integrate this into our everyday behavior.

We can use different words, but we are all discussing the same thing. You can say how much you 'care' and how much 'tolerance' you have or dress it up by saying 'acceptance.' We know this: everything matters, and even things you do not think matter are fueled by the love we give them or starved by the love we withhold. Billions of people, family, friends, and lost loves starve each other of life-giving, life-altering love, empathy, and forgiveness because of fear. People can be like deer in the headlights, frozen. They are frozen from the fear of moving forward and from the fear of turning around to heal and apologize in areas of their life needing forgiveness so they can move on, more whole. Depending on the day or the hour, this could be any of us who is weakened or tired enough to let fear, pride, or ego trick our minds into sidestepping the necessary healing we desire deep down. We must acknowledge that the world is undoubtedly rife with bad attitudes, narcissists, sociopaths, thieves, and manipulators of all kinds: the broken. We must remember that they have done nothing to heal themselves, nor have empaths prevented the conditions allowing them to thrive unchecked. Ultimately, without excuse, it will take all of us to heal all of us, irrespective of labels. That journey starts with respect, overcoming ourselves, and taking ownership of reality before judging people within arm's reach. The transformation of our behavior will be evidenced in the world by how we treat one another and the good we create.

The bridge we need to be brave enough to cross is deeper engagement and more meaningful conversations with each other personally and professionally. If we expect to improve culture, we cannot limit our engagement to factories, offices, and boardroom settings. Relative to this, collectively, our patience, empathy, and understanding must be exponentially greater. Especially if we want to grow humanity toward the dream our forebearers knew we could realize. To be clear, we are not talking about utopian perfection. We are talking about a human course correction that our great-grandchildren's children will approve of, looking back at us in the future. How much more motivation do you need? Despite the early cultural birth pains of transformation that we seem to be confusing with an approaching apocalypse, a clear opportunity to make leaps forward in behavior is the only leap that benefits everyone. We cannot afford to be cowards where love is concerned unless we desire to refuse love and become like that frozen deer in the headlights, refusing to act, who then is vaporized into memory. Is that what you want for those you love? I do not believe any of us do, ultimately. This is why we must question what motivates our life moment to moment: fear or love. Choose to imbibe love and do good if we want good to prevail.

Perhaps we humans have had enough lessons spiraling in circles, taking life's tests repeatedly, repeating the same lessons of history every twenty years over and over. Maybe we are beginning to see how remarkably close we are to realizing a significant cultural rebirth. Perhaps we are starting to tire of conflict, squabbling, and the fighting paradigms that have ravaged our planet's history for thousands of years. Maybe we are beginning to see that it is easier and more fulfilling to be good, do good, and cheer on the good in everyone, irrespective of cultural differences. Perhaps we are beginning to see and awaken to the fact that division in every form is wasteful. Maybe we are starting to see that each of us is an ambassador to the process of being human, like it or not. We are all accountable for the result we bring to the scribes of history.

Is having more joy, better health, greater longevity, safer communities, and more prosperity worth it? We still have so many natural challenges in life that if we were all more cooperative, we would still have much work ahead of us. Perhaps it is time for us humans to grow up, stop throwing cultural tantrums right down to the individual level, and learn to play nice with one another. It will take everyone choosing to take steps, make strides, and, with constancy, make the necessary leaps forward that will honor our humanity and perhaps save it. The first and most crucial step on our journey is to live with conviction to protect the love inside everyone. After that, anything is possible. The question is not whether we should do all these things; the question is: Do you have the courage to act?

Negative Behaviors

(Avoid these, and heal when these behaviors are apparent)

JUDGMENTAL	SILOS	CARELESS
THIEVERY	CONTROVERSIAL	SABOTAGE
DISTRUSTING	FEAR	NARCISSISM
IMPATIENCE	HARMFUL	CHEATING
DISHONESTY	SOCIOPATHY	DISMISSIVE
POOR PLANNING	SHALLOW	SUPERFICIAL
SELFISHNESS	MANIPULATION	HATEFUL
UNCOOPERATIVE	OPPRESSIVE	GREEDY
EGOTISTICAL	NEGLECTFUL	HARSH
HYPOCRITICAL	INCONSISTENT	APATHY
SELF RIGHTEOUS	POOR PLANNING	LETHARGY
TAKE SHORTCUTS	NEFARIOUS	AGGRESSIVE
INDECENT	IMPULSIVITY	JEALOUS
SCOPE CREEP	COMPLACENT	REJECTION
PROCRASTINATION	DRAMATIC	OBSESSIVE
POOR AWARENESS	ABANDONMENT	FAKE
UNMOTIVATED	BOTTLENECKS	GASLIGHTING
FAILURE TO ENGAGE	CONSTRAINTS	DISTRACTED

INDIFFERENT	PERFECTIONISM	HIDING
CODEPENDENT	HURT	WASTEFUL
UNAPPRECIATIVE	ANGRY	DECEPTIVE

Good Behaviors

(Exhibit these and other behaviors)

PERSEVERANCE	UPLIFTING	GRATEFUL
ACCOUNTABLE	TRUTHFUL	SELF AWARE
COMMITTED	INNOVATIVE	GENUINE
COLLABORATIVE	CREATIVE	AWARE
COOPERATIVE	SELF RELIANT	RESPONSIBLE
FLEXIBILITY	POSITIVE	SUPPORTIVE
TRUSTWORTHY	ENTHUSIASTIC	GRACIOUS
THOUGHTFUL	DRIVEN	OPEN
RELIABLE	STABLE	PROACTIVE
JOYFUL	ATTENTIVE	OWNERSHIP
HELPFUL	STEADFAST	DILIGENT
TIMELINESS	HIGH STANDARDS	TRANSPARENT
ADAPTABLE	PERSISTENT	LOYAL
RESPONSIBLE	EMPATHETIC	LOVING
ORGANIZED	KIND	PRUDENT
INSPIRING	INTENTIONAL	HARMONIOUS
RESOURCEFUL	CARING	FAIR
PURPOSEFUL	VULNERABLE	INTEGRITY

COACHABLE	RESPONSIVE	MOTIVATED
SYNERGISTIC	THANKFUL	HAPPY
HONEST	SELFLESS	COMPETENT
INTUITIVE	ENGAGING	MOTIVATED

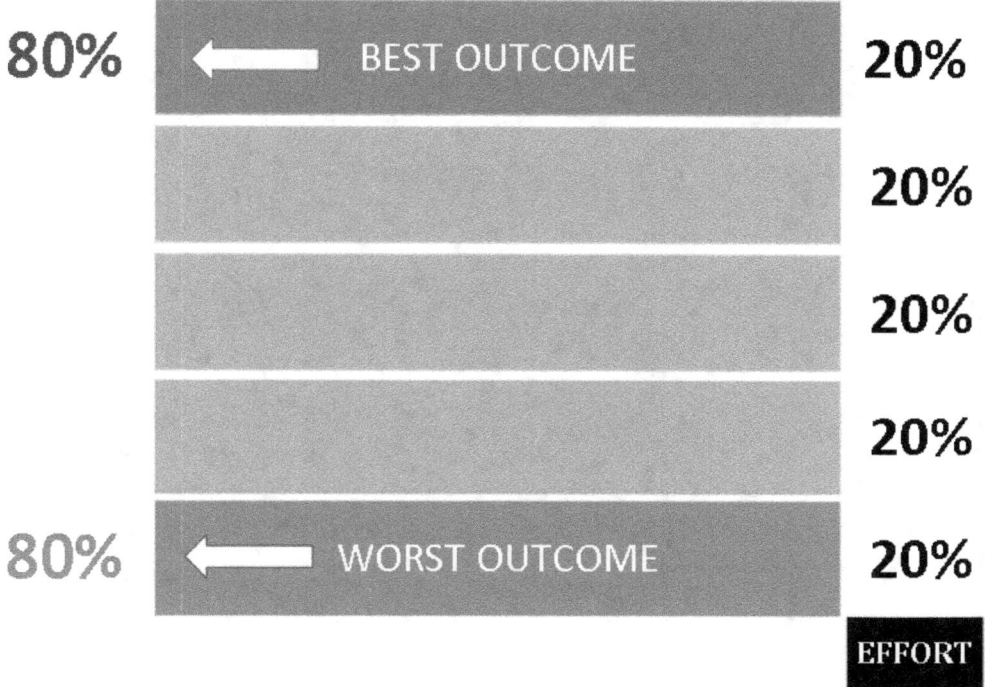

Figure A1

1. 80% of your best outcomes come from 20% of your effort.

2. 80% of your worst outcomes come from 20% of your effort.

3. The best or worst can be inside people individually too. They can be embodied more by those who rebel or are responsible for the best outcomes. These outcomes can also be organizations that succeed or fail to support, develop, grow, and lead.

(Desmos, 2024)

FORMING, STORMING, NORMING, PERFORMING

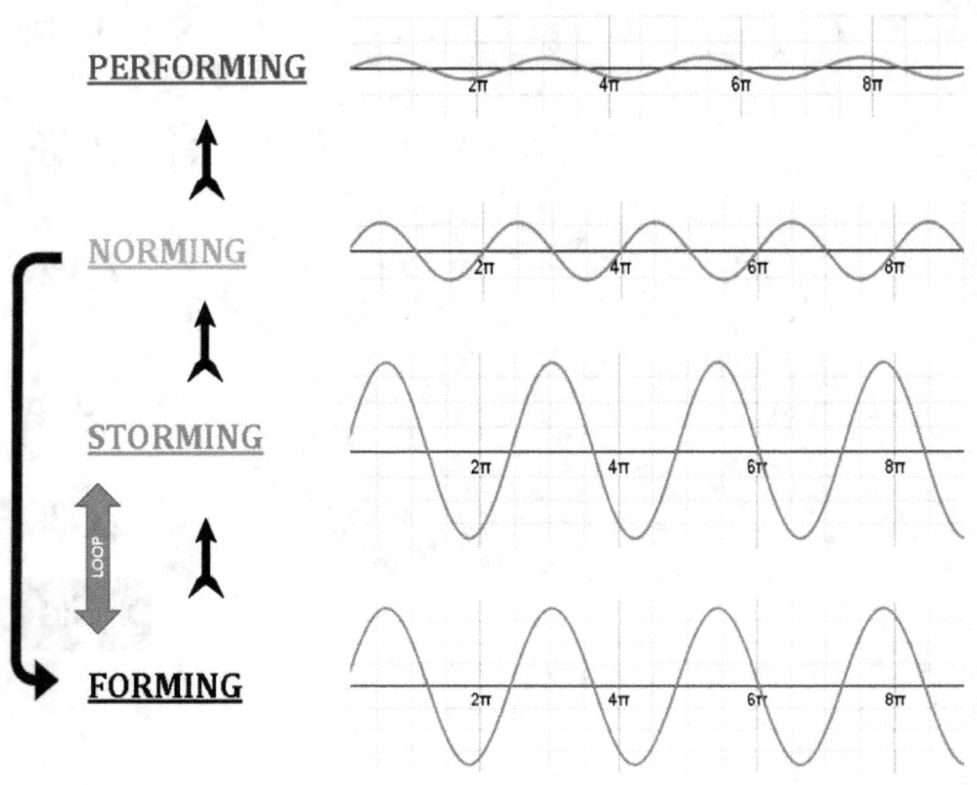

Figure A2

1. Teams FORM: Everything is new, and performance is not ideal.

2. As teams attempt to cooperate, differences emerge, and points of view, bias, and cooperation are a struggle. In this STORMING stage, performance can seem to worsen, not improve. It is incumbent on teams to overcome what holds them back from cooperating and find common ground, purpose, and vision. Leaders should build team

cohesion, so the team does not normalize getting stuck floundering between the FORMING and STORMING stages.

3. Once cooperation and performance are achieved, teams often enter the NORMING stage. There can still be struggles here, but the team knows better what to do, and the challenge becomes doing it with constancy.

4. Once the team is performing at a high level and being proactive in what they do is second nature, along with their communication skills, the team enters the PERFORMING stage. In this stage, cooperation, innovation, and continuous improvement are accepted, and there is a synergy in the team executing their efforts. Here, key performance indicators grow leaps and bounds, and the team has a customer-centric pride and professionalism from top to bottom.

5. Variability at each stage is an example. Ultimately, teams must achieve good results, reduce waste, and continually find ways to improve. Where constant prodding is required of the team, this is a sign your team is not breaking from norming into performing, and more coaching, developing, and building of your programs are required.

Organizational Assessment and Improvement Checklist

System and Administration

☐	Operations Plan
☐	Policy
☐	Processes
☐	Procedures
☐	ISO /Other & Regulatory Requirements
☐	Site Safety & Documentation
☐	Value Stream Map
☐	Lab/Product Inspection & Testing
☐	Quality: QM,QA,QI
☐	Management Review
☐	Facility/Grounds: Layout & Function
☐	Departments: Includes Supplier/Vendor Score
☐	Warehousing
☐	Shipping & Receiving
☐	Customer Service
☐	Training and Development Programs

General Data Collection and Assessment

☐	Climate Surveys & SWOT Diagrams
☐	KPI & Other Reports
☐	Manager/Supervisor Interview
☐	Other Interviews as Required
☐	Team Member Interviews:
☐	Maintenance Team Interviews
☐	Idea Inputs (Sticky Sheets)

Production Data Collection and Assessment

☐	Site and Process Video/Observation Timing
☐	Map the Value Stream
☐	Facility Machines & Equipment+ Safety
☐	ERP/MRP

Continuous Improvement Training and Opportunities

☐	5S
☐	Lean Methodologies
☐	Remove Wastes
☐	Gemba/Daily Management
☐	Facility
☐	Kaizen Review/ Event
☐	Single Minute Exchange of Dies (SMED)
☐	Visual Management

Note: Remove constraints and wastes, Reduce down times by improving response & repair/error correction times, Use radios to reduce response time in all areas, Increase tempo/cadence a little, don't procrastinate, take time to plan and prepare for the next day and/week and be more aggressive about working your plan.

Figure A3

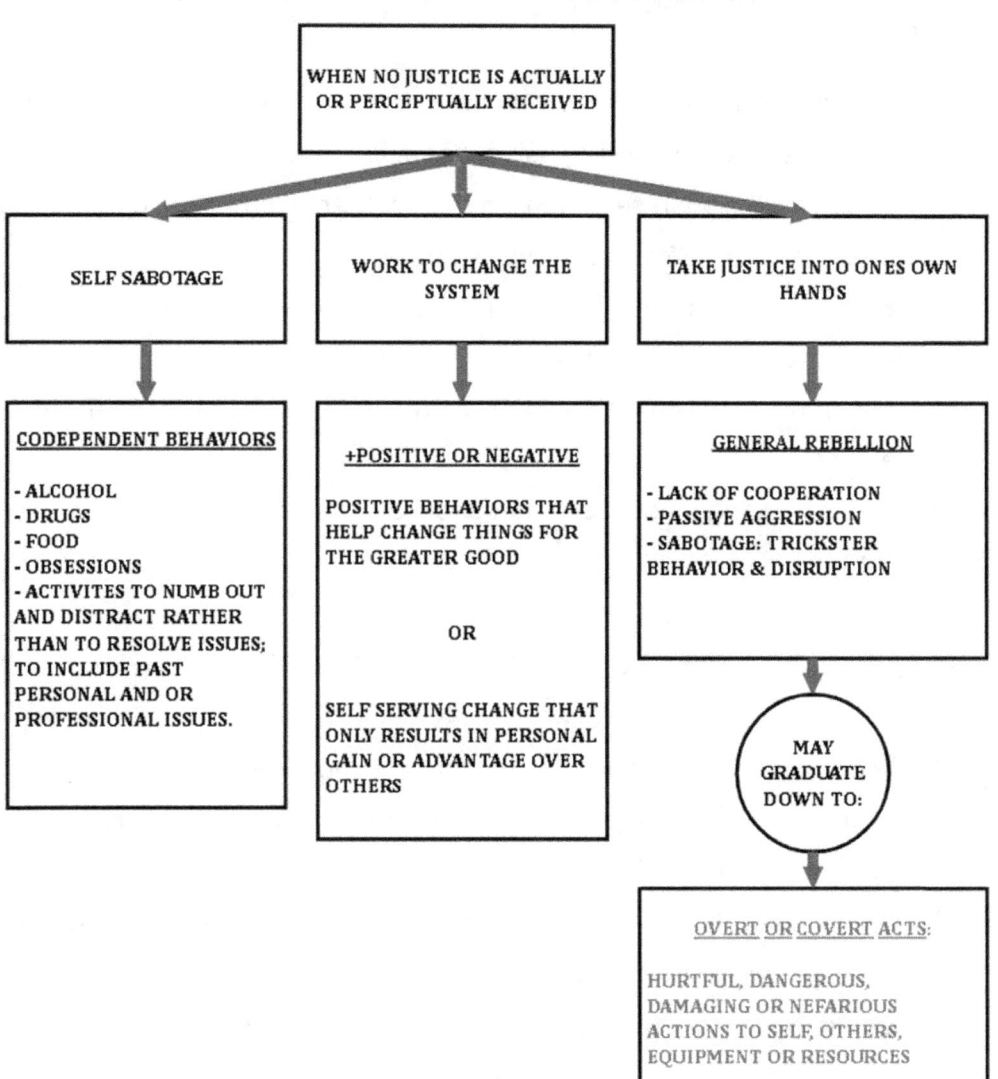

Figure A4

CONFLICT RESOLUTION

- <u>HUMILITY AND EMPATHY</u>:

    1. Be aware that everyone is suffering or has suffered from something.
    2. Some people are reliving their suffering every day, trying to break free from their own self-imposed mental & emotional prisons.
    3. Everyone thirsts for love and compassion.
    4. Everyone wants everyone to understand them while desiring to understand others less than they should.
    5. Everyone wants comfort and reassurance beneath hard superficial exteriors.
    6. Understanding these facets of people are first steps to resolving conflict.

- <u>ACTIONS TO TAKE TO BEGIN RESOLVING CONFLICT</u>

    1. Work to stop codependent behaviors. This includes personal obsessions and addictions as well as any emotional or professional validation codependence.
    2. Work positively to change internal & external systems to help heal & improve everyone and the environment for the common good.
    3. Do not overtly or covertly take justice into your own hands.
    4. Identify your rebellious nature and heal it from the source of pain, anger, fear, or frustration. Overcome your need or desire to rebel as a response to unfairness.
    5. Learn to cooperate and collaborate with others to find solutions that benefit the common good.

Align Purpose For The Customer

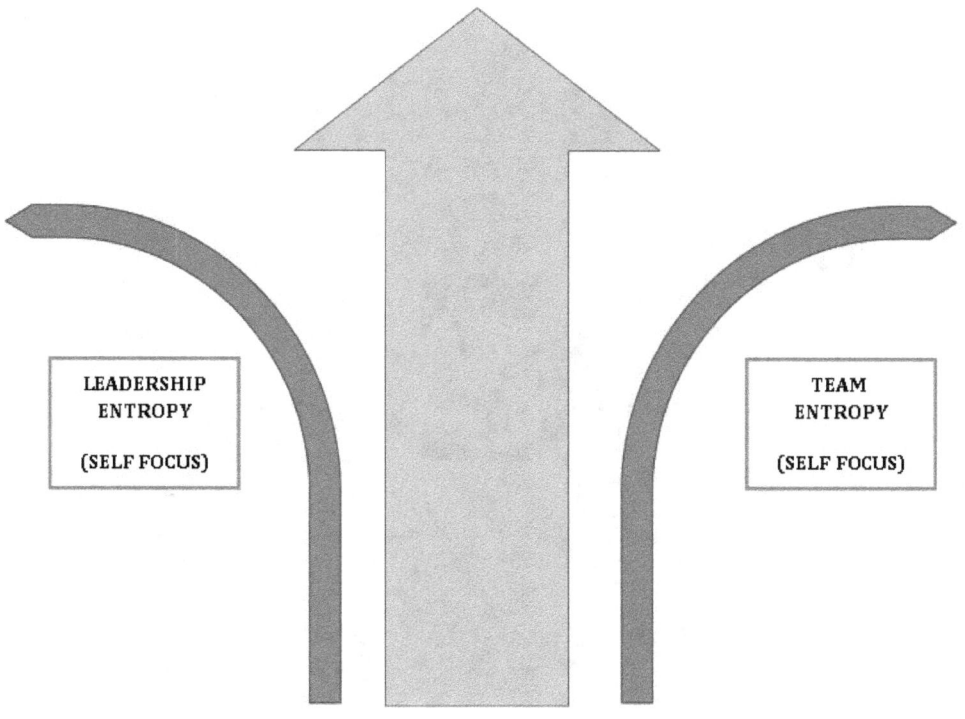

Figure A5

1. When the team or leadership becomes too self-focused, failures occur.

2. Realign focus on the customer and then the team. Customers and leadership will benefit if this approach is followed.

Who Are Your Customers?

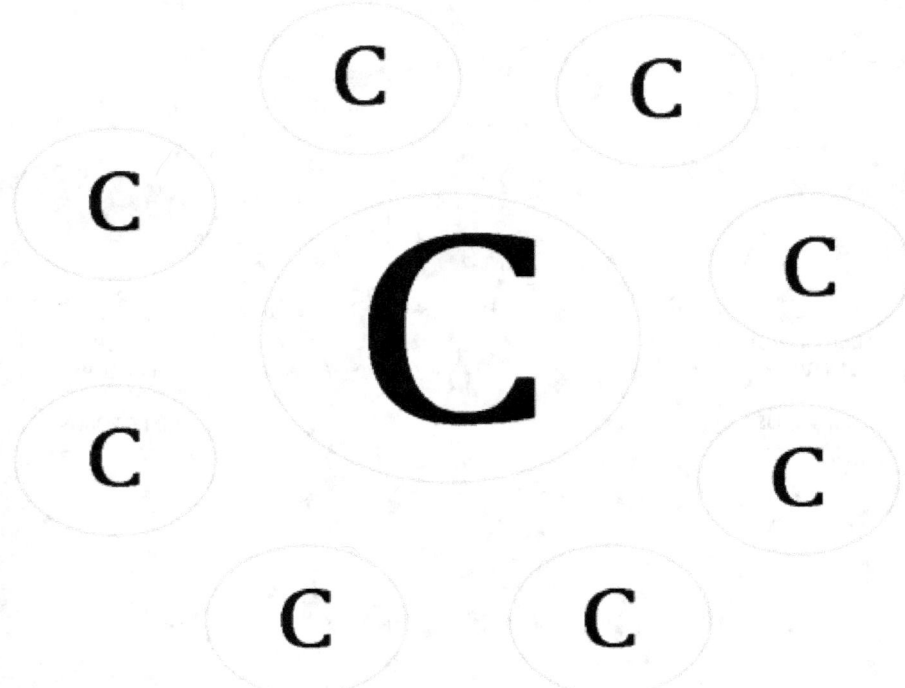

Figure A6

1. Identify the primary customers that the organization serves who make it possible for everyone to serve all secondary customers in their lives.

WINS DIAGRAM

WEAKNESSES	IMPROVEMENT OPPORTUNITIES
1	1
2	2
3	3
4	4
5	5
6	6
7	7
8	8
9	9
10	10

NEEDED RESOURCES	STRENGTHS
1	1
2	2
3	3
4	4
5	5
6	6
7	7
8	8
9	9
10	10

Figure A7

1. Honestly and critically list weaknesses, improvement opportunities, needed resources, and strengths. This will allow any person, team, or organization to stay focused on what challenges to overcome and turn into strengths.

Daily Management Board

	DAILY	WEEKLY	MONTHLY	YEAR	FOLLOW UP ACTIONS
SAFETY					
QUALITY					
DELIVERY					
COST					
People					

Figure A8

1. Update the daily management board with key performance data.

2. This can be an updated electronic document displayed on a TV screen or whiteboard. This is the first stop on a daily stand-up Gemba management walk in an open work area visible to the rest of the team.

Plan Do Check Act Worksheet

TEAM LEAD/EMPLOYEE							TEAM MEMBERS:		
VALUE STREAM:									
WORKCENTER:									
START & STOP DATE:									

WASTE IDENTIFIED	PROCESS / NOTES	PLAN	DO	CHECK	ACT	ACTION NOTES	COMPLETE Y/N

Figure A9

1. Use this as an improvement planning worksheet. This can be made into a whiteboard or electronic board for visibility during Gemba walks.

Performance and Hour x Hour Boards

PERFORMANCE	Current Day	Prior Day	Week Running	Week #1	WEEK #2	Week #3	Week #4	Month Running	Average / Day Running	Open	Operator	Sup / Mgr	QC / Maint	YEAR TO DATE	NOTES
PROD / Sales / Ship STANDARD															
PROD / Sales / Ship ACTUAL															
PERFORMANCE %															
SCRAP / RETURNS															
MECH Down Time HIST AVG															
MECH Down Time ACTUAL															
PCENTAGE +/-															

HOURLY	1ST SHIFT STANDARD	1ST SHIFT ACTUAL	SCRAP ACTUAL	2ND SHIFT STANDARD	2ND SHIFT ACTUAL	SCRAP ACTUAL	3RD SHIFT STANDARD	3RD SHIFT ACTUAL	SCRAP ACTUAL	SCRAP Return (ACTUAL)	Operator	Sup / Mgr	QC / Maint	DAILY TOTALS	NOTES
HR1															
HR2															
HR3															
HR4															
HR5															
HR6															
HR7															
HR8															
HR9															
HR10															
HR11															
HR12															
MECHANICAL Down Time															
CLOSE OUT TOTAL															

Figure A10

1. The performance whiteboard or electronic version can be used for a general product category. This should be visible to the entire team in an open area. This board should be a stop during your team's Gemba walk.

2. The Hour-by-Hour board below the performance board can also be a whiteboard or electronic board. This board can be a specific product line, for example. This board should be a stop during a Gemba walk by the management team to discuss performance status, resolve issues, and get feedback from the production team lead/s. Quality Assurance and supervisors should check the lines routinely and note those checks. The back of the board can be used to take more notes and put down issues or update waste details, supplies that are needed, and more. Make it applicable to your product or service-specific needs. This board serves as a scoreboard for the team. Take time to recognize, appreciate, and engage with the team where the work is being done. Use the board to update downtimes, record communications, and space for maintenance to update when repairs are complete to reduce the amount of downtime. Using radios in conjunction with the boards reduces time spent looking for support, which leads to reduced downtime.

Turtle Diagram

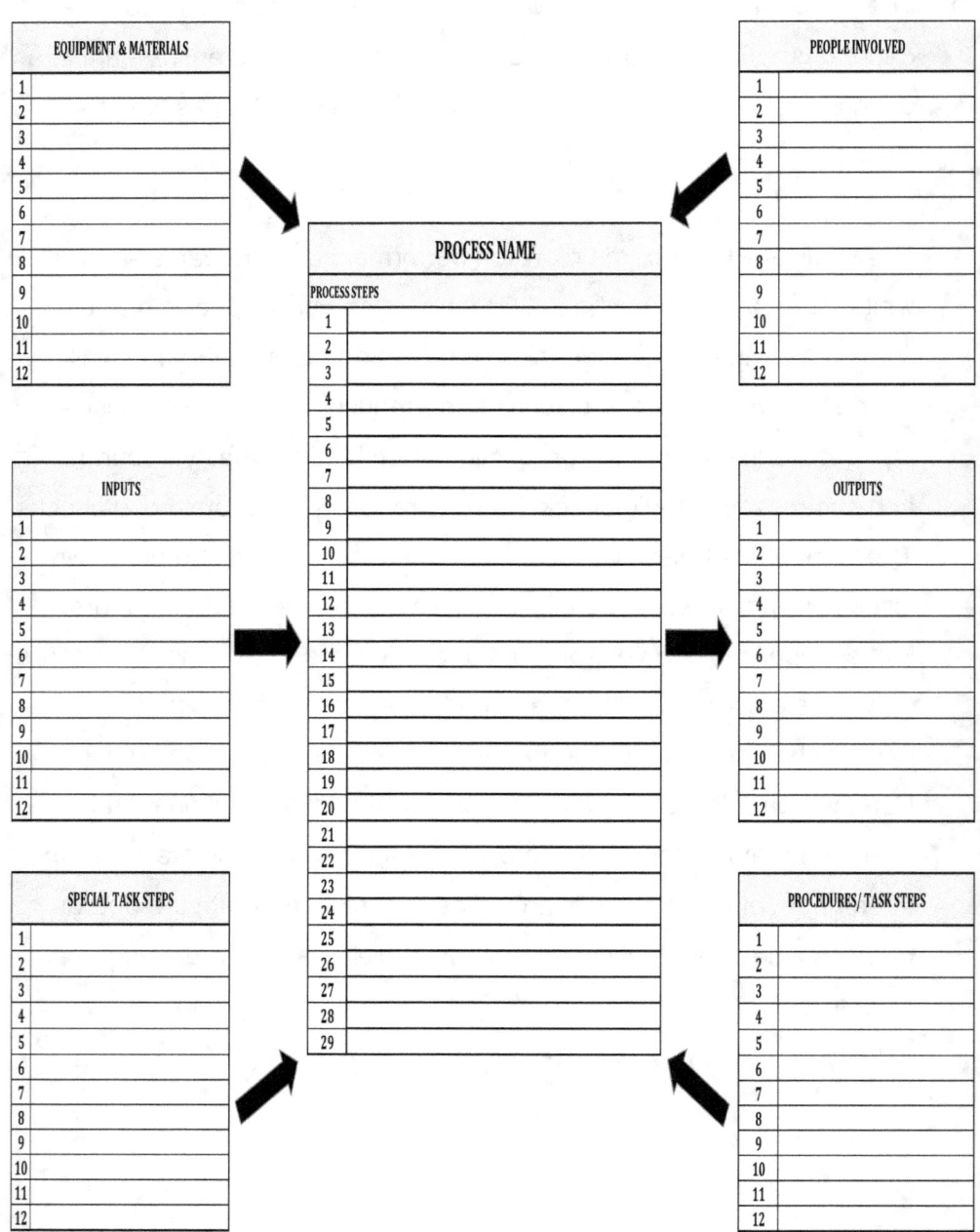

Figure A11

1. List required equipment and materials.

2. Write down the necessary inputs or conditions needed for the process.

3. List any special tasks required to be accomplished before the process.

4. Write down what roles are involved in the process.

5. Write down any sub-steps that are important to the process.

6. Write down the expected outputs specifically from the process.

7. Write down the detailed steps of the process.

8. This document, or worksheet, can be used to establish the current state of your process. Do one for each process. Once you have improved the process, you can either update this after making it a formal document or use it to build your standard work document. Ensure all processes are documented and formalized, which can aid in training as well.

9. As an exercise, you can have three different people do the same task and attempt to fill in a blank turtle diagram as accurately as possible. This will tell you how standardized your team is despite knowing it will not be a perfect result. You can use this as a discussion point to improve a process where references are not being used. When team members see that all three versions are not alike, explain why you need to have and use standard documents to ensure outputs are consistently repeatable. This can also help reduce waste when product or service quality is in question. In short, you can use this as a test sheet for any

organizational role. This should also give leadership teams something to consider regarding their processes, how well operations are being conducted, and areas where consistency and quality have been issues.

Idea Improvement Input Document

IDEA / SUGGESTION INFORMATION	DESCRIBE / DETAIL	MANAGEMENT: CONCUR / NON CONCUR				
IDENTIFY YOUR (WORK CENTER)						
WRITE THE IDEA OR SUGGESTION		SUPERVISORY: CONCUR / NON CONCUR				
WHAT PROBLEM DOES IT RESOLVE?						
WHAT ARE THE BENEFITS RESOLVING? PRODUCTIVITY / SAFETY / QUALITY / COST		QUALITY: CONCUR / NON CONCUR				
WHAT WASTES WILL BE REDUCED OR ELIMINATED? PLEASE LIST DATA TO BEST OF YOUR ABILITY						
PRINTED NAME	SIGNATURE / EMPLOYEE #	DATE OF FINAL APPROVAL				
PROCESS OWNER	IMPLEMENTATION DATE	PERFORMANCE MONITORING				
		Day/Avg	Week #1	Week #2	Week #3	Total
Example: Reduced Machine Down Time / Day	BASELINE PERFORMANCE PRIOR TO CHANGE 1/2/3					
	POST IMPROVEMENT 1/2/3					
Example: Reduced Scrap / Day	BASELINE PERFORMANCE PRIOR TO CHANGE 1/2/3					
	POST IMPROVEMENT 1/2/3					
Example: Increased Product/parts / Day	BASELINE PERFORMANCE PRIOR TO CHANGE 1/2/3					
	POST IMPROVEMENT 1/2/3					
Example: Increased Quality Parts/product/service / Day	BASELINE PERFORMANCE PRIOR TO CHANGE 1/2/3					
	POST IMPROVEMENT 1/2/3					
TOTAL PRE IMPROVEMENT IMPACT:	BASLINE PERFORMANCE TOTALS:					
TOTAL IMPROVEMENT:	POST IMPROVEMENT TOTALS:					

Figure A12

1. This document captures ideas constructively.

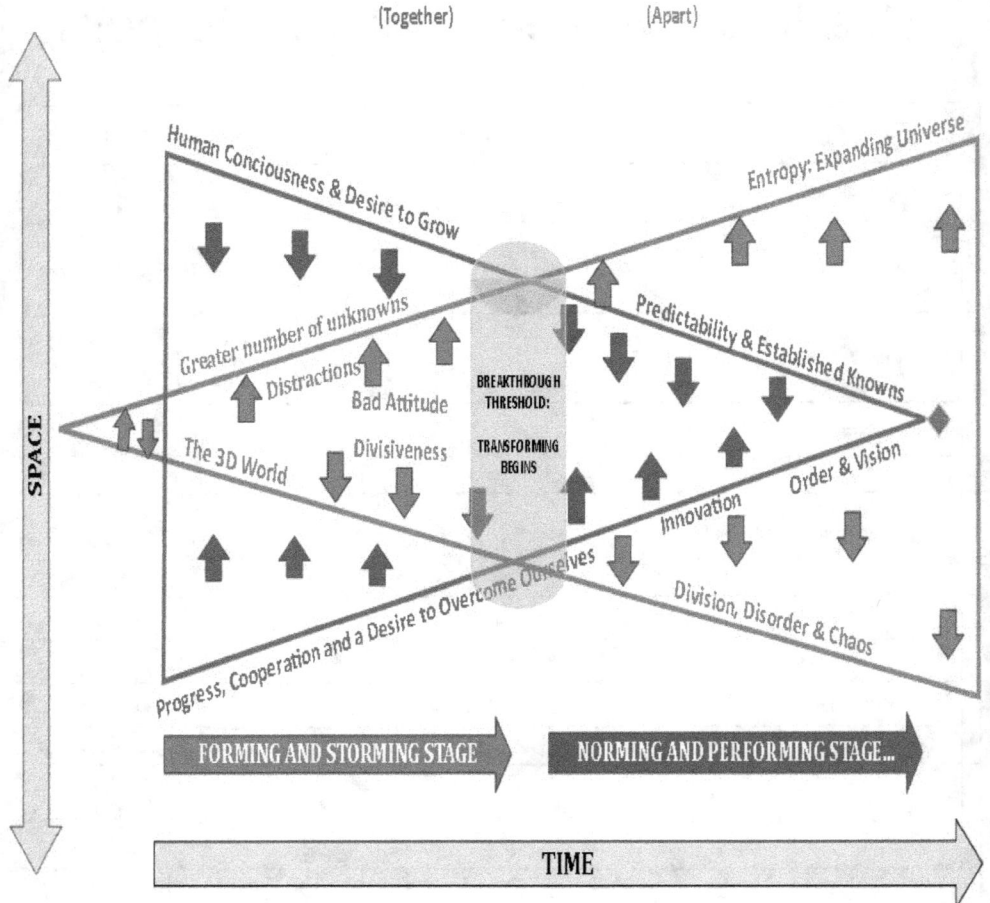

Figure A13

1. Entropy is in red; it expands in space and time. The energy of entropy pulls things apart and distracts our efforts, our focus, attention, and conscious awareness.

2. In blue, unlike entropy, the progression of our consciousness requires people, teams, groups, and cultures to expend conscious mental and physical energy to progress, cooperate, and overcome the entropy

inside and outside of us. Our consciousness's progression helps us resist entropy, disorder, and chaos. Everyone must consciously surge forward toward singularity, engagement, cooperation, agreement, and open communication.

3. The chaos we experience as we storm toward normalcy after not having it may initially feel apocalyptic. However, the process is a rebirth, the tension of a transformational birth to realize normalcy that will progress to perform in our lives and for our teams more efficiently.

4. People must see internal resistance as a force of entropy that thwarts progress distracts us, works against growth, and suppresses our desire to improve our lives. When your vision is clear about this, overcoming internal and external contradictions for yourself and your teams becomes easier.

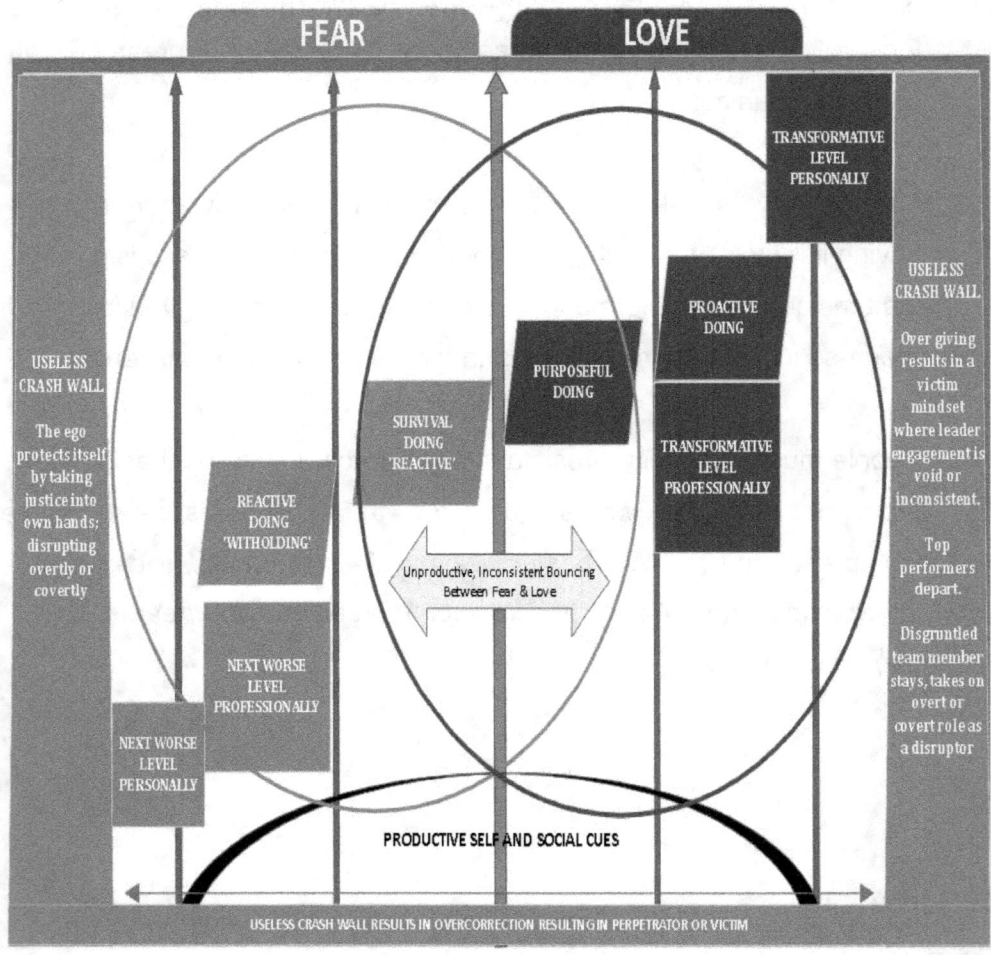

Figure A14

1. The boundary between living and working in a mind and heart space of love instead of fear is thin. It is the difference between being productive and being reactionary.

2. Bouncing back and forth on the line between love and fear leads to burnout and exhaustion, personally and professionally. Then people spiral down.

3. Transforming is recognizing when an individual or team operates in reactionary or withholding modes and deciding to become proactive. Personal and organizational self-actualization may be achieved when acting toward a personal, professional, or organizational vision.

4. When personal and professional behavior becomes inconsistent, then survival-doing becomes normalized. Failing to address and change the trajectory will result in reactionary doing where efforts are convenience-driven, silos are built, and walls of "Can't" become the bricks those walls are made. In reactionary modes, participation, customer service, team cohesion, and cooperation suffer.

5. In the extreme, withholding becomes an entitlement to convenience by a team member or a team. When challenged, this may hit the worst side of the useless crash wall, where behavior becomes a justified overt or covert disruption.

6. Conversely, the transformed high performer may not be appreciated or engaged with enough that it impacts progress. High performers may depart because of organizational distractions to repair dysfunction effectively.

7. Exhausted over-givers carrying more than an appropriate workload may feel unappreciated and depart. Some may hit the useless crash wall and, due to external factors, stay on and take on overt and covert

behaviors, riding the organization as far as possible to ensure its demise.

8. Engage, communicate, appreciate, counsel, and educate team members so that the most extreme crash-wall behaviors do not occur. Successful leaders should mentor the newest members, so cohesion is not taken for granted.

Bibliography

Abogodo, I. (2023). The archetype of the rebel. The Brain Blog. Retrieved from

https://thebrain.blog/the-archetype-of-the-rebel/

Ariella, Sky. (2023). 27 US Employee Turnover Statistics [2023]: Average Employee

Turnover Rate, Industry Comparisons, And Trends. Zippia.Retrieved from https://www.zippia.com/

Augustine, A. (430). What does love look like? Generosity Monk. (2015, October 14).

https://generositymonk.com/2015/10/14/augustine-of-hippo-what-does-love-look-like/

Cherry, K. (2023). 12 Archetypes: Definition, Theory, and Types. Verywell Mind.

Retrieved from https://www.verywellmind.com/

Cherry, K., & Mattiuzzi, P. G. (2010). Essentials of Psychology: An Introductory Guide to

the Science of Human Behavior.

Delgado, Jennifer. (n.d.). The 2 hour rule applied by Aristotle, Nietzsche, and Einstein.

Psychology Spot. Retrieved (2024) from https://www.psychology-spot.com/

Desmos, Inc. (2024). Desmos Graphing Calculator. Retrieved (March 25, 2024), from

https://www.desmos.com/calculator/w9jrdpvsmk

Ebert, R. (2000). Cast Away movie review & film summary. Roger Ebert. Retrieved from

https://www.rogerebert.com/

Garcia-Navarro, J. (n.d.). Escapism: Psychology and mechanisms. Psychology Spot.

Retrieved March 18, 2024, from https://psychology-spot.com/escapism-psychology/

Grohol, J. M. (2020). What is passive-aggressive behavior? Verywell Mind.

https://www.verywellmind.com/what-is-passive-aggressive-behavior-2795481

Gunderman, R. (2019). The Extraordinary Life of Nikola Tesla. Innovation. Smithsonian

    Magazine. Retrieved from https://www.smithsonianmag.com/

Hadley, D. (2021). 10 Fascinating Praying Mantis Facts. Retrieved from

    thoughtco.com/praying-mantid-facts-1968525.

Hill, B. (2021). What is the human hearing range in hz and db? Miracle-Ear. Retrieved

    from https://www.miracle-ear.com/

Karanjgaokar, Ruchir. (2021). Tuckman Model of Team Development: A Detailed

    Blueprint to Build Awesome Teams. AGILE KEN. Retrieved

    from https://agile-ken.com/

Leikvoll, V. (2023). How to Manifest Something: An Easy 5-Step Guide. Leaders.com.

    Retrieved from https://www.leaders.com/

Maxwell, J. (2001). The 17 Indisputable Laws of Teamwork: Embrace Them and

    Empower Your Team.

Maxwell, J. (2012). The Complete 101 Collection: What Every Leader Needs to Know

McLeod, S. (2018). Pareto Principle (The 80-20 Rule): Examples & More. Simply

    Psychology. Retrieved from https://www.simplypsychology.org/pareto-principle.html

McLeod, S. (2020). Maslow's hierarchy of needs. Simply Psychology.

    https://www.simplypsychology.org/maslow.html

McLeod, S. (2024). Maslow's Hierarchy of Needs. Simply Psychology. Retrieved from

    https://www.simplypsychology.org/maslow.html

National Nuclear Security Administration. (2018). Visible light: Eye-opening research at

    NNSA. U.S. Department of Energy. Retrieved from

    https://www.energy.gov/nnsa/articles/visible-light-eye-opening-research.

Nelson, C. (2019). Cortisol Hormone: Its Role In Stress, Inflammation, And Weight Gain.

    Retrieved from https://www.perfectketo.com/cortisol-hormone/.

Perkowitz, S. (2024). E=mc² equation. Retrieved from Encyclopedia Britannica.

https://www.britannica.com/science/E-mc2-equation

Pollack Peacebuilding. (2023). Workplace Conflict Statistics 2023. Retrieved from

https://pollackpeacebuilding.com/

Psychology Today. (n.d.). Neuroplasticity. Retrieved March 18, 2024, from

https://www.psychologytoday.com/us/basics/neuroplasticity

Raypole, C. (2021). What Are the Signs of Codependency? Psych Central.

https://psychcentral.com/lib/symptoms-signs-of-codependency

Riggs, J. (2021, August 26). First, do no harm and the Hippocratic Oath. ThoughtCo.

https://www.thoughtco.com/first-do-no-harm-hippocratic-oath-118780

Rodrigo, A. inviTRA. (2018). How many sperm make it to the egg? Retrieved from

https://www.invitra.com/en/faqs/how-many-sperm-make-it-to-the-egg/

Samuel, M. (2006). Creating The Accountable Organization: A Practical Guide to

Improve Performance Execution.

Siang, T. (2021). What is Ideation – and How to Prepare for Ideation Sessions. Interaction Design Foundation. Retrieved from https://www.interaction-design.org/

Sommer AP. Mitochondrial solar sensitivity: evolutionary and biomedical implications.

Ann Transl Med. 2020 Mar;8(5):161. doi: 10.21037/atm.2019.11.100. PMID:

32310246; PMCID: PMC7154450.

Usamani, F. (2024). 5 Whys for Root Cause Analysis: Definition, Example, and

Template. PM Study Circle. Retrieved from https://www.pmstudycircle.com/

Van der Molen MJ, Poppelaars ES, Van Hartingsveldt CT, Harrewijn A, Gunther Moor B,

Westenberg PM. (2021). Fear of negative evaluation modulates electrocortical

and behavioral responses when anticipating social evaluative feedback.

https://pubmed.ncbi.nlm.nih.gov/24478667/Front Hum

Vidor, K., Fleming, V., Cukor, G., Thorpe, R., Taurog, N., & LeRoy, M. (1939). The

Wizard of Oz. Metro-Goldwyn-Mayer (MGM).

Virtues For Life. (n.d.). Two wolves. Retrieved March 18, 2024, from

https://www.virtuesforlife.com/two-wolves/

Warren, M. (2021). Behavioral Management Guide: Essential Treatment Strategies for

Adult Psychotherapy.

Yuan, Lily. (2022). Guide: 12 Jungian Archetypes as Popularized by The Hero and the

Outlaw. Personality Psychology. Retrieved from https://www.personality-ps

Appendix A

Figure A1. Pareto Principle. (pg. 292).

Otherwise known as the 80/20 rule.

Figure A2. Forming, Storming, Norming, and Performing. (pg. 292)

A basic outlay of team development dynamics.

Figure A3. Organizational Assessment and Improvement Checklist. (pg. 296).

A simple checklist that demonstrates what to assess and improve in an organization.

Figure A4. Conflict and Conflict Resolution. (pg. 297).

Tributaries of conflict and some essential steps to resolve conflict.

Figure A5. Align Purpose for the Customer. (pg. 300).

Visual graph to demonstrate where alignment should be for teams and leaders.

Figure A6. Who Are Your Customers? (pg. 301).

Shows primary customers in the middle and all customers served by them.

Figure A7. WINS Diagram. (pg. 302).

Helps teams list, prioritize, and then improve in all areas.

Figure A8. Daily Management Board. (pg. 303).

This board helps to manage and communicate the history and status of programs and then come up with follow-up actions as part of daily management.

Figure A9. Plan Do Check Act Worksheet. (pg. 304).

Figure A10. Performance and Hour-by-Hour Boards. (pg. 305).

Maintains hourly, daily, weekly, monthly, and annual performance as part of team scoreboards. These are daily stops during daily management meetings/ Gemba walks.

Figure A11. Turtle Diagram. (pg. 307).

Helps the team build processes that will evolve into standard work documents later.

Figure A12. Idea Improvement Input Document. (pg. 310).

A document that can be used to collect improvement ideas based on current negative impact and serve as an approval and tracking document.

Figure A13. Singularity versus Entropy Diagram. (p. 311).

This diagram demonstrates the forces of entropy that pull on a team's ability to come together, cooperate, and improve. It reveals how cooperation aligns the team with their vision.

Figure A14. Duality Matrix of Fear and Love. (pg. 313).

This diagram demonstrates the dangers of the extremes of fear and apathy against love and high performance. It also shows the danger of what can happen when leaders do not engage, develop, appreciate, and communicate with the team.

www.ingramcontent.com/pod-product-compliance
Lightning Source LLC
Chambersburg PA
CBHW052142220526
45471CB00004B/1494